A PUBLICATION FROM THE JAMES FORD BELL COLLECTION
IN THE WALTER LIBRARY, UNIVERSITY OF MINNESOTA

MERCHANTS & SCHOLARS

ESSAYS IN THE HISTORY OF
EXPLORATION AND TRADE

Collected in memory of James Ford Bell, and
edited by John Parker

THE UNIVERSITY OF MINNESOTA PRESS · MINNEAPOLIS

The drawings on the cover and on the half-title pages are adapted from wind heads appearing in Gregor Reisch's *Margarita Philosophica*, Freiburg, 1503, and Claudius Ptolemy's *Geographia*, Strassburg, 1513.

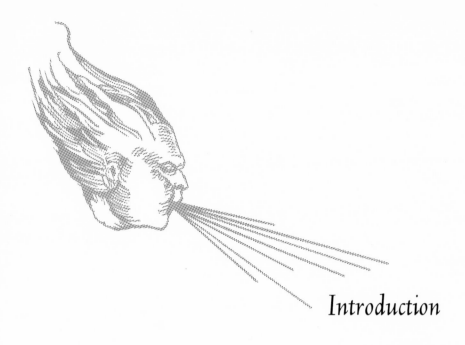

Introduction

by JOHN PARKER

THE AGE OF DISCOVERY and the incunabular age of printing both
had their origins in the technological advances of fifteenth-century
Europe, and both were stimulated by a spirit of inquiry that at once looked beyond
existing knowledge and back to ancient authorities. Less than two decades separated
the first printing of Ptolemy's great classical geography from the first voyage of Columbus. Strabo's view of the world and the voyage of Magellan were made known to
the inquiring public within one lifetime, yet their lives were separated by fifteen centuries.

In bringing the ancient world and the New World together, the explorer, the merchant, the scholar, and the publisher served each other well. The publisher with his
humanistic editors supplied the discoverer with all the knowledge of world geography
that had survived from ancient scholars and their medieval successors; the explorer,
in turn, provided the publisher with readily salable, exciting, and informative narratives of voyages to distant lands through unknown seas. Both the ancient knowledge
and the new stimulated merchants and scholars to inquire more fully into the reports
of products and peoples of hitherto unknown parts of the earth. Their enterprises
employed explorers, and their findings set publishers to work again.

It was the interdependability of these men of adventure and commerce with their
scholarly contemporaries that fascinated the late James Ford Bell, a merchant who
was interested in the origins of present world trade relations, and who viewed commerce as the major driving force in the modern world. He saw the student as an
essential partner of the merchant when he observed that "trade . . . searches for
that which serves its interests best," for the searching and interpreting of strange
skies, seas, and continents, as well as books and manuscripts which held the learning
of the past, were to him the basic research that liberated European commerce from
its medieval confines and launched the modern age of world trade. He was not content to merely know the methods and results of this research, since these did not bring
to him that intimate and personal relation with the past which constitutes the deepest
appreciation of history. To achieve this it was necessary to have the very books and

[3]

manuscripts that had been decisive instruments in the expansion of knowledge and commerce.

Founded by a merchant-industrialist who was a prominent figure in the modern economic history of Minnesota, the James Ford Bell Collection quite naturally had its origins in Mr. Bell's interest in the commercial penetration of North America which followed the three waterways flowing from Minnesota. The Mississippi River, the Great Lakes–St. Lawrence system, and the rivers that flow northward to find their outlet in Hudson Bay were all instrumental in opening this three-sided North American watershed to European commerce. It was this early emphasis on the region he knew best that brought to Mr. Bell's library the distinguished collection of French Americana and Hudson Bay material that still form the heart of the Bell Collection. Yet the merchants and explorers who followed these waterways could not be studied apart from their contemporaries who probed the Isthmus of Panama, the Amazon and Plate rivers, and the Strait of Magellan, for all of them represented national as well as private ambition in the New World. More than that, explorations in both North and South America often represented European commercial aspirations in Asia, as passages were sought through the American barrier standing between Europe and the Far East. To place these voyages and the books which resulted from them in their proper context, it was necessary to have contemporary descriptions of Asia which described Far Eastern trade and European participation in it. It became evident to Mr. Bell that a library concerned with the history of commerce had to be worldwide in scope, and that it had to contain the works of philosophers, geographers, navigators, merchants, and others who provided European readers with the knowledge essential to an enlarged sphere of commerce.

When the Bell Collection was made a part of the University of Minnesota Library in 1953 it was determined that its future growth should be related to the development of European overseas relations from the fifteenth to the end of the eighteenth century. This period saw the economies of far distant regions drawn together into an intricate commercial network, and witnessed the discovery, mapping, and describing of the major land masses and navigable waters of the world. With this scope settled upon, an acquisitions program was established to begin bringing together the materials needed by scholars interested in the development of European mercantile enterprise abroad, and a publications program was undertaken to provide encouragement and a suitable outlet for research in the history of commerce and exploration. This volume is the tenth in this series of publications, and represents in a limited way the scope and holdings of the collection.

In seeking the beginnings of the age of discovery, the Bell Collection has been led to fifteenth-century manuscripts, maps, and printed geographies which reflect the knowledge Europeans had of the outer world as navigators of Columbus's generation considered where the Western Ocean might take them. Those who formulated geographic thought were frequently not men of the sea, but scholars of humanistic tendencies who examined the theories of the ancients and sought to relate them to more recently acquired information. In Italy, Florence was a meeting point for all manner of artistic and intellectual currents, and in the first essay presented here Thomas Goldstein examines the background of geographic thought in that city which enabled Toscanelli to expound to Columbus the theory of the western route to the East. Here he finds the geographical works of Ptolemy and Strabo to have been crucial in the thinking of scholars gathered at the Council of Florence, as indeed they continued to be for another hundred years.

The humanists of the early sixteenth century who undertook the integration of newly-revealed geographical information into the European intellectual stream were, for all of their classical learning, heirs to much that was medieval, especially in their emphasis upon religion. In her study of the interrelations between the discoveries and humanistic thought Elisabeth F. Hirsch examines the writings of Erasmus, Damião de Góis, Sebastian Münster, and others to show how this kind of scholar grasped the significance of his own age, its debt to earlier learning, and the problems inherent in bringing unity to the world of Christendom which was steadily expanding into areas where avowed Christians had vastly different beliefs and practices.

While religious motivation for overseas expansion is not to be ignored, it is the impetus of commerce that is particularly emphasized in the Bell Collection. The wealth of the East was an undeniable attraction and it led us to inquire into the nature of the economic organization that produced and distributed it. Burton Stein has gone to temple inscriptions and other sources in India to discover the structure of the market communities of the Coromandel Coast and their hinterland, noting the closely-knit group of mercantile centers that gave impetus to a vigorous trade, but began to decline about a century before the Portuguese discovered the water route to India. Yet even as they declined and came under European dominance, the Indian cities held the attention of Western merchants who sent explorers into the most impossible seas and agents over inhospitable and unknown lands to seek the products of the East. From attempts to reach eastern markets by a northeast route western Europe acquired knowledge of its neighbors to the east, and in the last half of the sixteenth century the vastness of Muscovy, Tartary, and inner Asia became apparent on maps. John Webb has investigated the origins of one of these maps made by the Van Deutecum brothers, mapmakers of Antwerp, relating it to other cartographic works and itineraries of the period, and the gradual growth of knowledge about the regions it portrays.

The rivers of Russia and the Portuguese route to Asia were not adequate to the commercial ambitions of western Europe as nations sought to establish their own direct all-water connections with Asia. Toscanelli's generation had suggested the way, and Columbus had followed. The assault upon the American barrier which began with the sixteenth century was continued for another two and a half centuries by explorers who refused to believe there was not a navigable passage through North

America. Hudson Bay was the major focal point for English efforts to reach the Pacific Ocean by a northern route, and the voyage of Henry Hudson is the concern of Ernst Abbe and Frank Gillis, who find in their study of that voyage an opportunity to consider the history of the mapping of the east side of the bay — the part actually explored by Hudson — and to show the persistence of the earliest concepts as well as the variations that appeared in the period before the more frequent navigation of the bay after the establishment of the Hudson's Bay Company.

The hoped-for passages through the continent often led Europe's merchants to consider the potentialities of American goods. French sailors probing the St. Lawrence River found it easy to engage in trade with the Indians along its shores, as did fishermen who came ashore from the Grand Banks off Newfoundland. The possibilities of a settled trade inevitably produced thoughts favoring settlements, and in the last quarter of the sixteenth century an opportunity for taking walrus and cod from a base in the St. Lawrence, combined with religious troubles in England, led to an attempt at settling a group of congregationalists in the Magdalen Islands. David B. Quinn traces the story of this unsuccessful invasion of French and Basque fishing grounds, one of the earliest English efforts to establish permanent settlements in North America.

The reasons for the failure which attended many European undertakings abroad were numerous, and often involved political and religious differences in the settlements, poor management, and lack of a proper evaluation of the potentialities of the region which was to support the enterprise. In contrast to the English failure in the St. Lawrence, Ward Barrett provides a study of the successful management of English and French sugar plantations in the West Indies. He describes the efficient use of land, labor, and capital which was essential in this highly competitive industry, the major source of income from colonies in the West Indies. The sugar industry was also a link between three continents, creating a set of Atlantic commercial relations with far-reaching implications.

The African slave trade which grew with the sugar industry was primarily an appendage of the New World economy, yet in the 1680's, as the supply of slaves from the Mediterranean area began to prove inadequate to the needs of French naval policy, the Negro slave was brought into service in the French galleys, and even New France was looked to as a source of oarsmen. This problem of providing slaves for the galleys of Louis the Fourteenth is discussed by Paul Bamford, who shows how this ancient traffic in human beings was related to policies of state, religion, and foreign affairs.

Very early in the age of discovery it became apparent that the Atlantic and Indian oceans were to be the chief highways for an expanded European commerce. Yet for two and a half centuries after Magellan's voyage the attention of explorers and statesmen was often diverted to an imagined continent in the Southern Hemisphere which was believed to extend north into the South Pacific far enough to support a highly civilized population. Much of the early exploration in the vicinity of the Strait of Magellan was related to the belief in this Terra Australis Incognita, of which Tierra del Fuego was believed to be a northern peninsula. Helen Wallis has studied the early English interest in exploring the far southern latitudes, and presents an essay given largely to English knowledge and exploration of this tortuous waterway through a land believed to be peopled with giants. Beyond the strait lies a sprinkling of islands reaching ultimately the East Indian archipelago. It was this other side of the world that had set Spain and Portugal to debating early in the sixteenth century where their respective hemispheres of influence ended. The issue at stake then was the spice islands. In the 1740's the geopolitics of the Pacific was different, yet for small and even nonexistent islands large plans were laid, and the stake was still primarily dominance in commerce. De Lozier Bouvet, a French navigator and colonial governor, was the author of a grandiose scheme to give France a position of pre-eminence in the Pacific through the establishment of a series of island bases which would link up the trade of Europe, the East Indies, and South America. Professor O. H. K. Spate sees in this plan a truly global concept of mercantile and naval strategy that leads him to ask why we have arrogated unto our time the term "global century."

The worldwide aspect of modern commerce which is so frequently emphasized ought not to obscure the intricacies and far-flung nature of the trade of earlier centuries our age has fallen heir to. Indeed, we shall not fully understand the reality of a world laced together by bonds of commerce until we have learned more about the historic development of those bonds. This volume, diversified in its contents, is intended as a contribution and an encouragement to research into many areas of knowledge which will provide this background for an understanding of our own times. In acquiring source materials and in assisting in the publication of the results of research into the history of European commercial expansion, the James Ford Bell Collection hopes to continue the ancient tradition of cooperation between the merchant and the scholar.

Geography
in Fifteenth-Century Florence

by THOMAS GOLDSTEIN

F LORENCE in the quattrocento calls forth associations that have little enough to do with a fairly specialized branch in the history of science. The memories it evokes are of the unfolding of early Renaissance art; the flourishing of humanist studies; the cult of Plato; a setting of lovely churches and palazzi capped by Brunelleschi's cupola — one of the rare moments in history, in short, when a city rose to the heights of the enjoyment of living, amidst the loveliness of the Tuscan hills.

We are not used to thinking of this setting as sheltering scientific studies of major import, least of all a development in geographic theory that paved the way for the age of the great explorations. Nor do our notions of the age of discoveries include a phase of theoretical preparation in which Florence, about two generations before Columbus — at the very height of the early Renaissance — played a significant role. Standard ideas, in fact, have it the other way around: as though the explorers, thrusting into the unknown without benefit of any theoretical insights to speak of, were the cause of a geographic science that was a mere afterthought, crystallizing not before the sixteenth century, at any rate.

The lone exception these notions admit of is the famous "Toscanelli letter" containing the equally famous theory of the "westward route" from Portugal or Spain to the Indies. History presents this often-cited document essentially as a confirmation — one of many — of Columbus's own presumably highly fantastic scheme, in this instance by one of the most eminent and most highly respected scientists of his day. The modern reader is left with the inference that Toscanelli's theory must have been equally fantastic — and that geographic theory before Columbus was of no serious consequence.

Of late years, this image of a naive age — innocent of important scientific thought, steeped in a rarefied atmosphere of pure aesthetics, barren of any major theoretical contribution to the geographic discoveries — has been marred by a number of disturbing findings. To name just a few:

Our growing appreciation of the stature of medieval science makes it increasingly

NOTES for *Geography in Fifteenth-Century Florence* are to be found on pages 26 to 32.

difficult to overlook the sturdy role of geography, roughly since the twelfth century. Geography was by no means a neglected field either among the Arabs — from whom the West inherited an almost complete body of scientific practice and thought — nor among the thirteenth- and fourteenth-century scientific thinkers of the Latin West.[1] Why should this long-standing concern with geographic problems have failed to supply a consistent theoretical basis for the age of discoveries?

The Portuguese expeditions into the eastern Atlantic and down the west coast of Africa since early in the fifteenth century proceeded with such evident circumspection that a thorough grounding in geographic theory — assimilated at Prince Henry the Navigator's home base at Sagres — has by now been universally accepted.[2] Could the Sagres academy have worked in a vacuum, outside any significant context of contemporary European thought?

In 1410 — five years before the first of the Portuguese expeditions — a Florentine humanist, Jacopo Angelo de' Scarperia, completed his Latin translation of the most important compendium of ancient geographical knowledge and theory, Claudius Ptolemaeus's *Geography*. Modern Renaissance specialists have wondered whether the recovery of this vital classical work could really have had no effect upon the thinking of the explorers.[3]

The whole idea that the fifteenth-century Renaissance evolved in a climate of pure aesthetic delight, inhospitable to the rise of science,[4] has come in for serious challenge. Not only was the art of the early Renaissance grounded in solid mathematics, optics, perspective, and anatomy,[5] which had been thriving in Florence since the early quattrocento. Not only did the philological and historical studies of the humanists contribute important elements to the evolution of the modern scientific method.[6] Even the very roots of Renaissance art and architecture have been traced to a body of concepts with far-reaching implications for science — above all a philosophy of space based on a consistent mathematical world view.[7]

The beginnings of modern science, we see with increasing clarity, lie back in the later Middle Ages. The subject of geography — above all intense speculation about the shape of the earth — formed part of this evolution. Nor did the evolution cease during the fifteenth century. The idea of the discoverers groping about in the dark, with no more theoretical backing than a few rather absurd hunches, would seem increasingly to conflict with the perspectives of historical scholarship.

These considerations might be reason enough for a critical return to the available evidence. In point of fact, a close reading of the Toscanelli correspondence itself reveals a far more substantial body of underlying geographic knowledge than the offhand, theoretically worthless suggestion of a westward route would seem to imply. When examined against the background of the history of geographic thought, the purely practical suggestion that the "Indies" could be reached by sailing west proves to be underlain by a major theoretical premise. With one, or perhaps two lone exceptions, unknown to the West until the middle of the fifteenth century, this premise had never been stated before.[8] What it involved was nothing less than a complete revision of the basic concept of the earth: the theory, that is, that the ocean could be used as an intercontinental waterway. Added to this was a second equally revolutionary premise — equally subversive of the entire medieval tradition of geography: that the navigable Ocean Sea included the Southern Hemisphere. Taken together these premises meant the decisive abandonment of the traditional (ancient as well as medieval) concept of the *orbis terrarum* — the idea that a severely foreshortened three-continental land mass (Europe, Asia, and Africa) was forever confined within its own limits by an all-encircling Ocean Sea, conceived of very much as we today look upon outer space, as another orbit,[9] believed to be by its very nature inaccessible to the efforts of man. And it meant, by the same token, the abandonment of the idea that man's habitat was limited to the Northern Hemisphere. It meant the substitution of the modern concept of the earth for the one that — those one or two lone exceptions notwithstanding — had dominated geographic thinking ever since ancient times.

It seems axiomatic that the new concept, with all its psychological and practical implications, could hardly have occurred to Toscanelli out of the blue Florentine sky, while he was writing his letter. Behind it lay in fact an arduous intellectual development. Toscanelli's letter of 1474 represented no more than an exceedingly brief summary of a long and vigorous evolution of geographic thought, whose body had taken shape in Florence more than a generation before, during the earlier part of the fifteenth century, and which had culminated at the time of the Council of Florence.

It was this evolution during the early fifteenth century that formed the historical bridge between the medieval tradition of science and the age of the discoveries. The principal strength and primary inspiration of this process of thought lay in the revival of the best fruits of ancient geography — not the bare philological recovery and translation of the texts, but the active reintegration of the leading classical theories, in particular those of Strabo and Ptolemy. The intellectual conquest of the earth thus preceded Columbus's first voyage by more than half a century — a conquest based on classical sources, the legacy of medieval geographic theory and lore, and the systematic use of contemporary maritime experience and travelers' reports. It had been accomplished in the same place and at the same time that the Renaissance was directing man's senses toward other aspects of his earthly habitat, as an integral part of the process which Jacob Burckhardt has called the "discovery of the world."[10]

Paolo dal Pozzo Toscanelli's famous letter to Columbus is obviously the work of a tired and celebrated old man writing to a young unknown. In a few short lines, with somewhat perfunctory courtesy, "Paul, the Physician" advises young Columbus that some time before — on June 24, 1474, to be exact — he had written about the subject of Columbus's inquiry (that is, the theory of a new route to the spice areas) to an old acquaintance, the canon of the Lisbon cathedral, Fernão Martins. For the young man's benefit he enclosed a copy of that earlier letter as well as a copy of the sailing chart he had sent Martins to illustrate his theory.[11]

[13]

Yet even the letter to Martins, written in Toscanelli's seventy-fifth or seventy-sixth year, is clearly a tight-lipped summary of a highly complex theory, although designed expressly for the benefit of a layman. Reading it with this background in mind, one cannot help feeling that, because of his age and in view of this inexpert (though otherwise distinguished) audience — perhaps also because his own more intense concern with these problems lay by now more than thirty years back — the old scholar did not care to bother with a longer, more detailed explanation: The king of Portugal, he writes, Afonso V, through the services of the good canon, "now seeks from me some statement, or rather a demonstration to the eye, *by which the slightly learned may take in and understand*" [12] his suggestion of a sea route to the spice areas, shorter than the circumnavigation of Africa toward which the Portuguese were then bending their efforts. "I have already spoken with you respecting a shorter way to the places of spices than that which you take by Guinea, *by means of maritime navigation.*" [13]

The marked brevity of his style in dealing with a complicated subject may help to explain the astounding fact that historians have consistently tended to overlook the theoretical premise upon which his proposal was based. Besides, the originality of his thought is further obscured by the presence of two major "errors" in the westward-route proposal: Toscanelli's underestimation of the circumference of the globe,[14] and his obvious ignorance of the existence of the American continent — both common, if not inevitable errors in 1474 — combining, by understandable logic, into a vision of "the Indies" at the western end of the ocean, within a relatively short distance from Europe.

In point of fact, however, the understanding of his proposal required first and foremost an accurate conception of global geography (not just the knowledge that the earth was round, which had been familiar to geographers since antiquity. "Of all the vulgar errors connected with Columbus, the most persistent and the most absurd is that he had to convince people 'the earth was round,'" Samuel Eliot Morison said.) [15] Which was why Toscanelli seems at first to have thought of achieving the requested "demonstration to the eye" by sending a globe along with his letter ("I know this can be shown from the spherical shape of the earth," he writes), but had at last settled for a sailing chart, presumably because the old gentleman found the constructing of a globe a bit too cumbersome.[16]

Actually, despite the reluctant brevity of his style, he tries, as clearly as he can, to evoke a global concept in his reader's mind which is, at least in principle, altogether identical with that of modern geography. Instead of the traditional three-continental land mass of the *orbis terrarum,* surrounded by an impenetrable Ocean Sea, he clearly presupposes an ocean which had become an integral part of the earth, open to navigation, interspersed with habitable land formations. For Toscanelli's mind the entire earth had become accessible to man.

"You must not be surprised," he writes, trying to adjust his reader's vision to this new global view, "if I call the parts where the spices are west, when they usually call them east, because to those sailing west, those parts are found by navigation on the under side of the earth. But if by land and on the upper side, they will always be found to the east." Crucial, succinct, full of new meaning, the sentences look at first glance a little obscure. But for Fernão Martins, for King Afonso V, for Columbus, or for any other contemporary reader, they meant that he had to discard all at once the time-honored notion that the "habitable earth" was wrapped around with a kind of watery orbit. In his mind's eye, he had to link the two ends of the known earth by an enormous navigable waterway, thus in effect constructing a mental image of the modern globe (although still with a much smaller circumference, and as yet limited to three continents — plus whatever land formations the unknown ocean might still contain).[17]

But why "on the under side"? Toscanelli was evidently aware that the bulk of the Sunda archipelago — where most of the spice islands were — is in the Southern Hemisphere, to be reached at least partly "by navigation on the under side of the earth." His implicit premise is that the Southern Hemisphere was navigable, rather than covered by an unnavigable "torrid zone." Offhand one might assume that Portuguese navigation down the African coast had already demonstrated this fact beyond dispute. But in reality the Portuguese had crossed the equator for the first time only the year before, in 1473, under Lopo Gonçalves.[18] (The year is open to question; it may have been 1474.[19] Rui de Sequeira's expedition to Cape Catarina reached there on St. Catherine's Day, November 25, 1474 — possibly 1475,[20] but in any case later than the date of the Toscanelli letter.) What was more, the area covered by these pioneer expeditions extended over no more than one or two degrees S. Strictly speaking then, sufficient evidence did not exist by June 1474 to disprove the age-old belief in a "torrid zone" covering the entire Southern Hemisphere. Nor had the problem, patently of the highest importance for the Portuguese, been completely solved by Ptolemy, whose *Geography* contains some statements implying, mostly by inference and indirection, a rejection of the "torrid zone."[21] Since neither Portuguese maritime experience nor Ptolemy's inferences had firmly established the navigability of the Southern Hemisphere as a whole, Toscanelli's assumption that the spice islands of the Far East could be reached "by navigation on the under side of the earth" is remarkable in putting forth the idea of a navigable lower half of the globe.

Like the concept of a navigable Ocean Sea linking the continents, this assumption reflected a vigorous, original process of thought, synthesizing and transcending fragments of empirical evidence and hypothetical theory to reach definite and independent conclusions. It was the collective process of thought of a group of early fifteenth-century geographers which lay behind Toscanelli's brief but very bold statements.

Though a re-examination of his letter helps to clarify these implications and thereby to establish Toscanelli's precise contribution to the history of geographic

thought, he may in one sense have received too much credit.[22] As long as his letter
to Martins is considered the only important document of fifteenth-century geographic science, he necessarily appears to be the only outstanding scientist of his time
to delve into geographic problems. This view not only overlooks the role of the large
— albeit amorphous — group which had been carrying on geographic discussions (in
which Toscanelli may well have been a guiding spirit, due both to his early training
at the famous School of Padua and to his high achievement in other scientific fields).[23]
It also fails to give proper credit to the often highly informal (by rigid modern standards we might say "dilettante") ways in which early modern science sometimes
reached important results.

Without denying Toscanelli's role as the only known fully qualified scientist
among this motley group — or his apparently magnetic and inspiring personality —
one has to acknowledge that his fame in history rests on his having communicated the
"global" theory to the Portuguese, rather than on any substantial evidence that he
was its exclusive author. Though he was undoubtedly considered an authoritative
spokesman for the new theory, he makes no claim in either of the documents of having originated the new concepts all by himself.

The revision of geographic thought — from the traditional *orbis terrarum* cum
Ocean Sea to global — was unquestionably not the work of only one man. It was
evolved by an apparently sizable group of scholars and dilettantes, mostly with characteristic humanist leanings, between 1410 or shortly thereafter and 1439–1440,
the time of the Council of Florence (and possibly for a few years after that), in a
long series of discussions — informal "symposia" probably similar in setting and atmosphere to those held on loftier subjects at the Platonic Academy, almost half a
century afterward. We do not have a complete list of the participants, nor anything
like a consistent record of the proceedings.[24] In time more light may be thrown on
these discussions by new, more sharply focused research. Some aspects shall probably
remain forever lost to us — not only because of the notorious capriciousness of archi-
vistic history, but because there may have been reasons for conducting these meetings
under cover of relative secrecy.[25] Besides, the very informality of a lively intellectual
exchange — the kind of milieu in which the new concepts were undoubtedly worked
out — may be sufficient reason for the absence of any major geographical studies reflecting the thought processes of this group.[26] But the evidence suffices to show that
a number of well-known humanists took part in these talks;[27] that Florence soon became a center of geographic studies so that interested people from abroad, including
Portugal, would consult with the Florentines; that such eminent scholars as the Byzantine Gemistos Plethon took part in some of these symposia; and above all that the
discussions, however informal, followed a remarkably systematic approach to the
knowledge of the earth and showed vigorous conceptual progress.

The appearance in 1410 of the Latin version of Ptolemy's *Geography* (in itself
an indication in Florence of substantial interest in geography even before 1406, when

Scarperia began his translation)[28] had first loosed a spate of discussions leading to major revisions of the medieval picture of the earth.[29] The identity of the participants in these early discussions is lit up by little more than occasional glimpses — somewhat like faces carved out of the dark by the flicker of a candle. Poggio gives us such a glimpse when he sketches a picture of Niccolò Niccoli, Aeneas Sylvius, and Cosimo Medici bending their heads over a copy of the *Geography* ("Hos ego [i.e., Poggio] Ptolemei Geographiam inspicientes cum imprimis, ut mos est, salutassem").[30] Humanists vied to possess a copy of the Ptolemaic manuscript.[31] The study of the *Geography* stimulated a new interest in cartography which in time resulted in decisive cartographic reforms.[32]

The *Geography* was also studied at Henry the Navigator's Sagres academy. (Diogo Gomes, whose narrative of Henry's activities was later written down by Martin Behaim, reported that one of the Navigator's explicit aims was the exploration of the ocean beyond Ptolemy's scope.)[33] In mid-1428 Henry's older brother, Prince Pedro, came to Florence during a trip devoted to the collecting of maps and general pointers for his brother's enterprise.[34] By that time, the geographic symposia held at various places around Florence and attended by a number of the well-known humanists of the time were undoubtedly well enough advanced for Prince Pedro to find a group of deeply interested men, steeped in the essentials of Ptolemaic geography, enabling him to discuss his brother's enterprise in an unusually qualified group.

How decisively the Florentine group may have influenced Portuguese thinking during these meetings cannot be precisely established until the theoretical evolution of the Sagres school — and Prince Pedro's contribution to it — has been more fully reconstructed.[35] But the possibility might have to be considered in future Portuguese research that that influence may indeed have been marked. The Florentines were at any rate qualified to discuss the two Ptolemaic theories most relevant to the Portuguese project — the extension of the African continent beyond the equator, and the possibility that the Southern Hemisphere might be navigable.[36] Besides, the intense cartographic activities stimulated in Florence by the *Geography*[37] should have confronted Prince Pedro with a highly expert group of mapmakers, well versed in the mathematical implications of cartography, from whom he could get valuable advice on a subject of crucial importance for the Portuguese enterprise. Broadly speaking, what the Florentines had to offer Prince Pedro (and to Portuguese leaders on later occasions) was more than a mere familiarity with the Ptolemaic text. As the study of the evolution of Florentine geographic thought shows, the Florentines were intent upon collecting additional evidence for Ptolemy's theories, in order to have a complete picture of the earth. For example, Ptolemy's inference about the navigability of the Southern Hemisphere could be corroborated by a number of considerations about the navigability of the ocean in general — especially certain conclusions resulting from the geographic position of the spice islands, a problem uppermost in Florentine thought.[38] And the Florentines, out of the same preoccupation with the evolving of a new "global" geography, had reason to be especially interested in the Portuguese explorations of the eastern Atlantic island world (already well advanced by 1428).[39] The exchange of information and ideas on these subjects should have lent the talks with Prince Pedro a global dimension.

In fact, discussion between Florence and Portugal of problems of geography did not end with the Prince's visit. Throughout the fifteenth century Italian merchants in the Iberian peninsula were to act as middlemen in a lively two-way exchange of geographic information and theory.[40] When the Portuguese turned to Toscanelli in the time of Afonso V, through the good offices of Fernão Martins (and, later, when one of his younger associates, Piero Vaglienti, credited him with the original idea for the rounding of the Cape of Good Hope), Florence had been a kind of theoretical storehouse for the Portuguese expeditions, at least on crucial occasions, for quite some time.

In 1439 another distinguished visitor from abroad found himself drawn into the geographic symposia. Gemistos Plethon had come to Florence to attend the sessions of the Ecumenical Council in the entourage of the Byzantine emperor, John VII Palaeologus. During his many fruitful meetings with Florentine humanists he found their geographic interests so one-sidedly Ptolemaic that he decided to round out their view of classical geography with a forceful exposition of the theories of Strabo.[41] Even Plethon, however, succumbed to the Ptolemaic orientation of his Florentine friends with respect to a number of important concepts, so that the result was a lively give and take in which both sides ultimately managed to reconstruct and exchange the essential theories of the two leading geographers of the ancient world, creating an integrated picture of classical geography.[42]

Strabo's influence upon the course of Florentine thought — stemming from Plethon's vigorous advocacy — can clearly be traced, and was in fact highly important.[43] We find the Ptolemaic influence upon Plethon in his *Diórthosis* — or "Correction"; the full title is: "A Correction of Certain Errors Made by Strabo"[44] — written either while he was in Florence or immediately afterward, i.e., under the direct impact of his discussions with the Florentines.[45] One of the Ptolemaic theories he absorbed in this way was the principle of presenting the earth or its segments through spherical projection (which Ptolemy expounds in Book I, ch. XXIV, of the *Geography*).[46]

The critical sifting of Ptolemaic theories was to prove especially fruitful in the field of accurate projection of the earth's surface. Two Florentines, Leon Battista Alberti and Filippo Brunelleschi, pioneers both of Renaissance architecture and of the mathematical principle of perspective, were intrigued by the problem of applying the latter to cartography.[47] Alberti (who developed the final solution of perspective) introduced the principle of polar (or conic) projection in his *Descriptio Urbis Romae*.[48] A simplification of the spherical projection method, it had been suggested by Ptolemy as an alternative. Toward the end of the century both the spherical projection method and the text of the *Geography* itself (in which the method was set forth) combined to bring about the beginning of full-fledged modern cartography. A series of editions of the *Geography,* first in manuscript form, then printed, came to include maps drawn on the Ptolemaic principle; thus Ptolemy's text became, from the sixteenth century on,[49] the prototype of the modern atlas. Florence continued to play a leading part in this development: the terza rima version of the *Geography,* completed in Florence in 1482 by Francesco Berlinghieri,[50] contained a reproduction of the projection employed by Ptolemy himself,[51] and helped to establish the use of the Ptolemaic method in modern cartography.

Several elements predestined the Council of Florence to become the natural setting for a final synthesis of Florentine geographic thought. The council itself had been moved from Ferrara to Florence at Cosimo Medici's invitation, mainly for the purpose of raising the international prestige of Florence.[52] The pageant of delegates from Byzantium, Russia, and the Near and even Far East (as well as from all of Roman Catholic Europe) made Florence for one brief moment the capital of the Christian world. The council's efforts to effect a reconciliation between Western Catholicism and the Eastern church — culminating in a formal agreement to re-establish Christian unity [53] — clearly enhanced its ecumenical importance. By the same token the citizens of Florence were exposed to the dazzle of foreign civilizations. (Some of that exotic glamor has been captured in Benozzo Gozzoli's "Visit of the Magi.") Byzantine scholars such as Plethon made deliberate efforts to help the Florentines get the fullest benefit from this unique cultural opportunity. His geographic expositions were only a minor part of his effort to round out Western knowledge of the ancient legacy — to complement the West's knowledge of Aristotelian philosophy by expounding Plato, and to complement its one-sided Ptolemaic picture of the earth by expounding Strabo.

Geography-minded Florentines found themselves suddenly facing a microcosmic mirror of the known world, aided by an expert interpretation of a body of ancient geographic knowledge and theory that had until then been unknown to them. Toscanelli and his friends seized the opportunity to talk with foreign delegates to the council about remote parts of the earth, filling in details missing from their mental map of the world. In the symposia with Plethon on Strabo's and Ptolemy's major theories — one might imagine the talks with the delegates as taking place mostly in the daytime, during the proceedings of the council; the symposia in the quiet of the Tuscan night — they made spectacular progress in filling the larger gaps in the *terra incognita.*

One of the subjects in the foreground of both the discussions and the talks with the council delegates was the geography of the Far East. The entire land mass to the east of India had been hazy ever since antiquity. Strabo had thought of all Asia as an indistinct land complex, calling it "India" (the term "Indies" in the Toscanelli correspondence still reflects this traditional haziness; in fact, despite the clarifying efforts at the time of the council, maps into the sixteenth century still tend to fade out in the

Far East [54] — an indication of how very gradual was the focusing on that part of the world). Of the Southeast Asian island world Strabo merely mentions one major formation, "Taprobane," presumably a legendary elaboration upon reports about Ceylon. [55] Ptolemy — who wrote some hundred and fifty years later — was a great deal more specific in visualizing a distinct land mass to the east of India which he calls Sinae. He also saw a multitudinous island world. [56]

The Middle Ages had turned the whole world east and southeast of India into a vast, glittering stage for their exotic legends, though the more practical influence of travelers like Marco Polo can occasionally be traced on medieval maps. The Florentines had a particular reason for trying to clarify their picture of this remote part of the earth: their keen interest in the location of the spice islands. [57] Toscanelli appears to have taken copious notes from his talks with the council delegates, among whom was an emissary from "the country of the Great Khan," with whom he had a "long conversation . . . on many subjects, about the magnitude of their rivers in length and breadth, and on the multitude of cities on the banks of the rivers," as he was much later to recall in his letter to Martins. [58] Toscanelli amassed a great many notes about geographic subjects during his life (when the news of Columbus's discovery began to stir up the old interests, Ercole d'Este instructed his Florentine ambassador to recover Toscanelli's notes from his nephew). [59] The fate of his notes is unknown, but we may safely assume that his collection included those he took during the council.

Plethon too was keenly interested in the Far East. His "Correction" of Strabo shows that he absorbed important new information about the area while in Florence. [60] His sources may have been three: conversations with delegates, similar to Toscanelli's fact-gathering talks; the store of medieval travelers' reports (like Marco Polo's), available in the West; and Ptolemy's superior picture of Far Eastern geography. [61] The Florentines would have introduced him to the last two of these sources. Even if he was familiar with Ptolemy, as has been assumed, [62] before coming to Florence, the Ptolemaic imprint on his revisions of Strabo is so unmistakable that they clearly reflect the persuasive arguments of the Florentine followers of Ptolemy. But the whole Far Eastern problem was no doubt bandied about during their meetings. Part of his "Correction," incidentally, shows clearly that he too talked with delegates about various other parts of the world — with, for example, Isidore of Kiev and his fellow delegates about details of the geography of Russia. [63] Fact-gathering as well as the exchange of ideas was obviously intense on both sides.

Approximately at that time — probably during the council and while Plethon was there — the Florentines heard a report by a Venetian traveler, Niccolò de' Conti, who had been some twenty-five years in the East. [64] His detailed picture of the Southeast Asian island world [65] gave the Florentines important knowledge about an area they were particularly interested in. [66] When Toscanelli in the letter to Martins refers to an unspecified source of information about the Far East and its islands (in phrases like "it is asserted that . . . ," "they affirm that . . ."), the source was presumably Conti.

One listener was so fascinated by what Conti had to tell that he took detailed notes and later incorporated a transcription of them in his own works. As a reminder that these painstaking efforts to piece together a consistent picture of the earth were considered an exciting subject by eminent humanists we should note that the listener was Poggio Bracciolini.[67]

While the substance of these discussions (and their precise step-by-step evolution) remains somewhat shadowy in the absence of direct documentary evidence, we are aided by at least four major elements in reconstructing the essentials of Florentine geographic theory. They are (a) our knowledge of the discussions' point of departure; (b) our equally firm knowledge of the final result; (c) our knowledge of the major sources from which they drew their inspiration in piecing together a new concept of the globe; and (d) the inner logic of a thought process which, through several decades and many sessions of informal give and take (including, no doubt, countless trips over detours and up blind alleys), could essentially have followed only one course to arrive where it did.

The point of departure — to look ahead before tracing that thought process in more detail — was the Florentines' paramount interest in finding a new route to the spice islands. The final result, we know, was the premise of the Toscanelli letter: the theory of the navigability of the Ocean Sea, its place as an intercontinental waterway within a new, global concept of the earth. Their major sources, as we have seen, were first Ptolemy, then Strabo, and later the integration of these geographies, achieved during the exchanges between the Toscanelli group and Gemistos Plethon. Even without any more solid evidence on this point than the lively geographic communications between Florence and Portugal after Prince Pedro's visit, it is evident that the news of the progress of the Portuguese discoveries roughly till 1440 (i.e., up to the passing of Cape Bojador and a little further down the coast; and the exploration of the Madeira group, the Canary Islands, and the Azores) presented an additional vital source for the Florentines. We may assume with equal certainty that the Florentines studied the classical geographers principally for what they had to add to traditional medieval knowledge. Pierre d'Ailly's famous *Imago Mundi* (completed about 1410 and not yet influenced by Ptolemy's *Geography*)[68] can be considered a representative, up-to-date version of that tradition.

Lastly, while we are trying to retrace the thought process by which the Florentines arrived at a totally new concept of the earth, the other three elements will always have to be kept in mind.

Although the humanists were naturally attracted to the geographic symposia by the opportunity to delve into highly detailed aspects of ancient thought — and by a characteristic Renaissance pleasure in exploring foreign civilizations and countries, or in other words "the earth" [69] — the primary motive of the discussions was a great deal more pragmatic, if not downright commercial.

In both the letters Toscanelli stated the object of his proposal in unambiguously commercial terms — as a new "way to where the spices grow." Moreover, when writing to Columbus ("I perceive your magnificent and great desire to find a way to where the spices grow"), he implied that this desire had also been the object of Columbus's original inquiry. Both men had been active in the spice trade — Toscanelli as a member of his family's firm,[70] Columbus as an associate of several Genoese business groups.[71] And if it is not altogether certain whether Columbus, in his activities as an independent merchant on Porto Santo (where he established himself about 1480), continued to deal in spices,[72] he was definitely engaged in trade at the time he wrote to Toscanelli.

Most of the Italian businessmen in Portugal and Spain who transmitted geographic information between Italy and the Iberian Peninsula for the better part of the fifteenth century were also engaged in the spice business.[73] One of this group, Piero Vaglienti of Pisa (who collected reports on the voyages of discovery), commented upon Bartholomeu Dias's rounding of the Cape of Good Hope by neatly summing up the commercial result: "And thus an enterprise has been carried out that arouses the admiration of the whole world. The spices that should, or used to, go to Cairo by way of the Red Sea are now carried to Lisbon by this other route, and with this the Sultan has lost some five or six thousand ducats a year, and the Venetians the same." [74]

What Vaglienti was referring to was the historic reason behind the search for a new route, from the Florentines to the Portuguese and, finally, Columbus. By the fifteenth century the Turkish advances and other upheavals in the Near East had seriously dislocated traditional trade patterns, with the Turks imposing heavy tolls upon the European traders. Though a few privileged commercial groups faced with this problem succeeded either in offsetting their losses by virtually monopolizing the remaining import routes (like the Venetians),[75] or in avoiding the high tolls to the sultan through a kind of "most-favored-nation" agreement (like Lorenzo Medici's firm) — though a few solved the problem in these ways, less-favored business groups, in Italy and outside, were casting about for a more profitable business based on a direct access to the spice-producing areas.[76] It was this situation which led not only to a substantial transfer of Italian capital to Portugal and Spain,[77] but also to the intense intellectual efforts to find an alternative route, an effort that eventually required nothing less than a radical revision of the concept of the globe.

We shall have to envisage this background in order to appreciate why the recovery of first Ptolemy and then Strabo held such exciting new implications for the Florentines.

The first thing Ptolemy did for his fifteenth-century readers was to put the Far East, including its spice-producing island world, in sharper focus.[78] His notion of a great multitude of Southeast Asian islands agreed with Marco Polo's (and, later, Conti's) reports. But how could one reach these islands if not over the age-old spice routes across Asia, now the scene of intensified rivalry among the chief European economic powers? Traditional medieval notions offered no conceivable alternative. To the new approaches the fifteenth century was finally to work out, Pierre d'Ailly's *Imago Mundi* opposed three distinct traditional barriers.

Toward the east, Asia (including its island world) was blocked by the surrounding, proverbially impenetrable Ocean Sea. (D'Ailly restated this Homeric conception in authoritative terms in his chapter "De Mari" — although mentioning, with somewhat chilly sarcasm, that "quidam moderni philosophi" had begun to question this time-honored belief.) [79] The Far East, then, could certainly not be reached "by sailing west."

If the spice islands, on the other hand, were in the Indian Ocean (as d'Ailly — and with him, of course, the Florentine geographers — knew),[80] here was a second, additional barrier: for d'Ailly — in fact for virtually the entire geographic tradition from antiquity through the Middle Ages — the Indian Ocean appeared landlocked, blocked by a major land mass, toward the east. The only way to reach it was by an eastward voyage which d'Ailly thought would take about a year.[81]

As for reaching the spice islands by sailing around Africa, the very idea of the impenetrable Ocean Sea surrounding all three continents, obviously precluded that.

Ptolemy's *Geography* destroyed at least two of these traditional barriers. By introducing the concept of an African continent extending considerably south of the equator (i.e., to $16°25'S$) (Book VII, ch. V), he not only replaced the highly contracted northern sliver of the ancient — and later, again, medieval — maps by a far more accurate image, but, what was more decisive, he suggested that the Southern Hemisphere was at least partly inhabitable (Book IV, ch. VIII). To the early fifteenth century this meant the exciting possibility that the traditional "torrid zone" (in which ships would burn to a crisp and white men turn black) did not in fact cover the southern half of the globe. It gave impressive encouragement to Henry the Navigator's efforts to reach "the Indies" by sailing around the African continent.[82] And the Florentines might have detected at least an encouraging general implication: that an Ocean Sea without a torrid zone might perhaps be accessible to ships. The idea was startling enough to cause Plethon to correct Strabo on this point.[83]

Ptolemy is not, however, explicit in suggesting that the ocean could be used as a waterway (some modern scholarly assumptions notwithstanding).[84] Nor — again contrary to a modern assumption — did he doubt that the Indian Ocean was "landlocked." [85] It was Strabo through Plethon's advocacy, who on both these points supplied the missing pieces. Though Strabo had no clear idea of the Indian Ocean as such (the term does not even occur in his voluminous work),[86] nor of the Southeast Asian island world,[87] the startling idea fifteenth-century geographers did find in him was that the Asiatic land mass as a whole, south as well as east, was washed by the Ocean

Sea. ("But the Southern and Eastern sides [of 'India'] which are much greater than the other two, extend out into the Atlantic sea," he had said.) [88]

What this meant was neither more nor less than that Southeast Asia, including its island world (which the Florentines had come to see with growing clarity),[89] was accessible from the east — or, as Toscanelli was to put it in his letter, by "always sailing west." Provided, of course, that the ocean was indeed navigable in all directions.

The final, and all-important, conclusion that the Ocean Sea was open to navigation was prepared for by several cumulative pieces of evidence, and should therefore have been reached in a series of corresponding steps.

1. Portuguese navigation since 1415 demonstrated progressively that the eastern Atlantic, at least as far out as the Azores, as well as southward down the African coast, was indeed navigable, at least for a relatively short distance offshore.

2. Portuguese exploration of Atlantic island groups inevitably suggested the likelihood of additional land formations farther out. Since the discovered islands turned out to be habitable (permitting an island-hopping kind of sailing between them), the Ocean Sea was evidently not an alien element, destructive of human life (an assumption which a host of medieval legends had perpetuated).[90]

3. Strabo's over-all conception of Asia implied that its island world — instead of being situated in a landlocked Indian Ocean — jutted out into the surrounding Ocean Sea. Strabo actually said as much, at least regarding the one major island formation of which he was aware: "We have strong assurance that Taprobane is a large island *in the open sea, which lies off India to the South . . ."* [91] The open sea, south of "India," was for Strabo the surrounding ocean, as we have seen. The same assumptions (1 and 2 above) would have to hold true when the Ocean Sea was regarded from its Asiatic end, as from the eastern or "Atlantic." Before the discovery of the New World, the Atlantic and Pacific were of course thought of as one sea; in other words, the ocean must be navigable and its land formations accessible from both ends. Incidentally, the reasonable assumption of possible further, as yet unknown land formations was also true of the ocean when viewed from the Asiatic shore.

Speculation that the Ocean Sea might contain land formations, possibly entire continents — and thus be able to accommodate human life — was by no means altogether new. A thin thread of this kind of speculation had run from Plato's *Timaeus* through the late Graeco-Roman and medieval world all the way into the fifteenth century.[92]

The Middle Ages had made their own contribution to this age-old tradition by peopling the Ocean Sea with legendary islands. Our modern concept of "legendary" should not preclude our realization that the Middle Ages thought these islands were real.[93] Moreover, the *Timaeus,* with its assumption of a mid-oceanic continent, Atlantis, was well known during the Middle Ages.[94] During the fifteenth century all this long-standing speculation about oceanic land formations (including the idea that the ocean was accessible to man and hospitable to human life) generated a new spate of similar prognostications, culminating in Lorenzo Buonincontri's emphatic statement in 1476 that the existence of a "fourth continent" had become a foregone conclusion.[95]

If all these elements were by their very nature at best inferential and speculative (although undoubtedly influential for a systematic approach to the problem of the ocean's navigability), in Strabo the Florentines found at last the definite suggestion that the ocean could be crossed from east to west.[96] More importantly, Strabo's hypothetical statement to this effect (based on Eratosthenes) emerges from a distinctly global conception of the habitable earth, with the ocean forming an integral part of the habitable globe — and the further idea that it might contain habitable land formations, possibly entire continents. "The inhabited world," he wrote, "forms a complete circle, itself meeting itself; so that if the immensity of the Atlantic Sea did not prevent, we could sail from Iberia to India along one and the same parallel over the remainder of the circle." [97] Strabo explicitly points out in this context that the concept of the "habitable earth" (or *oikouméne*) should not be limited to the traditional three-continental land mass. "It is possible," he wrote, "that in the same temperate zone [i.e., that inhabited by us] there are actually two inhabited worlds, or even more, and particularly in the proximity of the parallel through Athens that is drawn across the Atlantic Sea." [98]

Strabo (basing his theories on a long tradition of Greek geographic thought which had assumed the sphericity of the earth since the time of Pythagoras in the sixth century B.C.) [99] conveyed to the Florentines his original — though inspired by Eratosthenes — concept of a navigable Ocean Sea embedded in a global concept of the habitable earth. The mere mathematical assumption that the earth was a sphere had of course not in itself affected the belief that the human habitat was limited to a small portion of the globe, a portion hedged in by a hostile and impenetrable element. Like Toscanelli's letter, Strabo's practical suggestion (tossed off as a mere hypothesis) formed part of a comprehensive theory of the globe. Just as for Toscanelli the novelty of his conception was in his emphasis upon the ocean as a potential intercontinental waterway, containing habitable land formations as well as being navigable — the navigability qualified only by a mention of the ocean's "immensity," and not specifying any inherently hostile properties.

For the process of global reconstruction in which the Florentines were engaged Strabo supplied a classical conceptual framework. But then the fifteenth century was ahead of Strabo's time in a crucial, practical way: Portuguese maritime experience had added an empirical element to classical theory.

Florentine thought in the fifteenth century had progressed by stages to a conception of the modern globe. The Far East and its spice islands had moved into sharper focus. The site of these islands — the Indian Ocean — had been mentally unlocked toward the east, made accessible across the Ocean Sea. Old *Oceanus* itself had been moved from its orbital status, integrated with the habitable world, tamed for the existence of human life, opened up for navigation. The Southern Hemisphere had been wrested from its "torrid" state — always by a mental combination of actual maritime or travelers' experience and classical theory — opened up for human life and navigation as well. The modern globe was ready, mentally and in outline at any rate. The spice islands could be approached "by navigation," sailing from east to west, even "on the under side of the earth."

All that was missing was an explorer's boldness to demonstrate the validity of the new theories, and, of course, such further details or refinements as an accurate measuring of the circumference of the earth (for which Magellan's voyage supplied the empirical basis); the discovery of the New World and its identification as a separate continent (for which Amerigo Vespucci supplied the data); the recognition of the separate identities of the Atlantic and Pacific oceans (based on Nuñez de Balboa's original observations); and the discovery and exploration in detail of the remaining continents — until the modern globe would at last be complete. Yet the fundamental principle of modern geography, even including a basically accurate cartographic method, had been developed in full, through a forceful adaptation of classical theory to fifteenth-century practical experience, by an impressive thought process, in the shadow of the quattrocento Renaissance.

NOTES

page 12

[1] See Boies Penrose, *Travel and Discovery in the Renaissance*, New York, 1962, pp. 11ff., for a brief, up-to-date survey. Pliny's *Natural History,* including its four books on geography, was used as a textbook throughout the Middle Ages (see A. C. Crombie, *Medieval and Early Modern Science*, New York, 1959, vol. 1, p. 11). Ptolemaic concepts had been reaching the West through the Arabs (through Edrisi's influence and through the *Almagest*, as well as through John of Holywood's abstract of the latter, the *Sphaera Mundi*) since the twelfth century. See Penrose, *op. cit.*, pp. 11f.; Philip K. Hitti, *The Arabs: A Short History,* Chicago, 1956, p. 149. For Albertus Magnus's, Roger Bacon's, and other thirteenth- and fourteenth-century scholars' mostly Aristotelian speculations on geographic subjects, see also R. Beazley, *The Dawn of Modern Geography*, Oxford, 1897–1906, vol. 3, p. 502 (and *passim*).

[2] See Penrose, *op. cit.*, pp. 45f. Carlos Coimbra, "O Infante e o objectivo geografico dos descobrimentos," in *Actas do Congresso Internacional de Historia dos Descobrimentos*, Lisbon, 1961, vol. 4, pp. 77ff., gives an idea of the extremely inferential nature of our information on this subject so far.

[3] Thus B. L. Ullman, *Studies in the Renaissance*, Rome, 1955, pp. 22f.: "Perhaps we should start anew to test, cautiously and scientifically, the impact of the Renaissance on the various aspects of civilization . . . Did the enormous influence of the translation of Ptolemy's Geography, finished in 1410 by Iacopo Angeli da Scarperia . . . have a bearing on the voyages of discovery?" See also *ibid.*, p. 23, n. 25.

[4] See, e.g., John H. Randall, Jr., *The Making of the Modern Mind*, Cambridge, Mass., 1940 (rev. ed. 1954), pp. 212f.

[5] See Rudolph Wittkower, *Architectural Principles in the Age of Humanism*, 2nd ed., London, 1952; Erwin Panofsky, "The History of the Theory of Human Proportions as a Re-

flection of the History of Styles," in *Meaning in the Visual Arts*, New York, 1955, pp. 55–107; Erwin Panofsky, "Das perspektivische Verfahren Leone Battista Albertis," in *Kunstchronik*, vol. 25, August 1915, pp. 504–516.

[6] See the valid survey in Myron P. Gilmore, *The World of Humanism*, New York, 1952, pp. 254ff.

[7] See Joan Gadol, "Leon Battista Alberti: The Renaissance of Geometric Space in Art and Science," Columbia University dissertation, 1963.

page 13

[8] I.e., Strabo (see below, p. 25), who, in his crucial passage, explicitly refers to Eratosthenes as the original author of the concept. Sporadic speculation about habitable parts of the globe, outside of the *oikouméne*, occurs in Greek thought since Plato; see also note 92 below. Some of this is echoed during the Middle Ages; see Penrose, *op. cit.*, pp. 12f. However, for the evolution of geographic theory one will have to keep in mind that all this speculation lacked Strabo's solid conceptual context. The same is true for Pierre d'Ailly's extremely casual remark about the navigability of the Ocean "if the wind be fair," in his *Cosmologiae Tractatus Duo*, c.1414. The fact that Columbus was excited about d'Ailly's remark — see Samuel Eliot Morison, *Admiral of the Ocean Sea: A Life of Christopher Columbus*, Boston, 1942, p. 93 — speaks for Columbus's fairly crude theoretical understanding, not for the importance of d'Ailly's revised theories for the evolution of a systematic concept of the earth.

[9] See below, p. 23, for Pierre d'Ailly's restatement of this classical concept in his *Imago Mundi*, c.1410. Lloyd A. Brown, *The Story of Maps*, Boston, 1950, mentions a Sumerian (or Akkadian) clay tablet, c.2300 or 2100, depicting the Oceanus river (p. 33) and discusses the Homeric concept (pp. 22f.). The idea of the surrounding Ocean river is entirely endemic to ancient and medieval cartography — the latter from Cosmas in the sixth century through the fifteenth century, up to Toscanelli's and Behaim's times — with a highly qualified implication in Ptolemy's *Geography* the only major exception (see below, p. 23), and, of course, Strabo's totally different concept (see note 8 above).

[10] For an argument in support of the continued validity of the Burckhardtian view of the Renaissance, see Thomas Goldstein, "Medieval Civilization from the World-Historical View," in *Journal of World History*, UNESCO, vol. 6, 1960, no. 3, pp. 503ff. (especially p. 505, n. 7).

[11] For a critical evaluation of the Toscanelli correspondence see Norbert Sumien, *La Correspondence du savant florentin Paolo del Pozzo Toscanelli avec Christophe Colomb*, Paris, 1927.

page 14

[12] The version used here is C. R. Markham's translation from the Latin in *The Journal of Christopher Columbus*, London, 1893, *Works Issued by the Hakluyt Society*, vol. 86 (italics mine).

[13] Toscanelli and Martins may have discussed the subject at length (and Toscanelli may thus have felt that he could rely on Martins's more elaborate explanations to the king) at the house of Nicholas Cusanus in San Pietro in Vincoli in Rome, where the three men met frequently during Cusanus's last years (Cusanus died in 1464). See Gustavo Uzielli, *La Vita ed i tempi di Paolo del Pozzo Toscanelli; ricerche e studi*, part V, vol. 1 of *Raccolta di documenti e studi pubblicati dalla R. Commissione Colombiana pel quarto centenario della scoperta dell'America* (from here on cited as Uzielli, *vita*), Rome, 1894, pp. 261ff. See also Paolo Rotta, *Nicolò Cusano*, Milan, 1942, pp. 111, 297. Martins together with Toscanelli witnessed Cusanus's testament.

[14] See the discussion of the circumference problem in Morison, *op. cit.*, pp. 64ff. Eratosthenes's near-accurate calculation had been lost in the tradition.

[15] Morison, *op. cit.*, p. 33. For the history and implications of the spheric concept since antiquity see W. G. L. Randles, *Quelques modifications apportées par les grandes découvertes à la conception médiévale du monde*, Lisbon, 1959, p. 5; Lloyd A. Brown, *op. cit.*, pp. 25ff.

[16] Toscanelli suggests two reasons why he preferred to send a portolano instead of a globe ("yet, to make the comprehension of it easier, *and to facilitate the work*, I have determined to show that way by means of a sailing chart"). One tends to suspect that the first reason is somewhat spurious — his global theory should

have been easier to demonstrate with the help of a globe than a portolano — so that the real reason should have been that the producing of a chart involved less effort.

page 15

[17] "Et non miremini, si voco occidentales partes ubi sunt aromata, cum communiter dicantur orientales, quia navigantibus per subterraneas navigationes ad occidentem semper illae partes inveniuntur; si, enim, per terram et per superiora itinera, ad orientem semper reperientur."

The scope of his theory becomes more evident if one compares Toscanelli's sailing chart with the earth as presented on earlier maps, still dominated by the notion of the surrounding Ocean Sea. Since both copies of his chart are lost, one might consult the reconstruction in Uzielli, *vita*. Both of Toscanelli's letters contain sufficiently specific references, including distances, to permit an essentially accurate reconstruction. See also the discussion in Sumien, *op. cit.*, p. 3; also H. Wagner, "Die Rekonstruktion der Toscanelli-Karte vom Jahre 1474 und die Pseudo-Faksimilia des Behaim-Globus vom Jahre 1492," *Goettinger Gelehrte Nachrichten,* Philosophisch-Historische Klasse (1894), pp. 208ff. (The Latin text of the letter to Martins can be found, e.g., in Sumien, *op. cit.*, pp. 9ff.) On the assumption of land formations inside the Ocean, see n. 92 and n. 95 below.

[18] See Penrose, *op. cit.*, p. 55; Damião Peres, *A History of the Portuguese Discoveries*, Lisbon, 1960, p. 48.

[19] Peres, *op. cit.*, places Gonçalves's and de Sequeira's discoveries between 1474 and 1475.

[20] *Ibid.*

[21] See below, p. 23.

page 16

[22] The principal studies about Toscanelli are by Gustavo Uzielli (see n. 13 for his monumental *vita*). Through a lifetime of enthusiastic devotion Uzielli managed to collect many essential documents and to establish Toscanelli's important contribution to the age of discoveries. Although subsequent historians have largely relied on Uzielli's work (see, e.g., Germán Arciniegas, *Amerigo and the New World: The Life and Times of Amerigo Vespucci*, New York, 1955), a critical re-examination of his conclusions and evidence would seem indicated

in view of his heavily apologetic bias, aiming at establishing Toscanelli's fame. Uzielli fully recognizes the role of the informal discussions of geographic subjects (in which Toscanelli participated) on which this essay is focused, and in fact has assembled most of the available evidence (Arciniegas's *Amerigo* contains additional significant material). He fails, however, to give a consistent reconstruction of the evolution of geographic theory in these debates, for which Professor Anastos's study has supplied a crucial element (see below, n. 42ff.).

[23] For Toscanelli's studies at the School of Padua, see Uzielli, *vita*, pp. 13ff. (See Uzielli, *vita*, pp. 22ff. for a detailed survey of his education.) The influence of the Padua tradition should be viewed in the light of John H. Randall, Jr.'s *The School of Padua and the Emergence of Modern Science* (especially ch. I, "The Development of the Scientific Method in the School of Padua"), Padua, 1961. For Toscanelli's only surviving manuscript, concerning problems of astronomy, geodesy, and geography (including the location of the manuscript in the Florentine Biblioteca Nazionale Centrale, which should be verified or relocated), see Uzielli, *vita*, p. 452.

[24] A detailed survey can be found in G. Uzielli, *Paolo dal Pozzo Toscanelli iniziatore della scoperta d'America*, Florence, 1892 (with appendix of documentary sources, "Osservazioni e documenti"), pp. 76, 208n, 209n. Also his *vita*, pp. 54ff., 72ff. Uzielli places these meetings in the Convento degli Angeli at Camaldoli in the years between 1420 and 1440. He lists Toscanelli, Leonardo Bruni, Palla Strozzi, Antonio Corbinelli, Filippo Pieruzzi, and Niccolò Niccoli among the participants. Arciniegas, *op. cit.*, pp. 45ff., discusses a continuation of these meetings at the Badia a Settimo. Unfortunately, his inspiring study works without consistent source references.

[25] Uzielli, *vita*, pp. 475ff. and *passim* assumes Toscanelli and his friends were conducting these discussions, at any rate after Cosimo's return in 1434, in the shadow of potential persecution by the Medici and those who shared the effective power over Florence with them. Uzielli's thesis seems to have been implicitly accepted by Arciniegas, *op. cit.*, pp. 85ff. Though Uzielli presents some telling evidence on the connection of the geographers with the anti-Medici opposition, the political undercur-

rents of fifteenth-century Florence may have to be clarified more thoroughly before the underground character of these meetings could be considered as established. However, economic motives for escaping the prohibitive Medici taxation through outside investments may have been strong (see below, n. 77); and it is noteworthy that the discussions seem to have been held consistently at some distance from the city. On the tendency of the contemporary governments to keep matters of geographic discovery a secret, see Jaime Cortesão, *The National Secret of the Portuguese Discoveries of the 15th Century*, London, n.d.; Morison, *op. cit.*, p. 344.

[26] See Pearl Kibre, "Intellectual Interests as Reflected in 14th and 15th Century Libraries," *Journal of the History of Ideas*, vol. 7, 1946, pp. 257ff., on the fact that fifteenth-century libraries contain little else on the subject of geography than maps or the texts of classical geographers. A careful study of the correspondence and other writings of the contemporary humanists (even on subjects not overtly related to geography) may yet produce a tenuous accumulation of supporting evidence through which the evolution of certain concepts — and, above all, the scope of humanist interest in these matters — might be more palpably traced.

[27] See n. 24 above. Specialized studies of the geographic interests of the fifteenth-century humanists, made on the basis of the available evidence, include Siegmund Günther, "Der Humanismus in seinem Einfluss auf die Entwicklung der Erdkunde," *Heffners Geographische Zeitschrift*, vol. 6, 1900, pp. 65ff.; Waldemar Sensburg, "Poggio Bracciolini und Nicolo de' Conti in ihrer Bedeutung für die Geographie des Rennaisse-Zeitalters," *Mitteilungen der K. K. Geographischen Gesellschaft in Wien*, vol. 48, 1905, pp. 257ff.; Alfred Berg, *Enea Silvio de' Piccolomini in seiner Bedeutung als Geograph* (Ein Beitrag zur Geschichte der Erdkunde im Quattrocento), Halle a.S., 1901. Besides these, G. Voigt, *Enea Piccolomini und sein Zeitalter*, Berlin, 1862, 2 vols., contains interesting material on Aeneas Sylvius's geographic interests. Arciniegas's cited study of Vespucci offers a wealth of material embedding Amerigo's education in the background of geographic studies in Florence since early in the fifteenth century. There seems little doubt that

humanist concern for geographic questions was first stimulated by the Florentine discussions; see below, pp. 17 and 20, for Aeneas Sylvius's and Conti's connections with this group.

page 17

[28] The possibility that the translation may have been begun by Chrysoloras has been suggested by Brown, *op. cit.*, p. 145. Scarperia may at any rate have been urged to undertake the translation by the man who introduced the study of Greek at the "Studio fiorentino."

[29] See below, pp. 18, 22, 23.

[30] Poggio Bracciolini, *De Infelicitate principis.*, op. 392 (cited in Sensburg, *op. cit.*, p. 342, n. 1).

[31] See, e.g., Sensburg, *op. cit.*, p. 342, about Poggio writing to Niccolò Niccoli concerning his desire to own a copy of the *Geography*.

[32] See below, p. 19.

[33] See D. Peres, *op. cit.*, pp. 24f.

[34] Prince Pedro, sometime around June, "tornò in casa di Matteo Scolari dall'albergo della Corona" (Uzielli, *Toscanelli iniziatore*, p. 73). See *ibid.*, pp. 73ff. and 208n for a discussion of Dom Pedro's probable moves in Florence.

[35] See n. 2 above. Also R. Beazley, *Prince Henry the Navigator*, London, n.d. The plain fact is that the reconstruction of Portuguese geographic theory, despite the intense interest of Portuguese historians, has made little headway so far. This is partly due to the scarcity of direct evidence, and partly, perhaps, to a general omission of attempts to reconstruct fifteenth-century geographic thought as a serious phase in the history of science.

[36] See also below, p. 20.

[37] See below, p. 17.

[38] See below, p. 21.

page 18

[39] By that time, the Portuguese had explored the Madeira group, the Canary Islands, and, in all probability, the Azores; see Penrose, *op. cit.*, pp. 46f.; D. Peres, *op. cit.*, pp. 30ff.

[40] See Charles Verlinden, "Les Découvertes portugaises et la collaboration italienne d'Alphonse IV à Alphonse V," *Actas do Congresso Internacional de Historia dos Descobrimentos*, Lisbon, 1961, vol. 3, pp. 593ff. (who discusses several instances of Italian contributions to fifteenth-century Portuguese discoveries). Actually, examples where Italian businessmen in

the Iberian Peninsula have played a crucial role in the transmission of geographic information are strikingly frequent and would deserve a special study: e.g., Columbus's contact with Toscanelli was arranged by Lorenzo Berardi (Morison, *op. cit.*, pp. 83f.), who belonged to a Florentine business firm with branch offices in Lisbon and Seville (cf. Uzielli, *vita*, p. 498). Giovanni (Gianetto) Berardi (friend of Amerigo Vespucci's first employer, Lorenzo di Pier Francesco de' Medici, and himself Vespucci's employer after 1492) brought about Vespucci's meeting with Columbus and may have helped finance Columbus's second voyage. The story, somewhat spread out through Arciniegas's volume, can be pieced together with the help of his index, by looking under "Berardi, Gianetto." Bartolomeo Marchionni, member of a Florentine house in Lisbon, was credited by Piero Vaglienti with having conveyed Toscanelli's support for Bartholomeu Dias's rounding of the Cape of Good Hope to the Portuguese court (Arciniegas, *op. cit.*, pp. 111f., 198). Piero Vaglienti, a Florentine with a small business firm in Pisa who collected reports on the Portuguese (and, later, Spanish) voyages, had grown up in the firm of Benedetto Dei, a Florentine businessman who was an authority on foreign travel, especially the geography of the interior of Africa (a subject evidently of primary importance for the Portuguese) (Arciniegas, *op. cit.*, pp. 111f., 125).

[41] See M. V. Anastos, "Pletho, Strabo and Columbus," *Annuaire de l'Institut de Philologie et d'Histoire Orientales et Slaves*, vol. 12, 1952, Brussels, *Mélanges Henri Grégoire, IV*, pp. 6f.

[42] Professor Anastos's highly stimulating study clearly establishes that Plethon, during his stay in Florence, met Toscanelli (and apparently others associated with the geographic symposia), and that, when confronted with the one-sided cult of Ptolemy among the Florentines, he countered by expounding Strabo's theories (especially where these conflicted with Ptolemy), thus bringing knowledge of Strabo to the West quite some time before Guarino da Verona's translation, completed in 1458, or that by Gregory Tiphernias (who finished his translation of books 11–17 of the *Geographikà* in 1456). (See Anastos, *op. cit.*, pp. 10, 11.) What Anastos fails to recognize is that the rather substantial corrections in Plethon's own

geographic concepts, as evident from his explicit corrections of Strabo's geography, clearly reflect Ptolemaic influence (except for some detail which he had obviously gathered from individual Council delegates) (see Anastos, *op. cit.*, p. 3). Therefore, the analysis of the substance of the theories which were assimilated by both sides on this occasion can leave no doubt that an extensive exchange of Strabonic and Ptolemaic views took place during the Council of Florence, and that the discussions between Plethon and the Florentines must have been thorough enough to allow what amounted to an essential integration of classical geographic thought.

[43] See Anastos, *op. cit.*, pp. 7, 13ff. for further discussion.

[44] See Anastos, *op. cit.*, pp. 1f.

[45] *Ibid.*

[46] See Anastos, *op. cit.*, p. 3, on Plethon criticizing Strabo for his un-Ptolemaic view that meridians may be represented by straight lines. Several of the other criticisms clearly reflect Ptolemaic concepts (see below). (Joseph Fischer, *C. Ptolemaes Geographiae Codex Urbinas Graecus 82 Phototypice Depictus*, Leyden-Leipzig, 1932.)

[47] See Günther, *op. cit.*, p. 86.

[48] See Gadol, *op. cit.*; Brown, *op. cit.*, pp. 69f.

page 19

[49] Brown, *op. cit.*, pp. 152ff.

[50] See Arciniegas, *op. cit.*, p. 94.

[51] Brown, *op. cit.*, p. 155.

[52] The role of the intangibles of prestige in Cosimo Medici's policy (and of Eugene the Fourth's and the Council of Florence's place within his scheme) is well presented in Ferdinand Schevill, *The Medici*, New York, 1949, pp. 70ff.

[53] Schevill, *op. cit.*, p. 74.

page 20

[54] Cf., e.g., the Mercator map of the world of 1538 (see A. E. Nordenskjöld, *Facsimile-atlas to the Early History of Cartography*, Stockholm, 1889, pl. XLIII).

[55] *The Geography of Strabo*; translated by H. L. Jones, Loeb Classical Library, London–New York, 1917, 8 vols., 2.1.14; vol. 1, p. 271.

[56] Book VII, ch. 3 ("Sinae"). "There are many islands around Taprobane," Ptolemy says

(Book VII, ch. 4), "which are said to number more than one thousand three hundred and seventy-eight."

[57] See below, pp. 22f.

[58] The reference in the letter to Martins is, somewhat vaguely (presumably in keeping with the whole tenor of the letter), to "the time of Eugenius," rather than to the Council. Eugenius the Fourth, 1431–1447, presided over the Council of Ferrara-Florence. See Uzielli, *vita*, p. 163, for Toscanelli's reference to the notes he took during the Council.

[59] Cf. Sumien, *op. cit.*, p. 7.

[60] Anastos, *op. cit.*, pp. 3, 5.

[61] See earlier discussion.

[62] Anastos, *op. cit.*, p. 6.

[63] *Ibid.*, p. 5.

[64] See Sensburg, *op. cit.* (n. 27 above). The date of Conti's return to Italy (and his stay in Florence) has been placed by Sensburg between 1439 and 1442, but with a good likelihood that he may have been there during the Council.

[65] Sensburg, *op. cit.*, pp. 257, 319ff., presents an extensive catalogue of the Southeast Asian islands identified by Conti. For a comparison, one might consult the thorough list of Far Eastern islands as identified by Marco Polo; see Leonardo Olschki, *L'Asia di Marco Polo*, Venice-Rome, 1957. Olschki's "island catalogue" has to be compiled with the help of the indexes — "Indice geografico ed etnografico" and "Indice delle cose notabili," *ibid*. See also, in English, *Marco Polo's Asia*, translated by John Scott, Berkeley, 1960.

[66] See below, p. 22.

page 21

[67] Sensburg's assumption that Poggio's relation was based on notes taken during Conti's talk seems more plausible than his alternative suggestion that it was based on dictation (*op. cit.*, p. 328). The oldest known manuscript of Poggio's relation dates from 1447–1448, but an older manuscript may have existed (*ibid.*, pp. 261f.). The report was finally incorporated into Book IV of Poggio's *Historiae de varietate fortunae libri IV* (see *ibid.*, p. 328).

[68] Latin and French text, ed. E. Guron, Paris, 1930, 3 vols. George H. T. Kimble, *Geography in the Middle Ages*, London, 1938, p. 211, has suggested that in his subsequent treatise, *Cosmographiae Tractatus Duo*, written c.1414,

d'Ailly made some major revisions in his geographic picture under the influence of Ptolemy's *Geography*, following the latter's Latin translation. Although Kimble's suggestion appears to have been rather generally accepted — see, e.g., Penrose, *op. cit.*, p. 13; Morison, *op. cit.*, p. 93 — some of d'Ailly's revised concepts are clearly Ptolemaic (such as the southward extension of Africa), but others are definitely not (such as the concept of an "open" Indian Ocean) (see below, p. 24). There is the possibility that stray concepts of Strabo were known during the Middle Ages and therefore may have influenced d'Ailly (d'Ailly's *Imago* in fact contains a doubtful reference to him; see Anastos, *op. cit.*, pp. 8ff., 10). On the whole, d'Ailly represents such a jumble of conventional medieval notions and surprisingly fresh concepts that a new critical study would seem indicated.

page 22

[69] See T. Goldstein, "Florentine Humanism and the Vision of the New World," *Actas do Congresso Internacional da Historia dos Descobrimentos*, Lisbon, 1961, vol. 4, pp. 195ff. (especially p. 203).

[70] See Uzielli, *vita*, pp. 504–511 (especially p. 506).

[71] See Morison, *op. cit.*, p. 22.

[72] *Ibid.*, pp. 39f.

[73] See above n. 40.

[74] See Arciniegas, *op. cit.*, pp. 111f.

[75] See Wallace K. Ferguson, *Europe in Transition; 1300–1520*, Boston, 1962, p. 425; Frederick C. Lane, "Venetian Shipping During the Commercial Revolution," *American Historical Review*, vol. 38, 1933.

[76] See R. Lopez and H. A. Miskimin, "The Economic Depression of the Renaissance," *The Economic History Review*, vol. 14, 1962, pp. 408ff.; R. de Roover, *The Medici Bank*, New York, 1948 (rev. ed. 1963); also see C. Barbagallo, "La crisi economico-sociale dell'Italia della Rinascenza," *Nuova Rivista Storica*, vol. 25, 1950.

[77] See n. 76, also Arciniegas, *op. cit.*, pp. 96f.

[78] See above, p. 20.

page 23

[79] *Imago Mundi*, vol. 2, pp. 542f.

[80] *Ibid.*, p. 140.

[81] *Ibid.*

[82] See above, p. 17.

[83] Anastos, *op. cit.*, p. 3.

[84] Ptolemy (generally far less boldly speculative than Strabo) makes no explicit statement about the navigability of the Ocean Sea. Kimble's assumption that d'Ailly's revised concept of an "open" Indian Ocean reflected Ptolemy's influence (see n. 68 above) implies that the spice islands could be reached both from the West and the East, the latter obviously by crossing the Ocean Sea. The crucial deduction would thereby have been made by d'Ailly, on the basis of a Ptolemaic theory — an assumption that seems generally to have been perpetuated in the literature (*ibid.*). Both theories are in fact alien to Ptolemy's mind, which is conservative rather than speculative on all major global concepts, original mostly in his cartographic — i.e., basically mathematical — ideas.

[85] In Book VII, ch. 5, Ptolemy says: "The Hyrcanium sea, called also the Caspian, is surrounded on all sides by land and has the shape of an island . . . *and we may say the same of the Indian sea, for with its gulfs . . . it is entirely shut in, like the Caspian, on all sides.*"

[86] See the index in vol. 8 of the Loeb ed., or the map reconstructed from the text, "The Inhabited World According to Strabo," by L. A. Lawrence, adapted from C. Müller's "Orbis Terrarum Secundum Strabonem" on the inside cover of vol. 1.

[87] See above, p. 20.

page 24

[88] Strabo, *op. cit.*, 15.1.11, Loeb ed., vol. 7, p. 15.

[89] See above, p. 20.

[90] See the fascinating collection of ocean and mariners' legends in W. Frahm, *Das Meer und die Seefahrt in der altfranzösischen Literatur*, Göttingen, 1914, especially pp. 21ff.

[91] Strabo, *op. cit.*, 2.1.14, Loeb ed., vol. 1, p. 271.

[92] See Goldstein, *Florentine Humanism*, pp. 199ff.

[93] See the perceptive discussion of "mythological" versus "empirical" geography in Leonardo Olschki, *Storia letteraria delle scoperte geografiche*, Florence, 1937.

[94] See P. O. Kristeller, *The Classics and Renaissance Thought,* Cambridge, Mass., 1956, p. 56; R. Klibansky, "The School of Chartres," in *Twelfth-Century Europe and the Foundations of Modern Society*, Madison, Wisc., 1961, pp. 6f.

page 25

[95] See Uzielli, *Toscanelli iniziatore*, p. 79. It is intriguing to note, in this context, that Toscanelli's chart — according to Uzielli's reconstruction (see n. 17 above) — contains a number of legendary oceanic land formations which in fact overlap with actual parts of the American continent. See Goldstein, *Florentine Humanism*, p. 206, n. 31.

[96] See Anastos, *op. cit.*, pp. 14ff. about the impact of Strabo's theory, according to Ferdinand Columbus, upon Columbus's cosmography. Professor Anastos's study demonstrates throughout that this — along with other major Strabonic theories — was conveyed to the Florentines by Plethon at the time of the Council.

[97] Strabo, *op. cit.*, 1.4.6, Loeb ed., vol. 1, p. 241.

[98] *Ibid.*, p. 243; the conceptual context, as well as the speculation about other "inhabited worlds," are presented as Strabo's own speculations.

[99] See above, n. 15.

The Discoveries and the Humanists

by ELISABETH FEIST HIRSCH

M Y LONG OCCUPATION with the life and intellectual development of Damião de Góis (1502–1574) was the source of this essay. I was not surprised to find the thinking of a Portuguese in many aspects inspired by the overseas adventures. In the course of my study it became clear, however, that not only Damião de Góis but his humanist friends in many other European countries followed the maritime conquests with immense curiosity. On the other hand, only a few modern scholars of humanism are prepared to deal with the stimulation the humanists received from the discovery of new worlds. Part of the explanation lies in the necessity for scholarly specialization; this has, as it were, locked up both the scholar of humanism and the scholar of the discoveries in their respective historical corners. It must be realized that such arbitrary separation does little justice to reality. Can one imagine any thinking person in the twentieth century not being a partner in the great scientific enterprises characteristic of our age? Can one imagine any thinking person in the sixteenth century not being excited about the news from overseas? Must not the opening of distant continents have affected the whole outlook of Europeans as space trips have affected ours?

It is needless to call attention to the fact that the imports from the East, available in much larger quantities than before, changed the daily life of Europeans from Lisbon to Cracow. Moreover, the spice monopoly held by the Portuguese king was a highly controversial topic. It kept the humanists busy arguing against it, as did the patriotic Italian Paolo Giovio, or defending it, as did Peutinger, the speaker for the great Augsburg merchants.[1] There were other experiences besides an immensely stimulated economy to bring the Orient closer to the imagination of Western man. It will be difficult for us to project ourselves into an age when elephants and rhinoceroses caused as much excitement and gave as much reason for discussion as our scientific inventions do for us. King Manuel received these exotic animals as rare gifts from India; in his pride he not only paraded them in the streets of Lisbon, but sent some specimens to Rome to impress the pope with his far-reaching power. Whenever they had a chance to look at them people rushed to admire the strange beasts; indeed such

NOTES for *The Discoveries and the Humanists* are to be found on pages 44 to 46.

"sophisticated" minds as Paolo Giovio and Sebastian Münster found the sight worthy of mention in their writings.[2] Furthermore, a German national residing in Lisbon sent a sketch of the rhinoceroses to Nürnberg where Dürer saw it and made one of his famous drawings from it.[3]

In the last part of the fifteenth century Italian humanists like Poggio and Angelo Poliziano had already displayed a keen interest in the discoveries.[4] It would be wrong, though, to conceive of a one-sided impulse leading from the adventurers to the humanists; humanist thinking inspired the discoverers no less. The daring explorers of the unknown seas were in many respects sharers of the same spirit that animated the humanists' intellectual explorations. Often the explorers made outstanding contributions to humanist learning.

It is an almost foregone conclusion, therefore, that the humanists must have looked upon the overseas conquests as an expression of their own outlook on the world. Thus the Portuguese humanist Damião de Góis thought that Henry the Navigator, who he believed was steeped in classical literature, was driven to his adventures on the sea by the desire to establish the veracity of ancient sources.[5] For our purposes it is less important to ascertain whether Góis's interpretation of the Infante's motives was right or wrong; rather his eagerness to couple the discoveries and humanist scholarship — the last field we would expect to yield connections — may reveal how in the mind of a humanist the two movements were closely identified.

It is necessary at this point to clarify somewhat the idea of humanist thinking. Humanism, like the Renaissance, had a long history before it reached its height, and when and where it came to that fullest flowering is a matter of widely differing opinion. Nor are scholars of humanism in agreement as to the best possible definition of it. Some prefer to define it as classical scholarship, whereas others consider this too narrow and too accidental to what may be called the humanist spirit. On the other hand, most scholars agree that a new period in history was inaugurated with the Age of Renaissance and Humanism. Can we not state with some accuracy when the new thinking was ready to encompass, in a seminal form, some basic concepts about modern man?

Since Jacob Burckhardt published his famous book, *The Civilization of the Renaissance in Italy*, one hundred years ago, his thesis of the individualism of Renaissance man may have been modified, but it has never been seriously disputed. The humanist wanted to be a widely educated man; that is why he embraced so many disciplines and why he gives the impression of being rather an amateur in many fields than a specialist in one. But there is another more disquieting side to this picture of a so-called well-rounded man. Hand in hand with the development of man's intellect went an understandable pride in man's manifold capabilities. Though people no longer think of Renaissance man as being unbridled, it is nevertheless true that the Renaissance produced a type of man dominated by his passions and his iron will — not only rulers like the Medici in Italy and France, but also the great heroes of the discoveries. We cannot conceive of them apart from the new spirit of daring and their enjoyment of power. Who does not immediately think of Hernán Cortés, the cruel conqueror of Mexico? Vasco da Gama's prayer before his departure was sincere: he believed that without God's help he would fail; without trust in his own strength and will power, however, he would not have defied the elements. Penrose, in his *Travel and Discovery in the Renaissance*, calls João de Castro "Portugal's universal Renaissance genius." [6] Castro, the last viceroy of India, was an adventurous traveler, an intrepid soldier, and a humanistic scientist who wrote down his observations in three "Roteiros." He was also the ruthless commander of the final battle of Diu in 1546, who, when the fight was won, ordered a slaughter of babies and children. Many humanists had no illusions about the darker aspect of the new man. Erasmus in a letter to Damião de Góis severely criticized cruelties against the Africans. Christianity's reputation was so bad, he pointed out, because Christians would rather command "beasts" than human beings.[7] It is an irony of history that, unknown to himself, the Dutch humanist had his share in the development of the new spirit.

For man in the Middle Ages, God and man's faith in God were the ultimate realities, and the bold adventurer would never have come into existence without a radical change in this attitude. It is significant that most leaders of the crusades remained unnamed: they were fighting God's cause, not their own. The discoverer, on the other hand, is proud of his achievement, which is credited to his great endurance, determination, and will power. On his homecoming, he is rightly celebrated as a hero; he has gained a position for himself by himself. The individualism of the Renaissance man, and his faith in himself, called also for a new kind of faith in God. Aware of it or not, the great adventurers had taken a leap onto a new religious base. Theirs was already the beginning of a man-centered world; together with its great promise for the future, that world also showed signs of danger. Like many explorers before them, the next generations indulged their lust for power more or less freely, though they remained professing Christians. The emphasis on man's unlimited abilities was responsible for the immense progress in the sciences, where it meant power over nature; but it also made possible the totalitarian rulers in the twentieth century.

It was the historic task of Erasmus of Rotterdam to express the new religious spirit behind the daring explorations. His Christian humanism represents the stage in humanist development where some essential features of modern man appear clearly: Erasmus's new insight into the relation between God and man, his emphasis on man as man, and his concept of scholarship.

Luther made a similar contribution to the new religious consciousness with his concept of justification by faith. But his roots reached deeper into religious grounds than Erasmus's. The German reformer realized man's dependence on God's grace for his faith and salvation. Luther, in Roland Bainton's words, "exulted God" and Erasmus "elevated man"; because of this difference they did not build the same future.[8] Without the Protestant revolutions we cannot envision our modern pluralistic societies; without the Dutch humanist the final victory of a world ordered and ruled by man would not have come to pass.

In Erasmus's view man was responsible not only for his own faith but for his own religious insight. This view is the source, I suppose, of the remark by C. A. Mayer, the great expert on Clément Marot, that Marot adhered to a "humane faith" (une foi humanitaire).[9] Hand in hand with this spiritual searching went a sincere hope for Christian unity.

It has often been said that the Erasmian humanists' desire for a united Christendom was a relic of the Middle Ages. Again and again the humanists argued that only a united Christian world would withstand the onslaught of the Turks and Arabs. On this basis one must also understand the discoverers' search for Christians on distant continents.

We must, however, ask whether the enlarged Christian world the conquerors and the humanists dreamed of was the same Christian world that existed in the Middle Ages. This can easily be answered with regard to the Ethiopian issue.

For our purposes it is not necessary to delve into the fantastic background that led to the final discovery of the Negus's realm. Suffice it to say that Henry the Navigator and his followers hoped to find a mighty Christian ally against the Moslem enemy. In 1514, "Precious" John dispatched to Portugal Matthew, an Armenian, who carried not only offers of a political alliance, but proof of the Ethiopians' true Christianity in the form of a crucifix supposedly made from the cross on which Christ died. This was the occasion for the Negus's first disillusionment. His claim of Christian orthodoxy was, for quite understandable reasons, received with great skepticism. Nevertheless, the Portuguese king sent the well-known legation to Ethiopia, which included the famous Father Francisco Álvares, who in turn became the Ethiopian ruler's emissary to the pope. The envoys from the Negus, led by Father Álvares, reached Bologna in 1533, where they paid solemn obedience to the Holy Father in the presence of Charles the Fifth.[10] But this was by no means proof of the full acceptance of the Ethiopians into the Christian community.

Zagazabo, one of the Negus's legates, spent many years in Europe trying to win friends for his country. In 1533 Damião de Góis was deeply touched by the Ethiopians' difficulty in being recognized as Christians, and it was not the first time his imagination had been captured by this question. When as a youth of twelve he met Matthew, the Negus's emissary, he was already interested in the religious issue. Many years later, serving as a diplomat for King João the Third, he talked about this thorny problem with his many humanist friends, and he made several missions to eastern Europe. On such occasions he stopped over in Danzig where the Portuguese king had important commercial interests, which gave him a welcome opportunity to meet John Magnus, the exiled archbishop of Upsala, an Erasmian humanist and historian. Magnus told Góis about the sad fate of the Lapps, and Góis talked about the Ethiopians. Magnus showed much interest in this problem, urging Góis to translate into Latin the letters brought by Matthew to the Portuguese king; this became Góis's first contribution to humanist writing when it appeared in Antwerp in 1532 as *Legatio Magni Indorum Imperatoris Presbyteri Joannis, ad Emanuelem Lusitaniae Regem, Anno Domini MDXIII* (Legation of the Great Presbyter John of the Indians).

Zagazabo, however, complained that Matthew's presentation of the Ethiopian faith was not accurate. With compassion for Zagazabo's religious difficulty and a bad scholarly conscience, Damião de Góis asked Zagazabo to give him a description in writing of his people's faith, promising to have it published in a Latin translation to make the whole complex issue known to Europe's cultured class. During his residence in Italy Góis received Zagazabo's manuscript; he added his own comments and some letters sent by the Negus to the Portuguese king and the pope, which Paolo Giovio, the Italian bishop and historian, had rendered into Latin and previously printed, and published the whole in Louvain in 1540 under the title *Fides, Religio, Moresque Aethiopium sub Imperio Pretiosi Ioannis* (The Faith, Religion, and Manners of the Ethiopians).[11]

Since the Ethiopian church belonged to the Coptic branch of Christianity declared unorthodox by Rome, it is highly significant that Zagazabo's pamphlet contained a plea for religious tolerance. It was a forceful appeal for the unity of all Christians regardless of dogma or ritual, be they Greek, Armenian, or Ethiopian. "We are all sons of baptism and feel the same about the true faith," Zagazabo exclaimed. Moreover, he supported his views by distinguishing basic from merely circumstantial religious facts. "There is no reason why we should argue so bitterly over religious customs; rather everybody should practice his own without suffering hatred and insult from others. Nor should anybody be excluded from the Christian community, if he observes native rites in a foreign country."[12] Zagazabo added his voice to the chorus of similar demands in support of religious liberty made in his age. One thinks of Sebastian Castellio, the famous adversary of Calvin, who, like the African bishop, stripped Christianity of much of its ritual and dogma.[13]

Góis sent his book dealing with the religion of the Ethiopians to his many humanist friends all over Europe, and from some letters we get an idea of the tenor of their reactions. Adamus Carolus, orator of Ferdinand the First of Hungary, made a typical comment in a letter to Góis thanking him for the essay: "We who confess Christianity should be greatly ashamed that the Ethiopians surpass us in the observation of religion."[14] Certain humanists gave little evidence of feeling superior to African Christianity. Erasmus joined many of his followers in requesting recognition of the Ethiopian faith. In his last writing, the *Ecclesiastes*, he deplored the pope's neglect of this outpost of Christianity.[15]

Among Europeans, curiosity about the Ethiopian emperor and the religion of his people had of course been of long standing. The eagerness with which Góis's essay was read gives further proof of this. Carolus complained that he had not yet been able to read the essay; the book had just arrived when Claudius Cantiuncula, a famous jurist and diplomat also known to Góis, was present in his home. The latter immediately snatched it from him and did not return it before he and other humanists had read it.[16]

The humanists, it becomes clear, thought of Christian unity in different terms than did the men of the Middle Ages. For them the idea of one Christendom exploded; they put in its place a Christian world composed of varied elements. The attitude of the Erasmians toward the Ethiopian question reveals an interesting relation of the discoveries to humanist thinking. A certain idealization of the Ethiopian religion that can be observed among the humansts was in all likelihood dictated by a widespread belief that moral degeneration was prevalent in the West. John Campensis, the Hebrew scholar of the university at Louvain who visited Rome in the 'thirties, was not alone in deploring the ignorance of religion and the immorality so apparent in the Eternal City.[17] But more than this was at stake. The opening of new continents and the acquaintance with new peoples had an effect on the intellectual horizon of the humanists comparable with the revival of classical learning. Both events are the consequence of the same inner forces and in turn strengthen those tendencies that were to become characteristic of modern man. To the Erasmians the Ethiopians taught a lesson in relative religious values, just as classical antiquity was regarded not only as an Age of Mankind never to be matched again by later centuries, but also as a worthy preparation for Christianity.

The Erasmians were the generation under whose observant eyes the most spectacular conquests and discoveries were made. They were close witnesses to the Golden Age of overseas adventures which opened up not only Africa and India, but China, Japan, and the American continent. As the imagination of the present generation follows the flight of the space ships into the cosmos, so the Erasmians had the fullest opportunity to witness an ever-enlarging world, and derived from the experience a thrill like the one that provoked their exhaustive travels. It has been observed that the humanists traveled all over Europe in the interest of their studies, but education was by no means the only reason for their arduous journeys. It makes an arresting story to follow the path of a Sigismund von Herberstein, the Austrian diplomat who described such outposts as Lapland and Tartary; of a Damião de Góis who followed similarly untraveled roads; of a Dantiscus who embarked in Venice on a boat headed for the Near East.[18] These ventures, borne on the wings of curiosity, were fact-finding trips often undertaken with the purpose of replacing legend with truth.

Europe's educated class was fully prepared to be greatly stimulated by the discoveries, the more so since there existed an intellectual interplay between the figures dominant in the conquests and the humanists, fostered by their common awareness of the importance of the discoveries. This awareness was the reason why most of the principal adventurers left journals, histories, or letters as records of their adventures. Whether we think of Afonso d'Albuquerque or of Las Casas, Cortés, and Columbus, their congeniality with the intellectual curiosity of the humanists is striking. Quite often scholars and adventurers knew each other well: their association deserves fuller scrutiny than has so far been accorded it. The example of Ferdinand Columbus, who went along on his father's fourth voyage and later enlisted the help of scholars in his famous library in Seville, may stand for many others.

Humanists throughout Europe anxiously awaited news about the discoveries. Thus, King Manuel's newsletters sent to Rome to inform the pope about his maritime successes were translated into many tongues. Impressive collections of topographies appeared all over Europe, prepared by such famous scholars as Sebastian Münster, Peter Martyr, Ramusio, Richard Eden. The important and widely circulated volumes were not restricted, as the titles often suggested, to nations overseas, but included, for example, Jacob Ziegler's and John and Olaus Magnus's descriptions of the Nordic countries, Damião de Góis's essay on Lapland, and Paolo Giovio's pamphlet on Russia. The discoveries were a strong incentive to the humanists' accumulation of a huge knowledge of the geography of the whole known world.

What was the humanist's conception of geography? This is an important question because many scholars of humanism still believe that Renaissance humanism, with its predilection for antiquity, retarded the development of modern science. As long ago as 1935 Atkinson, in his book dealing with French thought in the Renaissance, emphasized that the idea of progress in the sixteenth century was a direct response to the many new scientific facts.[19]

For the humanists geography was a descriptive science including some history and some treatment of the culture of the peoples in question. Travelers and sailors brought new information about distant countries which helped to replace the mere fantasies that had often been the only knowledge available before. It is not surprising that the humanist should stress observation and reliable facts in his topography, working hand in hand with the new method employed in other fields such as anatomy, where the method was used by Vesalius. Damião de Góis's argument with Sebastian Münster throws additional light on the issue of method. To Góis's great annoyance, Münster had, in his edition of *Ptolemy*, made some unfriendly remarks about the Spanish nation. In his *Hispania* Góis, soothing his injured patriotic feelings, answered and refuted most of Münster's statements. Cutting still deeper into the scholar's pride, Góis reproached him for having relied only on secondary information.[20] Münster, in turn, inserting in his celebrated *Cosmography* a long paragraph dealing with Góis's accusations, asked him whether he had been to Ethiopia before he wrote about events there.[21] Góis, as a matter of fact, was always careful to use what he thought were the most trustworthy sources, and he probably had meant that Münster had failed to be equally careful in his report on Spain. It is true, of course, that all the humanist topographical publications tried with more or less success to apply the same scientific ideal. What is important above all here is the principle. For reasons of accuracy Góis, before writing his description of Lapland, visited the country.[22] Whoever has looked through some of the big volumes on topography published in the sixteenth century must have noticed the new scientific spirit that pervades them, though it is still side by side with traces of fantasy.

As the first adequate expression of modern thinking was provided by Descartes's philosophy, so modern science revealed its true face only in the seventeenth century. And modern science, like Renaissance humanism, evolved slowly during several centuries. The great influence on the natural sciences of the Aristotelian school of thought dominant in Padua has been duly emphasized.[23] Less attention has been paid to the influence of maritime explorations, with their wealth of practical scientific experience. The strong mathematical interest in the circles of Vives and Thomas More might have been inspired by overseas navigation, which depended on careful astronomical observation and research. The accumulation of new insight into many cultural fields gave the humanists a feeling of pride in man's capabilities. Vives, a friend and correspondent of Góis, dedicated his *De Disciplinis* to the Portuguese king, João the Third, in 1531. In his dedicatory letter he spoke of the sailors "who open up distances over the heavens and the seas of which we have never heard before, who show us peoples and nations of great interest to us because of their extraordinary customs, their wealth, and crudity — truly to man was opened his plane." [24] Thomas More, visiting Flanders in 1515, was a frequent guest at the India house in Antwerp where, one story has it, his conversations with a Portuguese sailor gave him the idea for the locale of his Utopia.[25] Moreover, it may well be that More's interest in lands overseas was stimulated by his association with the Portuguese factors in Antwerp, and it may also well be that he caused his son John to translate into English Góis's first Latin publication about the Ethiopian embassy of 1514.[26]

The Erasmians showed an amazing understanding of Copernicus's astronomic theories. *On the Revolutions of the Heavenly Bodies* appeared in 1543 when its author was on his deathbed and therefore never aware of the injustice done his book by the Protestant Osiander, who, in an added preface, said that the book contained no truths contrary to tradition.[27]

Tiedemann Giese and Dantiscus, both bishops, humanists, and great admirers of Erasmus, were close to Copernicus for many years and defended his theories, the latter recommending the book in an epigram which, however, was not published.[28] Dantiscus's ready acceptance of Copernicus's theories may be not unrelated to his knowledge of the explorers' discovery of new astronomical facts. During his residence in Spain as Polish ambassador to Charles the Fifth, he had been on the most intimate terms with Hernán Cortés, a friendship in all likelihood responsible for Dantiscus's curiosity about the Spanish conquests; at any rate, when he returned to Poland after an eventful life abroad, leaving behind many friends among the humanists, he planned a notable library at his diocese at Heilsberg and therefore carried with him many documents relating to the American continent.[29]

In Portugal itself the maritime experiences were of great value to science. Though the experimental and the theoretical methods were still competing, certain outstanding scientists were able to combine the two. In the first decade of the sixteenth century Duarte Pacheco Pereira published his *Esmeraldo de Situ Orbis* in which he related his thirty years of seafaring, hoping that the account might serve as a guide to future sailors. Lacking a hypothesis upon which to base his observations, he nevertheless tried to bring order among his many facts.[30] Pedro Nunes, one of Portugal's great scientists, worked closely with João de Castro, the hero of Diu.[31] One outstanding example of the application of the experimental method was Garcia d'Orta's famous collection of medical information acquired in India. While he was there, this great Portuguese scholar even experimented on himself [32] with certain drugs.

The impressive maritime successes could not but have an influence on the idea Europeans formed of the place of their own time among the ages. Already Duarte Pereira believed that the present knowledge of the world was vastly superior to that of the ancients who had never traveled to the far regions.[33] Some French thinkers like Ramus and Louis LeRoy based their optimistic view of their era on its scientific success.[34] The Erasmian humanists believed that antiquity represented a high achievement by the human mind, but was antiquity superior to all other times in all respects? Erasmus gave, concerning the celebrated Ciceronian issue that plagued him for many years, a clear exposition of his belief in progress.[35] Moreover, in a letter to Góis he warned that Cicero spoke not as a Christian but as a pagan, and in his argument with Cursius Erasmus declined to accept Cicero's as the pinnacle of language, since he was after all only a human being with human imperfections.[36] Góis boldly claimed that the daring overseas exploits were a fit topic for a modern Homer who could derive his epics not from legend but from reality.[37] When he wrote those words, he was unaware that the Portuguese already had in Camões the poet who would one day do just that.

Even the minds of Bembo and Buonamico, two devoted admirers of Cicero, were open to the outstanding accomplishments of their own age. It was as a result of Bembo's encouragement that Góis told in Latin of the great events connected with the defense of Diu.[38] In a letter to Bembo, Góis compared events in his own time with the great deeds of antiquity; though the discoveries had not yet found the historian to describe them in the great manner of the ancients, they were, in Góis's estimation, as glorious as anything that had happened in antiquity. Buonamico, the humanist of Padua whose friends cardinals Pole and Sadoleto reproached him for his too strong inclination toward ancient paganism, had, in spite of this inclination, a full appreciation of his own period. In 1539 he wrote to Góis: "Do not believe that there exists anything more honorable to our recent age than the invention of the printing press and the discovery of the new world; two things which I always thought could be compared not only with Antiquity, but immortality" [39] — as much as to say that we are as good as the ancients. Beyond doubt, the discoveries were part of the reason for the humanists' admiration of their own age. Whether a particular humanist believed in historical progress or favored a cyclical process of history is of less significance; either view of history could be used to glorify the sixteenth century. Nobody has perhaps done this in stronger terms than Luis de Camões, the famous poet of the *Lusiads,* who proudly proclaimed the decline of ancient glory in the face of a "brighter valor in the West."

NOTES

page 35

[1] For Peutinger's views on the whole complex question of the monopolies see Clemens Bauer, "Conrad Peutingers Gutachten zur Monopolfrage" in *Archiv für Reformationsgeschichte,* 1954, vol. 1, pp. 1–43 and vol. 2, pp. 145–196.

page 36

[2] See Luis de Matos, "Natura intelletto e costumi dell 'elefante" in *Boletim internacional de bibliografia Luso-Brasileira,* vol. 1, Lisbon, 1960.

[3] See A. Fontura da Costa, *Deambulations of the Rhinoceros (Ganda) of Muzafar, King of Cambaia, from 1514–1516,* Lisbon, 1937.

[4] See Joaquim de Carvalho, *Estudos sobre a cultura Portuguesa do secolo XVI,* Coimbra, 1948, ch. 1, "Renascença e humanismo," pp. 25–29, and Antonio José Saraiva, *Historia da cultura em Portugal,* vol. 2, Lisbon, 1955, p. 73.

[5] See Damião de Góis, *Chronica do Principe Dom Joam, Rei que foi destes regnos segundo do nome . . .,* Lisbon, 1567, ch. 7, fol. 5v.

page 37

[6] See Boies Penrose, *Travel and Discovery in the Renaissance,* Cambridge, Mass., 1952, p. 67. For a discussion of the different concepts of Renaissance and humanism see Paul Oskar Kristeller, "Changing Views of the Intellectual History of the Renaissance since Jacob Burckhardt," in *The Renaissance: A Reconsideration of the Theories and Interpretations of the Age,* ed. Tinsley Helton, Madison, 1961. I should especially like to mention Professor Kristeller's extensive bibliography, included in the article.

[7] See letter written by Erasmus to Góis from Freiburg in 1533; "Proceres enim illi qui victorias praeda metiuntur malunt imperare beluis quam hominibus," in P. S. Allen, *Opus Epistolarum Des. Erasmi,* London, 1934, 11 vols., no. 2846, line 101.

[8] Roland H. Bainton, *The Reformation of the Sixteenth Century,* Boston, 1952, p. 69.

page 38

[9] See C. A. Mayer, *La Religion de Marot,* Geneva, 1960, p. 137: "La véritable foi de Marot fut une foi humanitaire."

[10] This fact has often been reported; see the letter written by João III to Pope Clement VII concerning this matter in Damião de Góis, *Fides Religio Moresque Aethiopum,* Coimbra, 1791, pp. 221–225.

page 39

[11] The Louvain edition was published by Rutgeus Rescius; a Paris edition was published by Chrétien Wechel in 1541.

[12] Góis, *Fides Religio,* pp. 262–263. "Nec est cause cur tam acriter de caeremoniis disceptetur nisi ut unusquisque suas observet, sine odio, et insectatione aliorum nec commerciis Ecclesiae ob id excludendus est, si peregre in alienis provinciis domesticos ritus observet."

[13] See Sebastian Castellio, *Concerning Heretics,* English translation and introduction by Roland H. Bainton, New York, 1935.

[14] "ut nos qui Christianismum profitemur pudere magnopere debeat quod ab ipsa Aethiopum gente religionis cultum observationemque superari quasi videmur." The letter was written in October 1540, and is published in *Epistolae Sadoleti, Bembi, et Aliorum Clarissimorum Virorum ad Damianum a Gois Equitum Lusitanum,* Louvain, 1544.

[15] See *Ecclesiastae sive Ratione Concionandi, Opera,* ed. John Leclerc, Leyden, 1703ff., vol. 5, p. 813. The religious question did not exhaust the complex issues related to the Ethiopians. Erasmus in referring to the pope's neglect may have had other aspects in mind. In several letters the Negus wrote to either the pope or the Portuguese king he asked for "technical assistance." The Ethiopian king had quite obviously the desire to westernize his country with the help of Western experts.

page 40

[16] Letter of Adamus Carolus to Góis; see note 14.

[17] See the letter written by John Campensis to Dantiscus from Rome, June 12, 1537: "Ego misere hinc abire cupio metuo tamen ne me rei indignitas cogat semel libere dicere quae sentio. Philippus videtur valde tractabilis et ratio revocandi non solum illum sed et Martinum ipsum Certissima inveniri posset idque cum gratia verum per alios quam hic Romae video ubi tanta est literarum sacrarum inscitia et tantum veteris inscitiae patrocinium ut nusquam fuerit quam maius." In Franz Hipler, "Beiträge zur Geschichte der Renaissance und des Humanismus, aus dem Briefwechsel des Johannes Dantiscus," in *Zeitschrift für die Geschichte und Altertumskunde Ermlands*, Braunsberg, 1891, vol. 9, pp. 541–542.

[18] For Dantiscus's biography see *Allgemeine Deutsche Biographie*.

page 41

[19] See G. Atkinson, *Les Nouveaux horizons de la renaissance française*, Paris, 1935. In regard to the Florentine humanists' thoughts about geography see Thomas Goldstein, "Florentine Humanism and the Vision of the New World," *Actas do Congresso Internacional da Historia dos Descobrimentos*, Lisbon, 1961, vol. 4.

[20] See Damião de Góis, *Hispania*, Coimbra, 1791, pp. 77–78. "quam Munsterus in suo novo Ptolemaeo praedicat ubi ad imitationem cuiusdam Michaelis Villanovani hominis mihi incogniti et hac in re non mediocriter lapsi, Hispanorum et Gallorum comparationem induxit. Puto eum cum Basileae profiteatur Gallis ad quos reliqua Basilea spectat excepta tertia ferme parte qua secundum Rhenum Germaniae adhaeret potius quam Hispanis adblandiri voluisse."

[21] See Sebastian Münster, *Cosmographiae Universalis Liber*, 1550, fol. [ ]5*r*, "Damiano in his quae de moribus Indianorum sub Preto Johanne agentium scripsit, in quorum tamen regionem nunquam venit nec aliquando venturus est."

[22] During his residence in Italy Góis wrote to Erasmus complaining about the hard winter. To this Erasmus replied, "What would you do at the Laplanders?" See P. S. Allen, *op. cit.*, no. 3043. Allen's explanation that the Dutch scholar knew of Góis's predilection for the Lapps and jokingly referred to this does not quite satisfy. Rather it should be assumed that Góis had mentioned to Erasmus his desire to visit the country. In his description of Lapland, Góis moreover, twice referred to his own observations of some pertinent fact.

page 42

[23] See J. H. Randall, "The Development of Scientific Method in the School of Padua," *Journal of the History of Ideas*, vol. 1, 1940, pp. 177–206. Also Eugenio Garin, *Der italienische Humanismus*, Bern, 1947.

[24] This is quoted in Antonio José Saraiva, *Historia da cultura em Portugal*, vol. 2, Lisbon, 1955, p. 531.

[25] On Thomas More see Felix Nève, *La Renaissance des lettres et l'essor de l'érudition ancienne en Belgique*, Louvain, 1890, ch. IV.

[26] See E. M. G. Routh, *Sir Thomas More and His Friends, 1474–1535*, London, 1934, p. 137.

[27] See Leopold Prowe, *Nicolaus Copernicus*, Berlin, 1883, 2 vols.

[28] *Ibid.*

[29] See *Allgemeine Deutsche Biographie* and the letter written by Lazzaro Buonamico to Dantiscus from Padua November 24, 1532, in which he asked him about literature on North and South America, in Franz Hipler, "Beiträge zur Geschichte der Renaissance und des Humanismus, aus dem Briefwechsel des Johannes Dantiscus," in *Zeitschrift für die Geschichte und Altertumskunde Ermlands*, 1891, vol. 9, p. 503.

page 43

[30] See Saraiva, *op. cit.*, pp. 458f.

[31] *Ibid.*, p. 465; Joaquim de Carvalho, "Influência dos descobrimentos e da colonização na morfologia da ciência portuguesa do século XVI," in *Estudos sobre a Cultura Portuguesa do século XVI*, vol. 1, Coimbra, 1947, pp. 21–73.

[32] On Garcia d'Orta see the recent study by Gilberto Freyre, "Garcia d'Orta: A Pioneer of Luso-Tropical Science," in *The Portuguese and the Tropics*, Lisbon, 1961, pp. 97–109. English translation by Helen M. D'O. Matthew and F. DeMello Moser. The title of d'Orta's essay is *Colloquios dos simples e drogas e cousas medi-*

cinais da India e assi de algumas frutas achadas nela.

[33] Saraiva, *op. cit.*, p. 461.

[34] See Bodo L. O. Richter, "The Thought of Louis Le Roy According to His Early Pamphlets," *Studies in the Renaissance*, vol. 8, 1961, p. 180.

[35] This controversy has often been studied. See Remigio Sabbadini, *Storia del Ciceronianismo*, Turin, 1886, and Izora Scott, *Controversy over the Imitation of Cicero as a Model for Style and Some Phases of Their Influence on the Schools of the Renaissance*, New York, 1910; in the latter Erasmus's *Ciceronianus* is translated into English.

[36] See Allen, *op. cit.*, no. 3043, "Dicas Christianum Ciceronem Loqui . . ." and "Responsio ad Petri Cursii Defensionem nullo adversario bellacem," in Góis, *Opera*, vol. 10, fol. 1751: "Quid mirum si Ciceronem habemus pro homine? Solus enim Deus est in quo nihil desideres."

[37] See *De Bello Cambaico Secundo Commentarii Tres*, dedicatory letter addressed To prince Luis, Coimbra, 1791, p. 298.

[38] See *Diensis Nobilissimae Carmaniae seu Cambaiae Urbis Oppugnatio*, Coimbra, 1791, p. 115: "Dum agerem Patavii ubi tua humanitate mire me totum devinxisti inter caetera quae ex Lusitanica ad me perferebantur accepi de bello Cambaico nonnulla quae (ut petisti) ex Lusitanica Lingua in Latinum sermonem converti." In the text Italicum wrongly for Latinum.

[39] See the letter written to Góis from Padua, September 1539, in *Epistolae Sadoleti, Bembi, et Aliorum Clarissimorum Virorum ad Damianum a Goes Equitem Lusitanum*: "Cave enim putes quisquam nostra superiorave tempora magis posse illustrare quam imprimendi rationem et novi orbis inventionem quae duo non modo cum antiquitate conferenda sed et cum immortalitate ipsa comparanda semper iudicavi."

Coromandel Trade in Medieval India

by BURTON STEIN

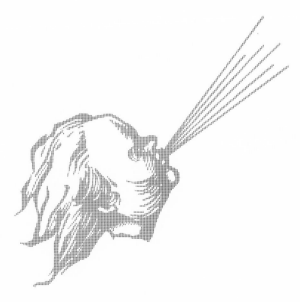

PENINSULAR INDIA'S mercantile activity on its east coast and in its eastern part has received just notice from historians of India,[1] but there has been no systematic study of the organization and functioning of this activity, nor any analysis of changes in the structure of the trade over its documented history of two millennia. As with many other aspects of India's long and complex history, the analysis of changes in the structure of trade may be approached from the vantage point of the medieval period, when the quantity of source materials permits detailed study and when, in the true sense of "middle ages," it is possible to look backward to an earlier period of India's history or to look forward to the epoch of European control and the beginning of India's modern period. Beyond the appropriateness and convenience of approaching the study of the Coromandel trade from the medieval vantage point, however, there is yet another reason to study this medieval trade system: the central and vexing problem of the decline of the widespread trade organizations upon which the system was based.

The antiquity of Coromandel trade has been established by a Chinese writer of the first century who reported commerce between China and Coromandel, notably the city of Kanchi (Conjeevaram, Chingleput district, Madras). This writer, Pan Kuo, spoke of the trade and the commodities of the city of Houan-tche, which has been identified as Kanchi.[2] Contemporaneous with this mention of Coromandel-Chinese trade is similar notice of trade between Coromandel and Rome in the *Periplus of the Erythraean Sea,* in which several Coromandel ports and inland trade centers have been identified; literary references to the trade have been confirmed by the discovery of the coins of Nero (A.D. 54–68), Trajan (A.D. 98–117), and Hadrian (A.D. 117–138).[3] Somewhat later, in the early seventh century, Kanchi is again mentioned as a great city by the most famous of the Chinese pilgrims to Buddhist sacred places, Yuan Chwang.[4] The early trade between China and Coromandel is further attested to by Chau Ju-kua, Inspector of Foreign Trade in Fukien during the thirteenth century, who refers to the interruption of early trade between Chu-lien (Chola dominion or Coromandel) and China.[5]

NOTES for *Coromandel Trade in Medieval India* are to be found on pages 60 to 62.

From settlements of Coromandel merchants in Southeast Asia comes archaeological evidence of substantial commercial and cultural relations during the first millennium of the Christian era. There were Hinou colonists from the Pallava kingdom of Coromandel in the modern state of Kedah on the western coast of the Malayan Peninsula during the period A.D. 550 to 750, and from this point of contact Hindu culture spread to other parts of the peninsula.[6] A more important area of commercial contact for Coromandel merchants was the port of Takuapa on the western side of the narrow waist of the Isthmus of Siam, which served as an entrepôt terminus for trade between India and China. Here, in the middle of the ninth century, a Tamil inscription from the reign of Pallava Nandivarman the Third refers to the activities of one of the famous mercantile associations of Tamil country, the Manigramam.[7] The contacts of Tamil merchants in Southeast Asia apparently became even greater during the period of the Chola kingdom, from which territory, Chola mandalam, the name "Coromandel" is derived. The significance of this contact is perhaps best exemplified by the construction of a Buddhist shrine in A.D. 1005 at Negapatam, the most important Coromandel port at the time — a shrine supported by grants from the ruler of the Malaysian kingdom of Srivijaya as well as from the Chola ruler Rajaraja the First.[8] In the following several decades, Dravida (Tamil) and Cholika (from Chola or Coromandel) merchants are mentioned prominently in the inscriptions of the Javanese ruler Airlanga (1006–1049).[9] In fact, as Coedes and others have pointed out, the greatest part of the heterogenizing impact of Indian culture upon Southeast Asia came from Hindu merchants of the Coromandel. And later, when the cultural influence became Islamic, Tamil Muslim merchants contributed to the further development of the civilizations of Malaysia.[10]

These early evidences of Coromandel trade do little more than substantiate its antiquity and its expansionist vigor. Its internal structure is revealed only later, in the body of Dravidian language and Sanskrit inscriptions of South India in early medieval times, from about the tenth to the thirteenth centuries. These inscriptions in stone give the impression of energetic and confident merchants organized in large, mobile groups carrying on business in a wide assortment of commodities from horses to precious stones.

Early South Indian trade organizations have usually been identified by the term "vira valanjigar" (Tamil; in Kannada "vira banajus"), meaning "valiant merchants," or by the more functional term "nanadesi," meaning "of many countries" or "itinerant."[11] Among the nanadesi several constituent trade organizations were famed for their mercantile activities. Of the most famous were the organization of traders of Ayyavole (modern Aihole, Bijapur district, Mysore state) and the Manigramam traders of the Tamil country, both of which pushed their trade into Southeast Asia. The scope of these organizations' activity[12] was wide: the Ayyavole traders centering in Mysore and ranging to the Coromandel coast and beyond, the Manigramam centering in the central part of Coromandel and ranging to the coast and beyond. For each, a number of towns appear to have been important focuses of trade, though as itinerant traders they traveled far. The time when these trade groups were most active and influential, judging from the frequency and tone of the inscriptions, was the eleventh to the thirteenth centuries.[13]

To illustrate the character of these early medieval trade organizations, a classic Ayyavole inscription may be cited. This inscription, dated A.D. 1050, suggests what the Ayyavole traders were like.[14] In its long introduction, which records a grant to a temple, the following facts appear: the traders are famed as the five hundred heroes, born to wander over the world to such places as Cera (modern Kerala state), Chola and Pandya (together making up Coromandel), Malaya, Magadha, Kausala (in northeastern India), Sauashtra (western India), Gauda (Bengal), and Parasa (Persia). The commodities they trade are elephants and horses; sapphires, moonstones, pearls, rubies, diamonds, onyx, topaz, emeralds, and corals; cardamon and cloves; sandalwood, camphor, and musk. Through the payment of customs they fill the ruler's treasury with gold and jewels and provide him with weapons. They confer gifts upon learned Hindu teachers and upon Hindu deities. Exuberantly the inscription concludes:

The five hundred svamis [lords] of the auspicious Aiyyavole, the best among their people, of unrivaled fame, of lofty and brilliant glory . . . like the elephant, they attack and kill; wise as Brhaspati [teacher of the gods]; fertile in expedients as Narayana [Vishnu, the great deity]; perfect in disputes as Narada Rsi [a divine sage] . . . clay they set fire to; of sand they make ropes; the thunderbolt they catch and exhibit; the sun and moon they draw down to earth . . . they are not ones to fall.[15]

The composition of the Ayyavole organization, about which the most is known of the early medieval trade organizations, is not clear from any of its inscriptions. The core of the organization apparently was made up of the nanadesi or itinerant merchants and, almost always, the swadesi or local merchants. Commodities were moved by water or overland on asses or buffaloes; goods were sold at wholesale or retail,[16] and the numerous merchant groups mentioned in the Ayyavole inscriptions were probably differentiated by the commodity traded and/or the mode of transport. One scholar has suggested that the Ayyavole organization was a federation of merchant groups associated with one of the major groupings of castes in medieval South India, the valangai, or righthand division of castes.[17] What this means is that these traders shared interests related to caste organization and function which supported the essentially economic relations of the trade. A consistent aspect of internal organization is the bond between the local merchants and the itinerant merchants, with the itinerants apparently the primary agents in the extensive trade network of the Ayyavole organization.

The Shikarpur inscription of A.D. 1050 and other inscriptions refer to important control by the Ayyavole organization over some of the towns where it traded and also to town officials who seem to be affiliated with the trading group.[18] This influence in towns went as far as the conversion of some settlements into special centers for trade, with specific regulations and privileges. Two Chola inscriptions deal with the converting of Coromandel settlements into such special towns, designated vira-pattana, one being Mylapore, now a part of the city of Madras.[19]

One of the best examples of the importance and strength of medieval Coromandel trade comes from the northern part of the coast in the thirteenth century. The port of Motupalli, some forty miles south of the delta of the Kistna River (Bapatla Taluk, Guntur District, Andhra Pradesh), received a charter in A.D. 1244, when it may already have been an important trade center, assuring its commercial ascendancy for at least a century. The charter was granted by a Hindu ruler of the Kakatiya kingdom of the Kistna-Godavari delta area of Coromandel; its introductory part reads as follows:

By [the] glorious Maharaja Ganapatideva the following edict has been granted to traders by sea starting for and arriving from all continents, islands, foreign countries, and cities. Formerly kings used to take away by force the whole cargo, *viz.* gold, elephants, horses, gems, etc., carried by ships and vessels which, after they had started from one country for another, were attacked by storms, wrecked, and thrown on shore. But We, out of mercy, for the sake of glory and merit, are granting everything besides the fixed duty to those who have incurred the great risk of a sea-voyage with the thought that wealth is more important than even life. The rate of this duty [is] one in thirty on [all] exports and imports. [This is followed by a list of commodities with a schedule of customs.] [20]

This edict of Ganapatideva was renewed in A.D. 1358 by the successor dynasty in this area, the Reddi kingdom, and renewed again with some modifications by the Vijay-anagar ruler, Devaraya Udaiyar, in A.D. 1390.[21]

Some ambiguity arises from the Motupalli inscriptions of this period in connection with the term mahasahasa, given to sea travel, which refers to the spiritually polluting effect of the sea and probably looks forward to the general prohibition of sea travel for Hindus in more modern times.[22] On the basis of this term in the A.D. 1244 inscription, Nilakanta Sastri suggests that overseas trade may have been in the ..ands of foreign merchants. There is no necessity for accepting this inference, however, and there is positive evidence of earlier and later sea trade by Hindus. Moreover, we have a perceptive witness to the Motupalli trade in Marco Polo, who visited the port in about A.D. 1293. He describes "Mutfili" as a great diamond and cotton emporium without mentioning, as he does in the case of "Coilum" (modern Quilon), on the western, or Malabar, coast of South India, that foreign merchants are important in the trade.[23]

The Motupalli inscriptions of the thirteenth and fourteenth centuries, combined with the earlier evidence of the activities of the Ayyavole Five Hundred, provide an impression of powerful and active Coromandel trade organization capable of establishing centers congenial to their trade and control and capable of eliciting cooperation and protection from Hindu warriors of the age. Without the ability to combine

the enterprise of the numerous constituent trade groups and without some cooperation from those with military power, trading organizations like that of Ayyavole
could not have operated over such a vast area for so long. Their accomplishment is
the more remarkable when we realize that the social and economic context they operated in was not urban and mercantile-oriented but dominantly agrarian. Vigorous
and powerful as they appear to be, the medieval trade organizations must be seen as
essentially integrated within the principal forms of social and economic organization
of medieval South India in general and Coromandel in particular.

The agrarian system of Coromandel was a patchwork of two basic types. One
type consisted of numerous nuclear areas of settled, village-based agriculture of a
low order of technological organization, served by simple storage irrigation, usually
from bunded reservoirs, and having a standard, simple division of labor within most
of the village productive units. These nuclear areas were integrated in administration, particularly during periods of important political and military consolidation,
as under the imperial Cholas from the late tenth century to the thirteenth; religiously,
through numerous settlements of brahmans, the priestly elite, and through the Hindu
temples; and socially and economically through caste groups and caste assemblies,
especially those of brahmans and such low but respectable castes as the vellelas, who
were the great agricultural caste of the Coromandel area, and some artisan castes.
Finally, integration was achieved through the activities of merchant organizations and
trade.

The second agrarian type, larger during most of the medieval period, consisted of
settlements in the forest and hilly tracts throughout the Coromandel area, which
were occupied by isolated, tribally organized peoples who carried on a mixed hunting
and shifting agricultural economy, augmented by stealing cattle and by other predatory activities.

The relation between these two agrarian types was continuously hostile, for,
throughout the medieval period, the more developed agrarian type pressed against
the wide and traditional preserves of the tribal people as more of the forests were
felled and more fertile lands brought under the plow. During this long hostile relation, in which the more primitive tribal peoples were a constant source of dread to the
caste-organized and village-dwelling peasantry and a constant source of fear to the
warrior families in these places,[24] tribal peoples were continuously assimilated to the
more developed structure of village society and economy.

Against this background of a peasant village–centered agrarian society expanding
from a number of older, settled, nuclear areas the early medieval trade organizations
of Coromandel must be examined, for these areas of settled agriculture and the so-
cietal forms associated with them provided the opportunity for profitable trade and,
at the same time, set the conditions under which this trade could take place.

The distribution of nuclear areas of settled agriculture, and the relation of trade
and trade groups to these areas during the Chola period, has not yet been studied.

Considerable evidence is at hand, however, which permits a preliminary reconstruction of the relation sufficient for the argument in this paper. The nuclear areas of settled agriculture were marked by cooperation between two kinds of village settlements. The most advanced forms of village organization, from the point of view of intensive use of agrarian resources, material and human, and a high degree of internal organization, were brahmadeyas. These were villages in which the brahmans dominated by means of control granted to them by warriors and others to support their teaching and ritual functions. In effect, brahmans were given most of the surplus village produce and the right to manage all aspects of village life through an assembly consisting of brahman residents, the mahasabha. Owing to the interest which has attached to these brahman assemblies as examples of early self-governing institutions in South India and the substantial number of stone inscriptions relating to their affairs,[25] it is possible to form a fairly definite idea of their distribution. On the assumption that the density of brahmadeyas is correlated with areas of relatively well-developed agriculture producing a surplus sufficient to support rather large populations of economically nonproductive persons, a rough mapping of nuclear areas is possible.

The second form of village in nuclear areas was that of lower-caste peasants, sudras, about which we know little. These villages were governed by assemblies called ur or urom,[26] and included the vast majority of settled villages in the nuclear areas as well as in the more peripheral areas of agrarian development.[27]

Nuclear areas of developed, settled agriculture were the focuses of medieval Coromandel life. Largely self-governing, the village units within the nuclear area were linked in a variety of ways — administrative, religious, social, and economic — as mentioned above. Recently, South Indian scholars have become aware of the existence of assemblies representing all the important elements within a nuclear area which met as occasion required to act together. These assemblies have been called periyanāttar (people of the region) or more particularly chitrameli, a word that frequently appears in the title of such regional assemblies as their affairs are described in stone inscriptions.[28]

The chitrameli assembly has received surprisingly little attention from historians, yet it is clear that these assemblies shared with the brahman assemblies control over the nuclear areas of Tamil country during the Chola period. It also seems clear that these assemblies were dominated by lower-caste farmers, especially the large Tamil caste of sudras called vellelas, though in all the chitrameli inscriptions there is the quite certain evidence of cooperation between the farmers and other important groups from the nuclear areas, including brahmans, artisans, Chola officials, and merchants.

A standard introduction, with some variations, opens most of the chitrameli inscriptions:

This is a record of the chitrameli, just and good to all people, the prosperous sons of the soil, those subsisting on cow's milk. Let this record, which is for the protection and strengthening of the sons of the soil, who are born of the fourth caste [sudras], prosper in this world.[29]

Meli means plowshare in Tamil, in conformity with the essentially fourth-caste, or sudra, character of the assembly, whose inscriptional records usually bear a sketch of a plow as well.[30] The significant integrative function of these assemblies may be measured by the various associations they formed with other important institutions and groups within the nuclear areas. There are references to groups of villages under the jurisdiction of the chitrameli comprising small regions called chitrameli periya-nadu; a number of Hindu temples are mentioned in inscriptions as under the special sponsorship of the chitrameli; some brahman villages, brahmadeyas, are similarly under the protection of the chitrameli.[31] In all, the existing evidence about the chitra-meli assemblies depicts bodies of particular vigor and effectiveness, and supports the view that the developed agrarian areas of the Coromandel region at this time were notably integrated.

Merchants were given a prominent place in chitrameli assemblies, contributing to their importance as an integrative institution. A series of Coromandel inscriptions of the late Chola period illustrates the relation between the dominantly agrarian assemblies and the merchant groups of the same nuclear area. From Tittagudi, in the Vriddhachalam taluk of the South Arcot district, an inscription of A.D. 1168 records an endowment by a chitrameli assembly to a temple whose deity, a soil goddess (bhumi-devi), is adorned with the symbol of the plow (meli) of the chitrameli. This gift was given by farmers, joining with a large group of merchants, some local (nadu and nagara), and some itinerants (nana desi); its purpose was to repair the temple and provide for festivals. This inscription says that the farmers are to give a set quantity of rice for each plow per year and the merchants a cash payment or a quantity of the specified goods they sell.[32] Another inscription of A.D. 1235 from Anbil (Udai-yarpalaiyam taluk, Tiruchirapalli District), the donative portion of which is damaged, says that the merchant group mentioned above and a number of other merchant groups of the area were subordinate to the chitrameli.[33] A long, interesting inscription from Piranmalai (Tiupattur taluk, Ramnad District), which contains no information about the date but begins with a variation on the introduction of other chitra-meli inscriptions, names thirty-nine commodities in the cases of which a group of merchants voluntarily levy upon themselves an assessment for the benefit of a temple. In addition to giving us another clue to the relation between the agricultural and the mercantile interests of the area, this inscription suggests the range of commodities traded — salt, food grains, spices, iron, elephants, and horses.[34]

These inscriptions and many others suggest high integration within the well-settled and stable areas of Coromandel (called nuclear areas here); they also point to the superiority in such areas of the low-caste farmers, the sudras, over artisans and merchant groups. These agriculturists, organized into assemblies, shared with the assemblies of brahmans control over the most essential aspects of life. Chola warriors in whose territories these organizations flourished appear never to have tried to take over their functions. On the contrary, a distinguishing characteristic of the Cholas was their support of these organizations through recognizing and maintaining the rights upon which the effectiveness of the organizations depended. It was essential to the Cholas that the areas of relatively high economic productivity be held and extended, for it was from these areas that the land revenue upon which the power of the Cholas depended came, with a minimum of strife, and where order was best maintained.[35]

The great vira valanjigar or nanadesi trade organizations such as that of Ayyavole and the Manigramam were active from the eighth to the seventeenth centuries, as determined by the earliest and the latest inscriptions referring to them. It seems clear, however, that the time of greatest activity and importance of both did not go beyond the thirteenth century. It has been argued here that the large, mobile trade organizations, with their widespread activities, were firmly rooted in the agrarian system of Coromandel, as evidenced by the chitrameli inscriptions of the same period. It is, in fact, not possible to conceive of trade activities of any sort or by any kind of organization which were not a part of the fabric of the dominantly agrarian society of the time; the chitrameli inscriptions make it clear that the various organizations of Coromandel merchants were integrated with and subordinate to assemblies representing the major interest groups in the more developed portions of Coromandel. These assemblies were made up of those who produced many of the commodities sold and consumed the largest part of the goods bought. Merchant groups, large and small, engaging in local or wider trade, were part of the changing agrarian order of Coromandel; their fate depended much upon the kind of development this agrarian order was passing through during the medieval period. Hence the decline and virtual disappearance of these great trade organizations after the thirteenth century points to accompanying changes in the agrarian order. Profound changes in the agrarian order did in fact take place from the fourteenth to the seventeenth centuries, and the nature of these changes provides a reasonable explanation for the decline of the great trade organizations.

The agriculture of early medieval Coromandel, that is from the tenth to the thirteenth centuries, corresponding with the period of Chola dominance, has been described as a patchwork of relatively well-developed nuclear areas based upon well-organized village units. Such village units of the nuclear area were dominated either by brahmans, priests, and teachers or by low-caste sudras — agriculturists. These units, together with merchants and artisans who were under their control, dominated the nuclear areas. Between nuclear areas, broad territories were inhabited by more primitive and dangerous forest and hill people who lived a hazardous life of hunting and shifting agriculture augmented by raids upon the settled communities of the nuclear areas. Through the early medieval period the nuclear areas expanded continuously though gradually and, on the whole, peacefully, as colonies of the older brah-

man or sudra settlements were established at the margins of the nuclear areas, as-
similating the primitive forest and hill people into caste-organized, settled villages.
This spread of the nuclear areas was abetted by the protection of the Cholas.

Two developments altered this largely peaceful growth. One was the decline of
Chola power in the early thirteenth century and with that decline the increased vul-
nerability of the nuclear areas to predatory warriors. The second was the great increase in such predatory warriors. The decline of the Cholas, after two centuries of
wielding power supreme in South India and felt even in Ceylon and distant Indonesia,
has been attributed mainly to the rise of two adversaries, both from poorer territories,
who descended upon their rich and developed lands. They were the Pandyas from the
south and the Hoysalas from the northwest. These were in addition to the increase
in warriors from the forests of Coromandel, such as the Kadava chieftain "who had
a vanguard of forest troops." [36]

The coming of warriors from the south and northwest and the irruption of forest
and hill chiefs inflicted irreparable damage upon the Cholas and began a decisive
change in the agrarian order of medieval Coromandel. The new order took a century
or more to mature, and, when it had been established, Coromandel was, along with
most of South India, a part of a different agrarian regime, under the control of Vijayanagar warriors who had extended their power from beyond the northern reaches
of Coromandel. [37]

The distinguishing characteristic of this regime, especially under the greatest of
the Vijayanagars, Krishnadevaraya (1509–1529) was its control by warriors. As
Nilakanta Sastri has noted, "Vijayanagar was perhaps the nearest approach to a war-
state ever made by a Hindu kingdom; and its political organization was dominated
by its military needs." [38] This fact is made abundantly clear by the Vijayanagar inscriptions, and confirmed by foreign witnesses who describe the large standing army
of Krishnadevaraya, supported by the ruler's treasury, and the division of most of the
territory of South India into more than two hundred military fiefs. [39] The military and
revenue requirements of this martialization of South India could only have been met
by a modification of the older agrarian structure. Inscriptions from the Vijayanagar
period suggest a marked decline in the previously independent and powerful local
assemblies of both brahmans and sudras as the local authority came increasingly to
be a powerful warrior, nayaka, or his military subordinates. [40] Some older warrior
families were left in control of their regions of established power, like the Pandya
family, for example — but only if they adapted themselves to the new martial regime,
with its more comprehensive control of human and material resources. This era saw
the rise of many new warrior families, however, some assuming power over the developed nuclear areas of Coromandel and others carving out and developing fiefs
from Coromandel's formerly marginal tracts. Many of these new families came from
these marginal tracts. Others descended upon Coromandel from the Telegu-speaking territory to the north — in part attracted by the opportunities of power, in part

simply following the spread of the Telegu-Vijayanagar warriors southward, and finally to some extent pushed out of their traditional territories in the north by the constant pressure of Muslim warriors under the Deccan sultanates.[41] The establishment and proliferation of this vigorous warrior control of Coromandel and many other parts of South India greatly intensified the colonization and settlement in villages of previously marginal regions in Coromandel, settlement based upon replacing forests with cultivated areas of stable agriculture to meet the needs of the warriors. On the whole, from the late fourteenth to the seventeenth centuries there appears to have been a vast expansion and consolidation of settlement in agricultural villages, but these new villages lacked both the integration and the self-government of the earlier ones.

This transformation of the agrarian order of most of South India and Coromandel greatly weakened the structure in which the great trade organizations of the earlier period had flourished. Each warrior, within the circle of villages that made up his fief (amaram),[42] zealously protected the resources of his territory and was likely to transform it into an isolated, self-sufficient economic unit which, among other things, in turn enhanced the status and scope of trade by local merchant groups at the expense of the formerly prestigeful itinerant traders. To some extent, too, considerable advantages in trade were gained by special groups of merchants from the "foreign" home territories of the new warriors as, for example, the komatis of Telegu-speaking territories who became one of the great trade groups of South India, presumably because they were supported by Telegu warriors. In addition, each of the new and powerful warriors encouraged the development of new urban centers by establishing pretentious headquarters and garrison towns and by supporting temples and centers for pilgrims in their new territories.[43] These new urban areas became the focus of activity for local trade groups, which contributed to the regionalization and narrowing of trade activities, to the detriment of the great networks of itinerant trade. The localization of trade was further marked by the efforts of the local warriors to attract communities of artisans to their territories by offering special privileges.[44] The tendency toward more localized trade as a reflection of more localized warrior power and the desire to maximize control over all resources did not eliminate the older diffuse trade network, but it limited the commodities in such trade to such essentials as salt, iron, and horses and such luxuries as fine textiles and precious stones.

One other influence in the new agrarian order probably militated against the formerly great trade organizations. This was the desire of warriors, great and small, to reduce the military and political power of these trade groups. Under the old order, trade organizations such as that of Ayyavole were able to establish centers of trade under their rule and supervision, as we have seen. Moreover, these traders, moving among the older nuclear areas with their wares, always had armed escorts to protect them while passing through the dangerous territories lying between the nuclear areas.[45] The military pretensions of these organizations can be seen in inscriptions which boast of their bravery, their sharp swords, and their honors as "sons of warriors." [46] The great itinerant trade groups must have been regarded as a threat to large and small warrior alike.

By the seventeenth century, the eclipse of the great trade organizations appears complete. From Portuguese and Dutch records of the sixteenth and seventeenth centuries we hear nothing of them, though the records contain long descriptions of trade and trade centers.[47] Nor do the copious records of the English in Coromandel in the seventeenth and eighteenth centuries refer to them. The major indigenous source for information about the medieval period, the inscriptions on stone, became less abundant during the seventeenth century, and they too are silent about the great trade organizations.

The course taken by the Coromandel agrarian system after the sixteenth century followed patterns evident from the fourteenth century. The warriors' control over agrarian life increased, especially after the collapse of Vijayanagar power in the middle of the sixteenth century when the Muslim sultanates of the Deccan combined to defeat the Vijayanagars. After this defeat, power over the countryside was even more firmly wielded by the many warriors who had held territories subordinate to Vijayanagar. Now these warriors, with only the slightest restraint from the few great nayakas of the earlier period of Vijayanagar greatness who established several large nayaka kingdoms, and even less restraint from the ominous presence of Muslim warriors to the north who looked covetously toward Coromandel, turned to a suicidal period of internecine warfare. This final period in the atomization of the warriors' authority in Coromandel made even local trade hazardous, to say nothing of commerce over the diffuse trade networks of the entire region.

The warrior-dominated agrarian order from the fourteenth century on destroyed the conditions under which the early medieval trade organizations had existed. In the three or four centuries before the fourteenth, the system of many nuclear areas of relatively advanced agricultural economy with independent assemblies capable of maintaining an advantageous balance against the more backward peoples who divided the nuclear areas from each other had been able to keep up a flourishing network of trade relations. Trade organizations of the early medieval period played a profitable and economically integrative role by cooperating with local merchant groups, by managing important trade centers, and by being prepared to protect their trade by force if necessary. Their inscriptions, which mention their support of Sanskrit learning and ritual, reflect the culture of the nuclear areas of Coromandel. Here the brahmans with their assemblies, cooperating with lower peasant castes, were islands of caste-organized Hindu society. Trade relations were thus re-enforced by a much deeper community of cultural interests shared by the brahmans, peasants, and traders of the nuclear areas. With the incursion of large numbers of warriors who took control of the nuclear areas came an extension of settled agriculture without the complex of institutions that had existed in the older areas. With warriors in power, the agrarian order of Coromandel was transformed from a two-part system of advanced and backward areas to a system of many small territories controlled by warriors jealous of their power and fearful of the designs of their warrior neighbors. The atomization of political and military power was accompanied by an atomization of economic organization which left no scope for the trade organizations of an earlier day.

NOTES

page 49

[1] The term "Coromandel" is taken from the ancient Tamil term "cholamandalam," designating the land of the Chola people, dating with certainty to the time of Asoka, in the third century B.C. In geographical usage the term has referred to the eastern coast of peninsular India from Cape Camorin to the delta of the Kistna and Godāvari rivers. My usage in this essay is an extension of the earliest meaning of Coromandel as a territory; in my sense Coromandel corresponds more or less with the territory of the Imperial Cholas of the tenth to the thirteenth centuries, extending from the southern tip of the peninsula to the deltaic region.

[2] K. A. Nilakanta Sastri, "The Beginnings of Intercourse between India and China," *Indian Historical Quarterly*, vol. 14, June 1938, pp. 385–386. This view of early Sino-Indian trade in Coromandel has considerable support, as noted by Nilakanta Sastri, but there is also some dissent: Elmer H. Cutts, "Chinese-Indian Contacts Prior to the First Century," *Indian Historical Quarterly*, vol. 14, September 1938, p. 496, using different sources, denies these early trade connections or even reciprocal knowledge during the early Han period.

[3] Relevant sections of the *Periplus* as well as numerous other fragments from the reports of foreigners about India to the fifteenth century have been collected and edited by K. A. Nilakanta Sastri in *Foreign Notices of South India; From Magesthenes to Ma Huan*, Madras, 1939, pp. 7, 59.

[4] *Ibid.*, p. 402.

[5] F. Hirth and W. W. Rockhill, *Chau Ju-kua; His Work on the Chinese and Arab Trade in the Twelfth and Thirteenth Centuries, Entitled, "Chu-fan-chi."* St. Petersburg, 1911, pp. 93–94.

page 50

[6] H. G. Quaritch Wales, "Archaeological Researches on Ancient Colonization in Malaya," *Journal of the Malayan Branch of the Royal Asiatic Society*, vol. 28, part I, February 1940, pp. 10–22, 69–72.

[7] G. Coedes, *Les États hindouisés d'Indochine et d'Indonesie*, Paris, 1948, p. 183.

[8] *Ibid.*, p. 239.

[9] *Ibid.*, p. 247.

[10] *Ibid.*, pp. 56, 410.

[11] T. V. Mahalingan, *Economic Life in the Vijayanagar Empire*, Madras, 1951, p. 31, and K. R. Venkatarama Ayyar, "Medieval Trade, Craft, and Merchant Guilds in South India," *Journal of Indian History*, vol. 25, 1947, p. 276.

[12] The importance of these two organizations is cited by among others A. Appadorai, *Economic Conditions in Southern India, 1000–1500 A.D.*, Madras, 1936, vol. 1, pp. 391–402, and K. A. Nilakanta Sastri, *A History of South India*, Madras, 1958, pp. 320–322.

page 51

[13] Appadorai, *op. cit.*, vol. 1, pp. 391, 399; see also his appendix table containing a topographical list of Ayyavole inscriptions, vol. 2, pp. 776–781.

[14] Mysore Archaeological Series, *Epigraphica Carnatica*, ed. B. Lewis Rice, Bangalore, 1886–1909, vol. 7, Shikarpur Taluk, no. 118.

[15] I have used the translation of this concluding section of the Shikarpur inscription no. 118 generously provided by Professor V. Raghavan of the University of Madras in a manuscript note on South Indian society and life.

[16] Venkatarama Ayyar, *op. cit.*, p. 276.

[17] S. Chandrasekhara Sastri, "Economic Conditions under Hoysalas," *The Half-Yearly My-*

sore University Journal, vol. 2, 1928, p. 220; Appadorai, op. cit., vol. 1, p. 395, concurs in this judgment.

[18] The Shikarpur inscription refers to the pattana swami (town leader); Appadorai, op. cit., vol. 1, p. 385, enumerates other examples.

page 52

[19] Government of India, *Annual Report of South Indian Epigraphy, 1912–13*, nos. 256 and 342 of 1912; also paras. 25 and 30. Hereafter cited as *ARE* followed by the number of the inscription or the page or paragraph of the report and the year collected.

[20] K. A. Nilakanta Sastri, "Foreign Trade under the Kakatiyas," *Journal of Oriental Research*, 1934, p. 319.

[21] *Ibid.*, p. 320.

[22] *Ibid.*

[23] Henry Yule and H. Cordier, *The Book of Ser Marco Polo*, London, 1926, vol. 2, pp. 359–363, 375–382.

page 53

[24] In many places in South India there are small carved stone monuments commemorating encounters between warriors of the settled village areas and raiding hill and forest people. These are viragal stones marking the death of such warriors.

page 54

[25] Among the best studies of the Coromandel mahasabhas are K. A. Nilakanta Sastri, *Studies in Cola History and Administration*, Madras, 1932, and R. Sathianathaier, *Studies in the Ancient History of Tondamandalam*, University of Madras, Sankara-Parvati Lectures, 1943–1944, Madras, 1944.

[26] K. A. Nilakanta Sastri, *The Colas*, Madras, 1955, pp. 492–494, and *ARE*, para. 34, 1910; *ARE*, para. 23, 1913.

[27] Appadorai, op. cit., vol. 1, pp. 152–154. These villages were generally designated by the term vellan-vagai, meaning "cultivator's share."

[28] The best discussion of these assemblies is K. V. Subrahmanya Aiyer, "The Largest Provincial Assemblies in India," *The Quarterly Journal of the Mythic Society*, Bangalore, vol. 65, 1954–1955, no. 1, pp. 29–47; no. 2, pp. 70–98; no. 4, pp. 270–286; and vol. 66, 1955, no. 1, pp. 8–22.

page 55

[29] I am indebted to Sri J. Sundaram, Epigraphical Assistant, Office of the Epigraphist for India for his help with this and other translations used in this essay though he is not responsible for the use I have made of them. On one point in the standard invocation there is disagreement which relates to the caste composition of the chitrameli members. Sundaram, Professor V. Raghavan, and Venkatarama Ayyar, op. cit., pp. 274–275, agree that this is a fourth caste or sudra assembly; Subrahmanya Aiyer, op. cit., vol. 15, no. 2, p. 75, suggests that the assembly included all four traditional caste groupings, e.g., brahmans, kshatriyas, vaishyas, and sudras. In another context, this distinction would be vital, of course; but in this discussion it is not essential to know whether agriculturists, or sudras, cooperated as a body in their assembly, the chitrameli. The standard introduction may be seen in either Subrahmanya Aiyer, op. cit., vol. 65, no. 4, p. 275, or *ARE*, p. 6, 1953–1954.

[30] *ARE*, p. 6, 1953–1954.

[31] These examples and other relevant inscriptional references are cited by Venkatarama Ayyar, op. cit., pp. 275–276.

[32] *ARE*, 21, 1903; *ARE*, 342, 1912; and *ARE*, 25, 1913 discuss the composition of this merchant group.

[33] *ARE*, 601, 1902.

[34] *ARE*, 154, 1903.

page 56

[35] The prospects of revolt in groups within such integrated nuclear areas was apparently not great since the brahmans, merchants, artisans, and sudras were relatively peaceful people considering the time. There is some evidence of risings, however, for example in the late thirteenth century in Chingleput district (probably in Uttirampakkam), where the brahmans, merchants, and sudras revolted at the time of the extension of Pandya rule from Madurai in the southern portion of Coromandel over the northern portion. *ARE*, 315, 1909; *ARE*, para. 34, 1910.

page 57

[36] Nilakanta Sastri, *The Colas*, pp. 421–422.

[37] Though the generalized irruption from within and beyond Coromandel in the thirteenth and fourteenth centuries may be re-

garded as the beginning of a significant change in the agrarian order, it was not the cause of this change as much as it was a symptom of changing relations within the older order where numerous ambitious chiefs, within and beyond Coromandel, owing to the experience of centuries at the edges of the caste-village complex of Hindu society, saw a way of enhancing their power and authority by becoming a part of that system and even ruling it. This process of assimilation of warriors is very ancient in India; it has recently been discussed with insight by D. D. Kosambi, "The Basis of Ancient Indian History," *Journal of the American Oriental Society*, vol. 75, no. 1, January 1955, pp. 35–45 and no. 4, October 1955, pp. 226–236.

[38] Nilakanta Sastri, *History of South India*, p. 297.

[39] *Ibid.*

[40] *Ibid.*, p. 298.

page 58

[41] The flight of warrior families from the Telegu-speaking portions of Coromandel in the face of Muslim pressure is a recurrent theme in the local histories recorded in the MacKenzie Manuscripts collected by C. MacKenzie in the late eighteenth century while he was posted as an engineer in the Madras Government. These manuscripts are now in the Oriental Manuscripts Library of the Government of Madras, Madras. Two major reference works in the collection are the Reverend William Taylor, *Catalogue Raisonnée of Oriental Manuscripts in the Library of the (Late) College, Fort St. George*, Madras, 1857–1862, 3 vols; and H. H. Wilson, *The MacKenzie Collection: A Descriptive Catalogue of the Oriental Manuscripts and Other Articles . . . Collected by the Late Lt. Col. Colin MacKenzie*, 2nd ed., Madras, 1882. Examples of references to Muslim pressure are "Account of the Badelapa Nayaka, Poligar of Rettayambadi in Coimbatore Country," Wilson, *op. cit.*, p. 419, nos. VI-1; Taylor, *op. cit.*, vol. 3, p. 290; "Account of Terumala Ponnappa Nayaka of Virupaksam Palayappattu," Wilson, *op. cit.*, p. 420, no. VI-3; Taylor, *op. cit.*, III, p. 299; "Kaifiyat of Kamaya Nayaka of Valaiyapatti," Wilson, *op. cit.*, p. 431, XXX-12.

[42] Mahalingam, *op. cit.*, p. 88.

[43] The development of temples reflected not only religious movements in this period which were of great importance everywhere in India, but also the greater status that supporting temples gave many of the warriors from low-caste groups eager to have their recent high status as warriors legitimated. Another possible reason for warriors' support of temples during this time was their recognition of economic activities which temples carried out, including irrigation and other agricultural development; see Burton Stein, "Economic Functions of a Medieval South Indian Temple," *Journal of Asian Studies*, vol. 19, no. 2, February 1960, pp. 163–176.

[44] Most notable of such migrations, perhaps, is that of the Sourashtrian weavers who settled in Madurai. A more general case would be the support given to weavers of Coromandel, kaikkolas, in order to induce them to move. See A. J. Saunders, "The Saurastra Community of Madura," *Journal of the Madras University*, vol. 1, no. 1, 1928, pp. 69–92; Appadorai, *op. cit.*, vol. 1, pp. 373–374.

[45] Nilakanta Sastri, *The Colas*, p. 597, speaks of mercenary armies under the Ayyavole organization.

page 59

[46] *Epigraphica Carnatica*, vol. 7, *op. cit.*, Shikarpur taluk, no. 118.

[47] These reports may be found conveniently summarized and with references in Mahalingam, *op. cit.*, pp. 118–140, to which may be added two useful Dutch works: Daniel Havart, *Op En Ondergang van Cormandel in Zijn Binnenste Geheel Open, En Ten Toon Gesteld . . .*, Amsterdam, 1693, in the James Ford Bell Collection, University of Minnesota, and Philip Baldaeus, *A True and Exact Description of the Most Celebrated Coasts of Malabar and Coromandel as Also of the Isle of Ceylon*, translated from the Dutch, Amsterdam, 1672. A recent study of Dutch trade may also be noted: Tapan Raychaudhuri, *Jan Company in Coromandel, 1605–1690; A Study in the Interrelations of European Commerce and Traditional Economies*, The Hague, 1962.

The Van Deutecum Map of
Russia and Tartary

by JOHN W. WEBB

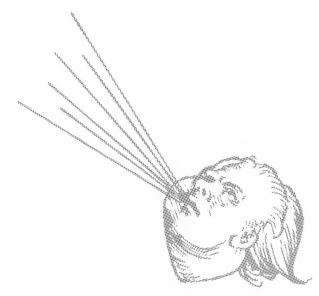

A LARGE MAP, in three sheets, of Russia, Tartary, and neighboring regions was printed in the Netherlands in the 1560's. Although the map gives no indication of author or date of compilation it is signed by the brothers Jan and Lucas van Deutecum. Apparently only one copy has survived to modern times: formerly in the Dashkov Collection in Leningrad, it is now preserved in the State Historical Museum, Moscow. There was no mention of the Van Deutecum map, as we shall call it, by students of the history of cartography until it was reproduced in 1906 by Kordt in his facsimile-atlas of the cartographical history of Russia.[1] The map was discussed by Michow in his summary of Kordt's work,[2] more recently by Bagrow in his general study of Russian cartography,[3] and by Keuning in a short article on maps associated with the English explorer Anthony Jenkinson.[4] The Van Deutecum map is a rich and impressive example of map engraving from sixteenth-century Dutch cartographers. Since it was drawn at a time of increasing interest among Europeans in eastern Europe and western Asia, the map deserves a fuller treatment than it has thus far had.

The names of two visitors to Russia appear in the title of this map: Herberstein, Austrian ambassador and self-styled "chorographer" of Muscovy, and Jenkinson, English diplomat, trader, and traveler, both key figures in the sixteenth-century revolution in European knowledge about eastern Europe and western Asia. But much, if not most, of this lifting of horizons resulted from the emergence of Muscovy as the center of Russian political organization and expansion; without this there would have been no ambassador from the Holy Roman Emperor in the West, and no Muscovy Company in London with its envoy seeking trading rights in the Tsar's dominions.

Ivan the Third (the Great), who succeeded as Grand Duke of Muscovy in 1462, was the real founder of the Russian state, for it was he who began to weld the Russian lands and peoples into a compact and centralized unit. He rejected Emperor Frederick's offer of a kingship, proudly claiming that he was sovereign in his own right. By absorbing Novgorod (*Novogardia**) with its large territories to the north

* All topographic and other names appearing on the Van Deutecum map are italicized in my text.
NOTES for *The Van Deutecum Map of Russia and Tartary* are to be found on pages 85 and 86.

and west of Moscow, Ivan laid a claim to Kiev (*Kioff*) more powerful than that of Poland-Lithuania. Perm (*Permea*), to the north and east, followed in 1472, and the principalities of Tver (*Twera*), Ryazan (*Resane*), and Vyatka (*Viatka*) were brought into subjection about 1485. On the southern and eastern margins of the Russian lands the Fabian strategy of Ivan and his successors confused the Tartars, whose divisions were skillfully played upon by Moscow, so that the Tartar grip was broken and the once all-powerful nomads subsided into a series of Khanates which were ineffectual in the newer and broader scale of state politics and warfare conducted from Moscow.

Ivan's confident claims and gradual methods were repeated by his son Vasili the Third (1505–1533), whose portrait we see facing the buildings at the bottom left of the Van Deutecum map, and whose patrimony is commemorated by a four-line poem in simple but direct terms: "I am the Emperor, the Lord and King,/ My own inheritance is sufficient,/ I have received and bought nothing from anyone,/ I have been baptized a Christian in the name of God." Vasili subdued Smolensk (*Smolenskia*) and Pskov (*Pleskovia*), further weakened the Tartars, and continued to organize and centralize the administration of his territories. Herberstein's mission in 1516 was peace between Vasili and Poland-Lithuania. His proposals were rebuffed, but he returned to Moscow in 1524, soon after the accession of Charles the Fifth as head of the Holy Roman Empire and of Suleiman the Magnificent as sultan of the Turkish Empire. But the Grand Duke was not interested in Herberstein's proposals for the defense of Christendom, and after two years' stay the Austrian left for home with a store of observations to include in his famous book *Rerum Moscoviticarum Comentarii*.

Ivan the Fourth (the Terrible) succeeded his father at the age of three, and took the government into his own hands when he was only fourteen. Soon he picked the fruits of Muscovite policy in the east: his conquests of the Khanate of Kazan (*Cazan Reg.*) and the Khanate of Astrakhan (*Astracan*) are commemorated on the map. The portrait of him on Jenkinson's map (see Figure 1, p. 68) with some of his titles – Ioannes Basilius Magnus, Imperator Russiae, Dux Moscoviae, etc. – is perhaps a remembrance from Jenkinson's encounters with Ivan while the Tsar was on the march in the west. Ivan began a war over the succession to Livonia in 1558, but here he became embroiled in a long conflict with Poland and Sweden; eventually he concluded a peace after a series of reverses had been inflicted on him by Stefan Batory, King of Poland.

But the great gains were to the east where Russia was at last attacking Asia. Despite the burning of Moscow by the Crimean Tartars in 1571, deliverance from the Mongol threat had come. The Volga was now a Russian river and with the prestige of the Tartars gone many peoples began to throw themselves under the protection of Moscow. Even the Khanate of Sibir over the Ural Mountains (*Orbis Zona Montes*) bowed before Ivan. The stage was set for the free-lance adventurers, such as Yermak, who spread Russian influence and power across Siberia to the Pacific Ocean within a century.

Sigismund von Herberstein was not the first ambassador to be sent from the Emperor's court to Moscow: Niclas Poppel, Georg van Thurn, and others had preceded him in attempts to sound out the Muscovite court on their attitude toward political and dynastic alliances.[5] Although Herberstein's diplomacy was unsuccessful, his notes about life in Moscow and personal observations about the western parts of the Russian lands, as well as material collected at second hand about the regions to the east of Moscow, were published some years after his return to Vienna in 1527. *Rerum Moscoviticarum Comentarii* forms by far the best of the early accounts of Russia, and it is not surprising that the authors of our map turned to it for a text to accompany their work.[6] Herberstein paid much attention to the rivers of Russia, which, flowing in interlacing patterns across the great plains of eastern Europe, made trade and travel far different from what they were in Europe further west. Frozen as they were in winter and suitable for fast horse traffic, and running full and fast in the spring, the rivers formed the only important highways. Herberstein concerned himself with the unraveling of the tangled skein of the main streams and their tributaries, and to noting the portages that connected their headwaters. He was at pains to point out the strategic location of the headwaters of the western Dvina (*Dwina*), the *Volga,* the Dnepr (*Borysthenes*), the Oka (not named on the map), and the Lovat (*Lowat*). In addition to many pages devoted to social, religious, and court life in Moscow, he also gives us the itinerary of a "journey to Pechora, into Yugra, and as far as the River Ob." Some of the many sixteenth-century editions of Herberstein's book include engravings of things seen in his travels, as well as maps of Russia and Moscow.

Anthony Jenkinson stepped onto the page of history during the initial stages of English expansion, in which he played an important role, for he was the greatest overland explorer from England in his age. The strong commercial ties which grew between Russia of Ivan the Terrible and the England of Elizabeth were, in good measure, due to his skill and courage. In 1553 Richard Chancellor and Hugh Willoughby set out to find a northeast passage to Cathay: Chancellor found instead the White Sea and a way to Moscow, and, after a second voyage in 1555, returned to Britain with a Russian ambassador and the promise of a lucrative trade with Moscow. By developing this new contact with the English, Ivan was hopeful of outflanking the political and commercial problems to his west. The Muscovy Company was formed at once, with Sebastian Cabot as governor, and in 1557 Jenkinson sailed with four ships filled with pewter and broadcloth. His instructions were to press for trading agreements in Russia and to explore the possibilities of an overland route to Cathay.[7]

Jenkinson returned to London in the autumn of 1560 after a momentous journey to Moscow by way of the White Sea and the northern Dvina (*Dvina flu*) and Sukhona (*Sughana*), to Astrakhan down the Volga, and to Bokhara (*Boghar*) by way of the Caspian Sea (*Mare Caspium*). He reported to the company that the overland route

Figure 1. Jenkinson's map of Russia and Tartary from Abraham Ortelius,
Theatrum Orbis Terrarum, London, 1606 (Bell Collection).

to Cathay was impracticable and suggested that the Caspian Sea and Persia might provide a profitable alternative to the Orient. While in London Jenkinson apparently drew a map of Russia, a version of which Ortelius included in his *Theatrum Orbis Terrarum* of 1570 (see Figure 1).

On this and later journeys Jenkinson spent much time in complicated diplomatic and commercial negotiations. Some years afterward he wrote for Hakluyt,[8] "The names of such countries as I, Anthony Jenkinson have travelled unto from the second of October, 1546. at which time I made my first voiage out of England, untill the yeere of our Lord, 1572, when I returned last out of Russia." After listing journeys made as a young man to the Mediterranean and the Levant, he continues,

I have sailed farre Northward within the *Mare glaciale*, where wee have had continuall day, and sight of the Sunne ten weekes together, and that navigation was in Norway, Lapland, *Samagotia,* and other very strange places. I have travelled through all the ample dominions of the Emperour of Russia and Moscovia, which extend from the North Sea, and the confines of Norway, and Lapland, even to the *Mare Caspium*. I have bene in divers countries neere about the Caspian Sea, Gentiles and Mohametans, as *Cazan, Cremia, Rezan, Cheremisi, Mordoviti, Vachin, Nagaia,* with divers other strange customes and religions. I have sailed over the Caspian Sea, and discovered all the regions thereabout adjacent, as *Cherkassi, Comul, Shafcall, Shirvan,* with many others. . . .

I have travelled 40. daies journey beyond the said sea, towards the Orientall India, and Cathaia, through divers deserts and wildernesses, and passed through 5. king-domes of the Tartares, and all the land of Turkeman and Zagatay, and so to the great citie of Boghar in Bactria, not without great perill and dangers sundry times.

After his journey to Bokhara Jenkinson returned home; the next year, in 1562, he went to Persia by way of the White Sea, Moscow, and the Volga, and returned again to Moscow in 1566 and 1571. "And thus being wearie and growing old, I am content to take my rest in mine own house."

Accounts of these and other journeys, copies of manuscript and printed maps, and other information relating to new discoveries and the widening of European geo-graphical horizons were accumulating in the workrooms of cartographers, engravers, mapmakers, and printers in the Netherlands. Indeed, by the 1560's, native and immi-grant mapmakers in the Low Countries had all but wrested supremacy in the business of cartography from the Italians. Among this distinguished band were the Van Deute-cum brothers. Jan and Lucas van Deutecum went to Antwerp from Deventer in 1559 to begin a long career as master engravers. They made a distinguished contribution to the golden age of cartography in the Netherlands, producing scores of separate maps, city plans, and town views. Much of their work was done for Christophe Plan-tin, the famous printer of Antwerp, a man of considerable business acumen who, with a fine company of engravers, was printer and distributor for such great cartographers as Ortelius and de Jode. He was to a considerable degree responsible for the Nether-lands' becoming the center of mapmaking in the late sixteenth century.[9]

The brothers' first important work was for Hieronymous Cock, who in 1559 de-signed and printed a gallery of thirty-one plates, engraved by Jan and Lucas, com-memorating the obsequies held in Brussels on the death of Emperor Charles the Fifth. Plantin printed the text of *La Magnifique et somptueuse pompe funèbre faite aus ob-seques et funeralles du très grand et très victorieus Empereur Charles V,* and the as-sociation of his name with this magnificent production brought him and his work be-fore the public for the first time.[10]

However, to judge from available lists of the Van Deutecums' work, it was some time before they began to work steadily at engraving maps. Most of the maps and atlases of that time passed through the hands of Plantin and are referred to in his accounts; it was not until 1563 that the brothers engraved a map of Portugal by Fer-nando Alvares Seco for Gerard de Jode.[11] This was followed in 1566 by a large map of the Netherlands.[12] Since Jenkinson's map and itinerary could not have been avail-able until 1562 it is possible, as Keuning says[13] that the map of Russia was the Van Deutecums' first attempt at engraving a map. Considering that other technicians were moving on to authorship and compilation (for example, Ortelius was formerly a map colorer and de Jode an engraver), it is not unreasonable to assume that the brothers were themselves the compilers, using whatever maps and texts were available to them in Antwerp. In compiling a map with three panels with an accompanying text, to be put on a wall for decorative purposes, they were following the format of the *Pompe funèbre du Charles V*, hoping, no doubt, to bring the quality of their work before mapmakers and geographers. Plantin's accounts and other map lists of the time, with the exception of a list printed by the bookseller Georg Willer, do not mention this map and, since only one copy is known to exist, it is impossible to estimate the number of copies printed and whether it was made available for sale elsewhere than at the Frankfort book fair.

But regardless of whether or not the Van Deutecum map dates from 1562–1565 or from a few years later, the brothers were soon engraving many maps. It is possible that they engraved some of the plates for the first editions of Ortelius in 1570. Their principal contributions were the plates for Gerard de Jode's *Speculum Orbis Terrarum*, published in 1578, and Lucas Jansz. Wagenaer's *Spieghel der Zeevaerdt*, published in 1584. About 1587 the brothers moved again, Jan settling in Haarlem and Lucas in Amsterdam. Jan attempted once or twice to bring out his own maps, but by 1592 both he and Lucas had retired from engraving. They died around the turn of the century, but not before Jan's sons, Jan the Younger and Batista, had succeeded to their father's profession.

The engravings of the Van Deutecum brothers were certainly equal in quality to those of their contemporaries. They used varying styles, but lines and inscriptions became less bulky as they experimented with new methods of engraving on copper. Although it is of generally high quality, being particularly notable for its calligraphy and for fine sketches of animals and human beings, the Van Deutecum map of Russia and Tartary was an early production and does not show the brothers at their best. Their finest engravings are the sea charts in Wagenaer's atlas, which is a monument to their genius as mature craftsmen.

The copy of the Van Deutecum map in Moscow is in three parts which measure 51.0 x 106.5 centimeters over-all. It is an unmounted black print from a copper engraving, and is not colored. The linear scale, at about one to eight million, is larger than for other contemporary maps of Russia, and the regions covered extend from Scandinavia and the Baltic lands on the first sheet, to the Urals and the Caucasus on the second sheet, as far as western Siberia and Turkestan on the eastern sheet. The title, which stretches across the top of the three sheets, runs REGIONVM SEPTENTRIONALIVM, MOSCOVIAM, RVTENOS, TARTAROS, EORVMQVE HORDAS CONPREHENDENTIVM, EX ANTONII IENKESONII ET SIGISMVNDI LIBERI BARONIS AB HERBERSTEIN ITINERARIIS, NOVA DESCRIPTIO (A New Description of the Northern Regions, including Muscovy, the Russians, the Tartars and their Hordes, from the Itineraries of Anthony Jenkinson and Freiherr Sigismund von Herberstein). (See Figure 2.)

Though it is not possible to give an exact date for the making of this map, con-

Figure 2 (this and the following two pages). The Van Deutecum map, 1562.

SEPTENTRIO   CIREMISSI

MARE GLACIALE

CONDORA

DVINA

PERMIA

VS

TI

VGE CEREMISE

VIATKA   VACHIN

MEROS LAW

LOW GOVOI   CAZAN REG.

DIMVR   SERMISE

CO   RESANE   BVLGARIA

VIA   MORDVA

SEVERA PRO.   CRIME   COSONCHA TER

CVMANA TER   HORDA   VSEZVCANI TER

MARE DE ZABACHÆ   CIRCASSI   INAGACHI TER

PONTVS   CAITACHI   COLCHIS   PERICORCHI TE

EVXINVS   MENGRELIA   IBERI   IBERI

GIORGIANI

BOLI   ARMENIA

AMASIA

NATOLIA   PEGIAN

MERIDIES

TVMEN

NOGAI TER

TVRB LACVS

OCEANVS SCYTHICVS

TVRBI

MOLGOMZAIA

VZESVCANI

BAIDA

MACRITI

IOVGHORIA Y E D A COLMARCK DOBSAN

14

KITAIA

LACVS

13

IVGORIA HORDA

CASSACKIA

HORDA

BASCHIRDI

KIRGESSI

TARTARIA PARS

HORDA

17

CHESELITI TAR.

SIBIERAI PRO

TVRQVSTA

HORDA

TVRCK MEN

NAGAIA

HORDA

Bophar

10

Tashent

ZAGATAI

8

Samercadis destructa

Asson

MARE CHVVALIS COMORIA

Corasan perua

Urbs Corasan à Rege Persia adiacentibus Tartaris anno 1555 expugnata fuit.

Korshy

MARE CASPIVM

Corasan magna

MARE BACHV

MARE CORVZV

Belach

SERVAN GILA

STRABAT TER

GVMENT PRO

MEDIA DIAR

O R I E N S

temporary evidence allows us to place it in the 1560's. Bagrow discusses a catalog published in 1573 in Augsburg by the bookseller Georg Willer[14] which lists books, atlases, and maps sold by Willer at the Frankfort book fair in 1572. The part of the catalog devoted to decorative wall maps contains the only contemporary reference to the Van Deutecum map I have uncovered: it is listed as "Regiones Septentrionales ex Antonii Ienkonsenii & Sigismundi ab Herberstein itinerariis." Willer does not give any dates for the maps on his list, but most of them were produced in the middle 1560's. In any case the map was certainly not drawn before 1561, the year that Jenkinson returned from his journey to Bokhara. It probably appeared before Mercator's world map of 1569, certainly before the second edition of Mercator's map of Europe appeared in 1572.

At first sight the map appears to be organized on the basis of a simple plane projection. A series of check marks, representing the positioning of lines of longitude, appears along the lower border. Longitudes are at intervals of ten degrees, running from 30° to 110° and based on Ptolemy's prime meridian at the Fortunate Islands. However, it is not clear what kind of projection was used. Perhaps the makers of the map were as yet unschooled in the mysteries of map projection and attempted to put together three sections with unconnected grid patterns, each of the sections corresponding to one of the three sheets. The meridians on each sheet may be parallel to each other, and meet the parallels at different angles from sheet to sheet. Thus the meridians on the western sheet are pitched slightly to the east, those on the center sheet run north and south, and those of the eastern sheet are pitched to the west. If this unusual (and rather crude) procedure was used it will help to explain the confusion in the representation of the shore of the *Mare Glaciale*. The center section, which is designed roughly on the principle of Mercator's famous projection, has an overly long north coast (made wider by the overextended east–west measurements of the Black Sea) which has had to be filled in with imaginary islands and coasts. This would help to explain the easterly position of *Nova Zemla* (Novaya Zemlya) and the existence of two *Vaigatz* Islands on the map (one is named *Vaigate*).

The claiming of the two itineraries as sources (rather than the maps associated with Jenkinson and Herberstein) perhaps indicates that the title refers as much to a text accompanying the Van Deutecum map (examples of such a text have not survived) as it does to the map itself. This indication is strengthened by the existence of the numerals 1 to 15 in different parts of the map, which probably refer to sections of a text. Also, the main body of the map is derived not from Jenkinson's and Herberstein's maps (with which some features of the eastern sheet and the inset of Moscow respectively are associated), but from other maps current in the 1560's, most notably the map of Europe published by Mercator in 1554.

The cartographic history of the Van Deutecum map is long: I shall here summarize briefly the growth of knowledge about Russia and neighboring regions as shown on maps and atlases up to the time of its publication.[15]

The legacy which cartographers of the Renaissance received from Ptolemy includes the Tanais (*Don, Tanais vel Don fluvius* on the Van Deutecum map) flowing into the Palus Maeotis (Sea of Azov, *Mare de Zabachae*) and the *Borysthenes* (Dnepr) flowing into the *Pontus Euxinus* (Black Sea). The *Mare Caspium* of Ptolemy was roughly elliptical, with the long axis running east–west; it was very large, and too far to the east, extending as far as the proper position of the Aral Sea, which did not appear on his maps. Into the Caspian flowed the Rha (Volga, *Volga Russ, Edel Tarta: Rha*), the Daix (Yaik, *Iaick*), and, mistakenly, the Oxus (Amu-Darya) and the Jaxartes (Syr-Darya, *Chassel vel Loxarte*). Regional maps in Ptolemy's atlas (in, for example, the Ulm edition by Lienart Holle of 1482) show a number of towns in Bactriana and Sogdiana, many of which were ancient predecessors of more modern cities along the old route from China to the West.

From the Catalan atlas of 1375, which recorded some of the results of the journeys of Marco Polo, we get D'Organçi (Oxus), Urgence (Urgendzh, *Urgense*), Bagar (Bokhara, *Boghar*), Samarchan (Samarkand, *Samarcandia*) and Carachora (*Karakorum*).[16] Fra Mauro, who filled his mappemonde of 1459 with many place names and much information, gives us Balch (Balkh, *Balach*), Cagatai (Zagatai), Organca (Urgendzh), Sarayzuch (*Serachick*) — the diminutive of Sarai, a tent city of the Tartars, Raxan (Ryazan, *Resane*), Permia (*Permea*), *Mordva*, and many others.[17] From the globe of Martin Behaim (1492), and from the revisions of Ptolemy's atlas by Martin Waldseemüller (1516) and Batista Agnese (1525) came some further information which further modified the classical inheritance.

The remarkable map of Anton Wied, first published in 1542, gives us much new information specifically about Russia.[18] Wied's map, which was printed in both Russian and Latin, identifies the Abdoriani (*Obdo*), Yugoriani (*Ioughoria*), Condoriani (*Condora*), and Voguls; Velikaya Perm (*Welikiprem*) and Tumen Veliki (*Tumen*); Kitaisko (Cathay, in this case associated with the Obi River, which appears as *Kitaia Lacus* on the Van Deutecum map), and a number of other places. The map also contains many drawings of animals and human beings and is notable for the representation of woodlands and forests, cities and towns.

The map associated with the various editions of Herberstein's account of Russia appears in two places: in the earliest edition of *Rerum Moscoviticarum Comentarii*, from Vienna in 1549, and in a version by Giacomo Gastaldi made for the first Italian edition, from Venice in 1550. Figure 3 is a photographic copy of the earlier map from the copy in the James Ford Bell Collection of the 1557 German edition from Vienna. Although the 1557 map appears to be rather crude in detail, its main purpose was to make clear the relations among the main rivers of Russia and the location of their courses relative to the principal cities. Gastaldo was also the compiler of a series of maps of various parts of the world which were often bound up into atlases; some of these deal with regions covered by the Van Deutecum map. Mercator's large map of Europe, published in 1554 and revised in 1572, attempted to sum up what was

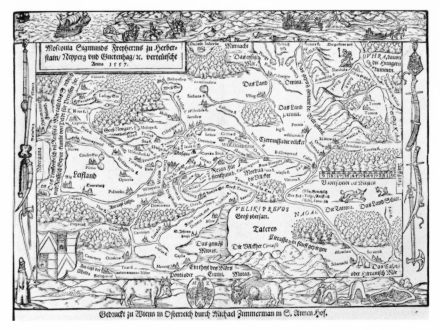

Figure 3. Herberstein's map of Russia from his *Moscovia der Hauptstat in Reissen*, Vienna, 1557 (Bell Collection).

known about the continent up to that time. On a different scale came Mercator's large world map of 1569, again a fine compilation of current geographical information.

Lastly for our purposes in this essay, Anthony Jenkinson drew, or had drawn, a map of Russia and Tartary. A version of this map was later included by Abraham Ortelius in his *Theatrum Orbis Terrarum*. Figure 1 is taken from the copy in the James Ford Bell Collection of the first English edition of Ortelius, printed in London in 1606. The date of Ortelius's version of this map (1570) and the date of the original (apparently 1562) create some difficulties when the Van Deutecum map and the version produced by Gerard de Jode (1578) are considered: these difficulties will be discussed later. In any case the Van Deutecums (or whoever the authors of our map may have been) could call on a substantial body of material to use in preparing their map.

In dealing with the content of the Van Deutecum map, particular attention will be paid to those parts which offer new features or new interpretations of information shown on maps published previously. Since the texts have not appeared in the previous literature on the map, an English translation will be given here.

We find that the plan of Moscow and drawings similar to each of the figures in the inset also appear in the earliest edition in German of *Rerum Moscoviticarum Comentarii*, published in Vienna in 1557 by Michael Zimmerman. The streets and houses shown on the plan are only a stylistic representation of the center of Moscow, for, though Herberstein wrote: "six years before my arrival at Moscow, the houses were counted by order of the prince, and the number was 41,500," [19] he treated this estimate with reserve, observing: "The city itself is built of wood, and tolerably large, and at a distance appears larger than it really is, for the gardens and spacious court-yards in every house make a great addition to the size of the city." [20]

Jenkinson's description of the Kremlin[21] as he saw it some thirty-five years after Herberstein increases our respect for Moscow as the metropolis of a growing empire:

The citie of *Musko* is great, the houses for the most part of wood, and some of stone, with windows of yron, which serve for summer time. There are many faire Churches of stone, but more of wood, which are made hot in the winter time. The Emperour's lodging is in a faire, and large castle, walled four square of bricke, high, and thicke, situated upon a hil, two miles about, and the river on the Southwest side of it, and it hath 16. gates in the wals, and as many bulwarks. His pallace is separated from the rest of the Castle, by a long wall going north and south, to the riverside. . . . In the Church doores and within the Churches, are images of golde: the chiefe markets for all things, are within the saide Castle, and for sundry thinges, sundry markets, and every science by it selfe. Also in the winter there is a great market without the Castle, upon the river being frozen, and there is sold corne, earthen pots, tubs, sleds, etc. The Castle is in circuite 2900 pases.

Both Herberstein and Jenkinson were struck by the unusual methods of travel in the Russian winter. The figures above the city plan are a composite made from engravings in the Vienna edition of Herberstein, although all have been made to face to the right (as have the three armed horsemen) to improve the artistic quality of the map. Of winter travel Jenkinson wrote: "the people travel with sleds, in Towne and Countrey, the way being hard, and smooth with snow: the waters and rivers are all frozen, and one horse with a sled, will draw a man upon it 400 miles, in three daies." [22]

Gazing across Moscow is the grand duke, Vasili the Third, who had been dead for many years by the time this map was drawn. He holds a metal-pointed staff like the one carried around the Kremlin by his father, Ivan the Third, who would certainly have approved of the sentiments expressed in the four-line poem. The poem (see p. 66 above) is a German version of a Latin verse which can be found in some editions of Herberstein, including the Venice edition of 1550.

The two animals standing on the bank of the Moskva River appeared first on Wied's map, but the full-scale engravings from which the Van Deutecums made these versions appeared first in the 1557 Vienna edition of Herberstein. On the left is the aurochs, a wild European ox which was eventually exterminated in the seventeenth century by forest-clearing and hunting. The other animal is the European bison, the hunting of which Herberstein describes as needing "men of great strength, agility and cunning." This species was numerous in the sixteenth century and managed to sur-vive until modern times; it is now under government protection in eastern Europe. Herberstein wrote an extensive account of both animals.[23]

The cartography of the rivers of Russia is much improved on the Van Deutecum map over that of the Ortelius version of Jenkinson's map. With regard to European Russia, Jenkinson's map appears to have reverted to the state of knowledge that existed before Herberstein's map appeared. The Van Deutecums give a more correct representation of the headwaters of the *Borysthenes* (Dnepr), *Dwina* (the western Dvina), and *Volga*; although the *Tanais* (Don), *Sem* (Seym), and Oka are still joined through *Lake Plotho* as they were on Wied's map. In the north the *Onega, Dvina, Sughana* (Sukhona), *Voijchogda* (Vychegda), and *Mesena* (Mezen) are remarkably good likenesses. However, the *Pechora* is far to the east of its proper position, and a large stream called the *Yug* flows north to the *Mare Glaciale* (Arctic Ocean) to fill up the resulting space. The *Volga* receives a number of tributaries, including the *Mologa*, the *Mosko* (Moskva)–Oka–*Desna* (Klyazma) system, the *Kastroma* (Kostroma), and *Samara* (Samar).

The Kama system is represented well enough, although the Vetluga is misnamed the *Viatska*, the Vyatka the *Kama*, and the Kama the *Viscora*. The headwaters of the Kama system are correctly placed in the Urals, called *Orbis Zona Montes*, but much extended to the south from the short range that appears on the Ortelius map with the same name. The Urals run in the proper direction on the Van Deutecum map, and extend from about 72° to 58° north, which is roughly correct. Over the mountains are indications of rivers to the east of the *Obij fluvius* (Obi), perhaps an early guess at the Taz or Yenesei. The Obi itself flows to the *Mare Glaciale* from *Kitaia Lacus* (the Lake of Cathay): this whole conception is from Herberstein and is contradictory to the statement in the southeast corner of this map that Cathay is thirty days' travel to the east from Cascara.

The hydrography of the southern half of the eastern sheet is a composite of tradition, speculation, and new information. The traditional view, as in Ptolemy, was to have the Oxus and Jaxartes rivers flowing into the Caspian Sea; this is shown on the Van Deutecum map, with the Oxus unnamed and the Jaxartes called *Chassel vel Loxarte*. The roughly elliptical shape of the Caspian is also traditional. On the Ortelius map the Caspian is shaped very differently; that representation was not used by the Van Deutecums.

The brothers also failed to follow the Ortelius solution to the Oxus-Jaxartes problem. On the Ortelius map are two Oxus rivers. The first is the Amou (Amu-Darya) which we see flowing into the Sur (Syr-Darya) and then northward into Kitaia Lacus. Assuming that Jenkinson himself completed the map published by Ortelius, it is likely that he himself had no doubt of the existence of Kitaia Lacus, which he mistook for the inland drainage region we know as the Aral Sea. The second is the Ougus (i.e., Oxus), which flows from the south, and, according to Jenkinson's narrative, "falleth into another river called Ardocke, which runneth toward the north and consumeth himself in the ground." Since he had been there, some scholars believe that Jenkinson could have done better than this; perhaps he should have, but his confusion is not unreasonable when one remembers that he shows an "Amou" and a "Syr" flowing north (he was unaware that "Amu" was the Chinese name for the Oxus) to a lake that was thought to be a fact, and also that he talks about an old bed of the Oxus and discusses a channel flowing north into the desert.

Another explanation might be that the eastern part of the Ortelius map was not drawn until 1570, and was based on sources other than the original map of Jenkinson. In any case the Van Deutecums give us two streams, one of which is called *Sur* and flows northward. Since it is possible that their map antedated the eastern part of Jenkinson's map as it appears in Ortelius, the Van Deutecums may have been the first to attempt a mapping of these rivers, which the compiler of the 1570 map continued as best he could. The implications of these possibilities will be discussed below.

When considering the inaccuracies in the representation of the rivers of Turkestan on the Van Deutecum map, one can hardly blame the authors for not solving the riddle. Over a century later the celebrated map of eastern Europe and Asia by Nicholas Witsen (1687) still showed an elliptical Caspian Sea.[24] It was not until the early eighteenth century that the Caspian-Aral-Syr-Amu complex of inland seas and rivers was surveyed and reproduced on maps with tolerable accuracy.

Jenkinson's text contains the following description of the Caspian Sea; interestingly, it makes no mention of either the Oxus or Jaxartes among the list of streams entering the sea.

This *Caspian sea* (to say some thing of it) is in length about two hundred leagues, and in bredth 150, without any issue to other seas, to the East parte whereof, joyneth the great desert Countrey of the *Tartars,* called *Turkemen*: to the West, the Countreyes of the *Chyrcasses,* the mountains of the *Caucasus,* and the *Mare Euxinum,* which is from the saide *Caspian* sea a hundred leagues. To the North is the river *Volga,* and the land of *Nagay,* and to the South part, ioyne the Countries of *Media,* and *Persia.* This sea is fresh water in many places, and in other places is salt as our great Ocean. It hath many goodly rivers falling into it, and it avoideth not it self, except it be under ground. The notable rivers that fall into it, are first the great river of *Volga,* called in the *Tartar* tongue *Edell,* which springeth out of a lake in a marrish, or plaine ground, not farre from the Citie of *Novogrode,* in Russia, and it is from that springe to the sea, above two thousand English miles. It hath divers other goodly rivers falling into it, as out of *Sebaria, Yaick,* and *Yeim*: Also out of the mountaines of the *Caucasus,* the rivers *Cyrus,* and *Arrash,* and divers others.[25]

In company with many of their illustrious contemporaries the compilers of the Van Deutecum map did not acknowledge the work of others when they used it. Gerhard Mercator's map of Europe, published in Duisburg, in 1554, was the source of much of the central and western sheets, including Scandinavia south of the latitude of Trondheim, the coasts of the Baltic and the south of the coast of the Gulf of Finland, the upper Volga as far downstream as Kazan (but not the tributaries of the Volga flowing in from the north), the Don region, the Dnepr and Pripet drainage systems, and the coasts of the Black Sea and the Sea of Azov.[26] The outline of the Caspian Sea and the names of towns and rivers in the Caucasus region closely follow a map by Giacomo Gastaldi published in 1561. In northern Scandinavia and the large stretches of country to the north and the east of the Volga we have what appears to be a distinct attempt to include evidence that had recently been collected by Herberstein and Jenkinson or displayed on maps by Wied and others.

Within those parts of the Van Deutecum map where Mercator's Europe of 1554 was used as a guide are some inscriptions and drawings. The reference to the battle near the Dnepr River ("Here Sigismund the King of Poland slew 80,000 Muscovites in the year1554") was transcribed directly from Mercator, unfortunately with an error: the date should be 1514. Elsewhere we are told that "The Crimeans are Mohammedans who carry on war in earnest with the Muscovites": John Stow recorded that in 1571 "The 24 of May, being assention day, ye kinge of ye Crimmes came to the Citie *muscovi* with above 120,000 horsemen and men of warre . . . and ye *Moscho* being unprovided, the sayd Tartars set a fyre the citie, subbarbs, and both castels." [27]

The many coats of arms which decorate the west and southwest of the map are taken from the map of Europe by Caspar Vopell, first published in 1555. Vopell's map of Europe is known only through a single copy of a nine-leaf woodcut made in 1566 from the copper-engraved original. The quality of the engravings on the Van Deutecum map implies that they were taken from the 1555 version rather than from the cruder woodcut.

The peoples of the north were as fascinating to the sixteenth-century mind as they are to us today. The cartouches and drawings on the map give us information about their life and some legends associated with them. "The Permians and Condorians were once independent tribes, and are now governed by the Russian Tsar. For the most part they embrace Christianity. In winter they travel through the snows in sleighs which are drawn either by dogs or reindeer. They eat the good parts of venison, they do not use bread. The reindeer move in herds. Their clothing is the skin or pelt of wild animals." This is a précis of a lengthy discussion in Herberstein.[28] The note that "The Duchy of Yugoria is the region from which the Hungarians are said to have come" is similar to a statement found on Wied's map. In the northeast corner of the map is an account of certain tribes — the same statement that is on the Ortelius version of Jenkinson's map. But the illustrations on the two maps are different. "The Molgomzaiana, the Baidans, the Colmacky are independent tribes. They worship the sun or a red cloth hung from a lintel. They live in camps, and they eat the flesh of all living things, of serpents and worms, and they use their peculiar speech."

The legend of "the golden woman," worshiped by the Abdorians near the mouth of the Obi River, appeared on Wied's map, and Herberstein devotes some space to it.[29] The version on the Van Deutecum map is taken from Mercator's map of Europe of 1554, and is different from the version on the Ortelius map: "Solateia baba. From this comes the 'golden old woman'; it is worshiped here as an idol. But it is the figure of an old woman, holding her son in her lap, and having another child near her, who they say is her nephew."

The northern lands also have many fine drawings of reindeer in different attitudes, wolves, and sleds drawn by reindeer and dogs. A number of these engravings have a heraldic flavor. Near the Volga are drawings of "bears climbing the trees" (probably for honey), of bear-baiting, and of a hunter using the protection of a tree while attacking a bison; all of these are derived from Wied's map. The way of life of the northern nomads and their dependence on animals is amply displayed. The map sums up the life of the "Samoyeds" (a general name applied collectively to the northern peoples) thus: "This picture presents to our eyes the nature of the inhabitants of these regions, who are commonly called Samoyed, who are idolaters and who live in the wasteland."

The then recent subjugation of the Tartar Khanates along the lower Volga by Ivan the Terrible is recorded: "Kazan, a kingdom of Tartary, was assailed and subjected in the year 1551 by the Emperor of Russia. Astrakhan, a kingdom of the Tartars, was conquered and added to the kingdom of the Russians in the year 1554."

The expansive power of Russia as described by Vopell on his map of Europe is repeated here: "Moscow, which is 400 miles long, has a duke so rich in silver that he can lead an army of about 300,000 horse."

On his map of Europe Mercator had taken Wied's suggestion and tried to clear up the question of the columns of Alexander, which appeared in many of the newly printed versions of Ptolemy's *Geographia* (Secunda Asiae Tabula). The Van Deutecums' version is the same as Mercator's: "Ancient geographers placed the columns of Alexander here, but today nothing of such a kind is found to survive."

The Christian Circassians were intriguing to Europeans, surrounded as they were by powerful Islamic peoples: "The Circassians profess Christianity and they have their own language. They live in camps and in the funerals of relatives they have parades and they richly celebrate the rituals, and sometimes as a memorial of the deaths of friends they cut off parts of their ears." The engraving of a monarch seated before his tent and surrounded by warriors (just north of the Caucasus Mountains) is similar to an engraving on Vopell's map. It also bears resemblance to the engraving of Ivan the Terrible on Ortelius's version of Jenkinson's map.

The Van Deutecum map has a substantial body of text and many drawings which illustrate the life of the Tartars, Turks, and Persians. Vopell's map of Europe was the source of the following text (it is somewhat longer in the original): "The Tartars are a nomadic people, and, well-known to be eternally distinguished in warfare, are divided into hordes." Reports of the huge tent cities of the Tartars, especially that of Sarai on the left bank of the Volga below Kazan, no doubt inspired the following: " 'Horde' is said in the language of the Tartars 'hommum,' that is, a body drawn together in the form of a city, which, vagabond-fashion, wanders here and there."

East of the territory of the Volga Bulgars a space is occupied by a military chase, perhaps the Russians in pursuit of a retreating horde. Further east we see a series of scenes of domestic life among the Tartars, including a small flock of sheep, the milking of mares, the slaughtering of herd animals, the preparation of food, perhaps dice-playing and dancing, and many tent settlements. The line of four camel-drawn wagons is depicted as it appears in the version of Jenkinson's map published in 1578 by Gerard de Jode.

The Ortelius version of Jenkinson's map tells us the story of "ritus quidam Kirgessorum," the text of which the numeral 12 probably refers us to:

The Kirghiz lives in a body (that is, in hordes) and it has a rite of this fashion: when their priest celebrates divine service he takes blood, milk, and the dung of oxen and mixes it with earth, pours it into a certain vessel, and he climbs a tree with it, and, an assembly having been gathered, he sprinkles it on the people, and this sprinkling is worshiped as a god. When someone among them dies on a day they suspend him from trees in the place of burial.

On the same map of Ortelius we find a long text dealing with the group of figures appearing near the numeral 12 on the Van Deutecum map: "These stones representing the shapes of men, cattle, camels, pigs and other things were once a horde of people and a feeding flock, which by some astounding change stiffened into stone, losing in no part its earlier shape. This prodigy happened about 300 years ago."

Jenkinson's itinerary as published by Hakluyt in 1589, and the map published by Ortelius, gave the sixteenth-century information about the cities of Turkestan. The Van Deutecum map gives us *Taskent* (Tashkent); *Arsow* (the Acsow of the Ortelius map, perhaps Ak-su in Chinese Turkestan but usually taken to be the Akhsi associated with Babar the Great); and *Casara* (Cascara on the Ortelius map, now Kashgar), whose prince, we read, "is a Mohammedan and attacks the Kirghiz." We also find *Caracoll* (Karakul); *Urgence* (Urgenduzh); *Cosin* (perhaps Wan Ghazi); *Chant* (possibly another town mistaken for Samarkand); and *Corasan parva* ("The city of Khorassan was taken by the Persian king in the year 1558 from the advancing Tartars"). *Corasan magna* (perhaps the old Persian province of Khorassan); *Kirmina* (Kӱrmina on the Ortelius map, now Kermina); *Mangusla* (Mangyshlak); *Serachick* and *Shakeshick* (both Tartar encampments, the former name being the diminutive of Sarai) are other entries. From Gastaldi's map come *Lahaziobet, Otera, Frimouch, Cosmai, Rauore, Salacinit,* and *Simian.* Towns omitted from the Van Deutecum map but present on the Ortelius map are Andeghen (Andizhan), Kirshij (Karshi), Shaysure (Sellizure, now Shahr Vezir), and Mary (Merv).

The description of *Samarcadia distruicta* (Samarkand) is the same as that on the Ortelius map: "Samarkand was once the greatest city in all Tartary, and it lies in twisted ruins, together with many traces of antiquity. Here is buried Tamerlane, the man who led the captive Baiazite Turks bound in cages with chains. The inhabitants are Mohammedans." Samarkand is one of the world's great historic cities. After Alexander's eastern conquest in 329 B.C. it became a meeting place for Orient and Occident. It boasted a paper mill (the first outside China) in A.D. 751, had a water system, paved and tree-lined streets, and many palaces and mosques. The city was destroyed in A.D. 1220 after a long period as a center of Arabic culture and trade, but by A.D. 1300 had become the capital of Tamerlane's empire. Its silk and iron industries attracted suppliers and buyers from China, India, Persia, and the West.

Boghar (Bokhara) must have been a welcome sight to the thirsty and robber-harried traveler. It is recorded on the Ortelius map that "From Mangyshlak to Sellizure it is twenty days journey without any settlements, with great dearth of water. From Sellizure to Bokhara the same distance is infested with robbers." On the Van Deutecum map we read: "This is Bokhara, which was once subject to the Persians. The citizens embrace the Mohammedan heresy and speak Persian. Commercial intercourse is frequent here from Cathay, India, Persia, and other regions of the earth." Under its emirs Bokhara had been an important center of Islamic culture. This was as far as Jenkinson reached on his journey, Hakluyt tells us. "Wee have bene as far as Boghar, and had proceeded farther on our voyage toward the lande of Cathay, had it not bene for the incessant and continual warres, which are in all these brutal and wilde countreys, that it is at this present impossible to passe, neither went there any Caravan of people from Baghar that way these three yeares." That Jenkinson's route showed the way to Cathay is reported thus (the corresponding text on the Ortelius map is slightly different): "The desert stretches eastward to Cathay thirty days' journey from Kashgar (where begin the boundaries of the Empire of Cathay)." Jenkinson also reported on the items of trade: "From the Countries of *Cathay* is brought thither in time of peace, and when the way is open, muske, rubarbe, satton, damaske, with divers other things." [30]

The text dealing with the government of the Turkmenians is a summary of a longer account in Jenkinson's narrative.

The kingdom of the Turkmenians has been divided among five brothers of which the one that holds the first place has the title Azin Khan; the rest are called Sultans. They hold only five towns or rather castles under their empire. Of these Urgendzh holds first place. The inhabitants hold the Mohammedan sect, and they live according to the custom of the Nogai, and they are continually at war with the Prince of the Persians, commonly called the Sophy.

Concerning the Persians we read:

The Medes and Persians are Mohammedans and they fight enthusiastic battles with the Tartars. This is so mainly because of different customs since they are unwilling to shave their upper lips as do the Turks and Tartars. In these regions there is a great number of Chinese. [31]

Of the numerals on the map some have already been referred to, and others probably led the reader to expanded statements about peoples and places already noted in the text translated above. The numeral 1 no doubt refers to a text on the North Cape region, perhaps similar to that of Jenkinson's narrative. [32] Engraved in mirror image is 6, the text for which perhaps dealt with the rivers of Turkestan or contained additional facts about the Tartars. Similar information may also have been given in the texts referred to as 8, 9, and 10.

It remains to discuss the relative chronology of this map; the "original" map of Jenkinson which Ortelius dates as 1562, and the two other maps ascribed to Jenkinson: the Ortelius version of 1570, and the de Jode version of 1578. The Ortelius map is dated 1562, and gives Jenkinson as author and London as the place where the original was made. Assuming for a moment that the Ortelius map is an emended or altered version of an original map, it becomes evident that there are no exact copies of the original.[33] In 1562 Jenkinson was on his journey to Persia, having left London in May 1561 for Russia and the Caspian Sea after only a short stay of six months following his return from his journey to Bokhara. This raises the possibility that Jenkinson was not the author of the 1562 original, since he could not have been in London at the time. William Borough claimed in 1581 that he had drawn a map of Jenkinson's journeys; he said, however, that he had shown routes of the journeys to Russia *and* *Persia*, which would not have been possible in 1562.[34] Another possibility is that Jenkinson did not draw the original map until 1564 or 1566, and that the date given by Ortelius is an erroneous speculation.

But regardless of whether Jenkinson was the author of the original map, it is unlikely that the Ortelius map is the same as the original map. Certainly the Van Deutecums did not use a map similar to the Ortelius version; their coastlines and rivers in both Europe and Asia are different, especially in the north and east, where we would expect them to use any new maps that might have been available to them. Both Keuning and Bagrow thought that the de Jode map was more like the original map than the Ortelius version; place names are closer to Jenkinson's text versions as printed by Hakluyt, and the Ortelius map has all the appearance of a map made in the Low Countries.[35] Also it is obvious that Mercator did not use a map like the Ortelius map as a model for his world map of 1569: his Caspian Sea has the conventional elliptical shape.

Since the title of the Van Deutecums' map makes no mention of a map by Jenkinson, referring only to an itinerary (that is, a text), it is possible that they did not use the original version of Jenkinson's map, and also that Jenkinson's map had no texts. If this is true then it becomes possible that some of the Ortelius version was based on the Van Deutecum map, especially the texts in the eastern part. When one adds the texts of the Van Deutecums which are missing to those printed on the map he might justifiably conclude that the brothers' work contained all the texts found on the Ortelius map, plus many more that were not included in 1570 because of inappropriateness or lack of space. The argument that the de Jode map is closer to the original thus gains some support from this assumption, for it has almost no texts.

Whatever the solution to these problems, the authors of the Van Deutecum map must have had available a description of Jenkinson's journey to Russia and Bokhara. This description must have been different from the version published later by Hakluyt, for it obviously included extra information on which the brothers based some of their texts. For example, the descriptions of the religious rites of the Kirghiz and the legend of the stone statues (which appear on the Ortelius map) are not found in Hakluyt.

The Ortelius map was probably prepared by adding a new eastern section covering the Caspian Sea and Turkestan to Jenkinson's original map. This suited the format of the 1570 atlas and, incidentally, saved Ortelius the cost of engraving a separate plate covering those regions. The Van Deutecum map may have historical importance in addition to its intrinsic value, for it appears to be the earliest extant cartographic record embodying information collected by Jenkinson, and may well have been a source for the Ortelius map.[36]

NOTES

page 65

[1] V. Kordt, *Materialy po istorii russkoy Kartografii*, part II, vol. 1, Kiev, 1906. The Van Deutecum map is reproduced in plates IV, V, and VI, from which the photographic copy (Figure 2) was taken.

[2] H. Michow, "Weitere Beiträge zur älteren Kartographie Russlands," *Mitteilungen der Geographischen Gesellschaft in Hamburg*, vol. 22, 1907, pp. 127–172.

[3] L. Bagrow, "History of Russian Cartography," to be published as a supplement to *Imago Mundi*, the manuscript of which was examined at the British Museum by permission of the superintendent of the Map Room and editor of the supplement, R. A. Skelton.

[4] J. Keuning, "Jenkinson's Map of Russia," *Imago Mundi*, vol. 13, 1956, pp. 172–175.

page 67

[5] A standard work on early travels and accounts concerning Russia is the compilation by Friedrich von Adelung, *Kritisch-Literärische Ubersicht der Reisenden in Russland bis 1700*, St. Petersburg, 1846, reprinted by N. Israel, Amsterdam, 1960.

[6] *Rerum Moscoviticarum Comentarii* was published in Vienna in 1549; other Latin editions were published at Basel (1551, 1556, 1571), Antwerp (1557, 1557), and Frankfort (1560, 1600). An Italian edition was printed in Venice in 1550. The first edition in German came from Vienna in 1557; other German edi-

tions were published at Basel (1563, 1567), Prague (1567), Frankfort (1576, 1579, 1589), and Vienna (1618). An English edition of Herberstein was included by Richard Eden in his *History of Travayle in the East and West Indies, Etc.*, published in London in 1555 and 1577: from Eden's version is taken the nineteenth-century edition issued by the Hakluyt Society, *Notes on Russia . . . by Baron Sigismund von Herberstein*, ed. R. H. Major, London, vol. 1, 1851, vol. 2, 1852.

[7] The initial English voyages are included in Eden, *op. cit.*, 1555, and some subsequent journeys in Eden, *op. cit.*, 1577. Hakluyt contains an extensive body of material on English voyages and travels by Jenkinson and other servants of the Muscovy Company: see *The Principall Navigations, Voiages and Discoueries of the English Nation . . .*, London, 1589. See also E. D. Morgan and C. H. Coote, *Early Voyages to Russia and Persia by Anthony Jenkinson and Others*, vols. 1 and 2, London, 1886.

page 68

[8] Hakluyt, *op. cit.*, 1589, p. 436.

page 69

[9] See Colin Clair, *Christopher Plantin*, London, 1960.

[10] A. J. J. Delen, *Histoire de la gravure dans les anciens pays bas et dans les provinces belges des origines jusqu'à la fin du xviiie siècle*, Paris, 1934, vol. 2, pp. 118–119.

[11] J. Denucé, *Oude Nederlandsche Kaartmakers in betrekking met Plantijn*, Maatschappij der Antwerpsche Bibliographilen, 2 vols., Antwerp, 1912, 1913.

[12] F. Van Ortroy, *L'Oeuvre cartographique der Gerard de Jode et de Corneille de Jode*, Ghent, 1914.

[13] J. Keuning, "XVIth Century Cartography in the Netherlands," *Imago Mundi*, vol. 9, 1952, pp. 35–63.

page 74

[14] L. Bagrow, "A Page from the History of the Distribution of Maps," *Imago Mundi*, vol. 5, 1948, pp. 52–63.

[15] The principal works on the history of Russian cartography include not only those previously cited but also Kordt, *op. cit.,* part I, Kiev, 1899; Michow, "Das erste Jahrhundert russischer Kartographie 1525–1631" und die Originalkarte das Anton Wied von 1542," *Mitteilungen der Geographischen Gesellschaft in Hamburg*, vol. 21, 1906, pp. 1–63; John F. Baddeley, *Russia, China, Mongolia* . . . London, 1919, 2 vols.

page 75

[16] The Catalan Atlas is preserved in the National Library in Paris, and was reproduced by A. E. Nordenskjöld in *Periplus: An Essay on the Early History of Charts*, Stockholm, 1897.

[17] A sumptuous facsimile edition of Fra Mauro's map was edited by Roberto Almagia and published in Venice in 1956.

[18] See Michow, *op. cit.,* 1906, and "Die ältesten Karten von Russland," *Mitteilungen der Geographischen Gesellschaft in Hamburg*, vol. 4, 1884, pp. 100–168.

page 77

[19] Major, *op. cit.,* vol. 2, p. 5.
[20] *Ibid.,* p. 338.
[21] Hakluyt, *op. cit.,* 1589, p. 337.
[22] *Ibid.,* p. 338.
[23] Major, *op. cit.,* vol. 2, pp. 95–97.

page 79

[24] See *Monumenta Cartagraphica*, ed. F. C. Weider, vol. 5, The Hague, 1933. A map in the series titled "From a Secret Atlas of the East India Company," drawn by Witsen and dated 1655, shows a Caspian Sea about as long as it is broad. It is obvious that Italian as well as Flemish cartographers of the sixteenth century were unaware of reasonably accurate portolans of the Caspian Sea drawn in the late medieval period by Italian mariners. See L. Bagrow, "Italians on the Caspian," *Imago Mundi*, vol. 13, 1956, pp. 3–10.

[25] Hakluyt, *op. cit.,* 1589, p. 358.

[26] Reproduced as part of *Drei Mercator-Karten in der Breslauer Stadtbibliothek*, Gesellschaft für erdkunde zu Berlin, 1891. See the articles by A. Heyers in *Zeitschrift für wissenschaftliche Geographie*, Weimar, 1890, vol. 7, pp. 379–389, 474–487, 507–528, and the monograph by H. Averdunk and J. Müller-Reinhard, "Gerhard Mercator die Geographie unter seinen Nachkommen," *Petermann's Mitteilungen*, Erganzungsheft 182, Gotha, 1914.

page 80

[27] Morgan and Coote, *op. cit.,* vol. 2, p. 338.
[28] Major, *op. cit.,* vol. 2, pp. 45–48.
[29] *Ibid.,* p. 41.

page 83

[30] Hakluyt, *op. cit.,* 1589, p. 356.
[31] Morgan and Coote, *op. cit.,* vol. 1, pp. 68–73.
[32] Hakluyt, *op. cit.,* 1589, pp. 333–335.

page 84

[33] In his "History of Russian Cartography" (MS) Bagrow notes that there is mention in Plantin's accounts of a map of Muscovy that has not been accounted for. In Denucé, *op. cit.,* vol. 2, p. 25 we read that Reynald Wolff "painter of the English King" (Elizabeth was queen at the time) asked (in 1573) if he could send twenty-five copies of a map of Muscovy to Plantin. Bagrow thinks that this could refer to copies of Jenkinson's original map.

[34] See E. G. R. Taylor, *Tudor Geography: 1485–1583*, London, 1930, p. 30.

[35] *Imago Mundi*, vol. 13, 1956, pp. 173–175, and Bagrow, *op. cit., passim*.

page 85

[36] I am indebted to Karl Morrison of the Department of History at the University of Chicago for help in translating Latin inscriptions.

Henry Hudson and the Early Exploration
and Mapping of Hudson Bay, 1610 to 1631

by ERNST C. ABBE *and* FRANK J. GILLIS

"A long, long way divides the Chinese [from us] with a
    long sea [voyage]
    And the noble mind is impatient of a lengthy wait,"
Said Hudson; and lacking a vestige of fear sought the Indies in the West
    To gain renown by a shorter course.
Now, now in his boldness, he began to conquer the unknown strait,
    Now to promise rewards to his men and almost to see [the rewards];
When the unruly mob of sailors forced him to halt in those great
    undertakings, nor did they, with knowledge, refrain from injuring
    a man who intended no harm.
But our hero persists on his way, either certain of overcoming the
    halting or (O may the holy divinities avert this!) to die.
Hear, God, our prayers, and add this day to the calendar of England,
    In view of the recent glorious saving of our Prince.

From Hessel Gerritsz's map, "Tabula Nautica," translated
by Professor Norman J. DeWitt

HENRY HUDSON'S NAME, with justice, adorns a great and gracious river, a long and tortuous strait, and a vast and forbidding bay — the last also giving his name to the longest-lived of the ancient companies of adventurers. We know little of his early life.[1] That he probably came from a family which showed an interest in both commerce and the sea is fairly certain. At the same time, we lack detailed knowledge of his activities in the brief, tempestuous, and final period of his life, from 1607 to 1611, during which he made four arduous voyages into cold and unfriendly areas in search of a passage to the East. Throughout these celebrated expeditions he was supported by English and Dutch financiers whose capital, venturesome spirit, and informed enthusiasm, animated by the Anglo-Dutch cooperation of the late sixteenth and early seventeenth centuries,[2] encouraged them to take the long chance.

So impelling was Hudson's vision and so intense his desire to find a way to the rich spice lands of the Orient that, the records lead us to believe, he would have sailed under the flag of any nation that would finance and equip him.[3] And his interest was more in science than in the economic and political power struggle among the English, Dutch, French, and Spanish.

Hudson rose to prominence in 1607 on completing his first voyage for the Muscovy Company — an unsuccessful voyage in search of a passage to Asia, exploiting Robert Thorne's will-o'-the-wisp theory of an open polar sea between Spitsbergen and Greenland. His second voyage, also for the Muscovy Company, was made the following year. An attempt to find a northeastern route above Russia, through the Barents Sea, it also failed in this chief purpose, but accomplished important exploration of a part of Nova Zembla.

In the winter of 1608–1609 Hudson visited Holland and, while there, talked with members of the new Dutch East India Company; with the Reverend Peter Plancius, the Netherlands' leading geographer and adviser to the company; and perhaps with such renowned geographers and cartographers as Abraham Ortelius, Jodocus Hondius, and Hessel Gerritsz, at that time a little-known but talented and promising car-

NOTES for *Henry Hudson and the Early Exploration and Mapping of Hudson Bay, 1610–1631* are to be found on pages 112 to 116.

tographer and publisher who was to play a large part in making Hudson's name prominent a few years later. After this meeting with enterprising merchants and learned scholars, Hudson, equipped with ship, crew, and fresh geographical data, set sail on his third voyage to the Arctic in April 6, 1609, this time in the pay of the Dutch. When his mutinous men and the heavy Arctic ice blocked the northeastward attempt near Nova Zembla, he sold the crew on an alternative plan by which they would sail to the west in search of a passage through America. This voyage became the famous one which resulted in extending Captain John Smith's map of Virginia to the north, recording new observations and discoveries in the area of Delaware Bay, the Hudson River, and adjacent coasts. On the way home, after consulting the still partly mutinous crew, some of whom were inclined to seek the Northwest Passage through Davis Strait, Hudson decided to spend the winter in Ireland before attempting such a bold move as that; he therefore landed in Dartmouth, England, on November 7, 1609.[4]

His fourth and final voyage was made in the service of Sir Thomas Smith, Sir Dudley Digges, and John Wolstenholme, three men willing to invest in Hudson's experience, energy, enthusiasm, and judgment, for the fabled riches of the East would be the reward of success. Hudson's seaman's mind was apparently intrigued by George Weymouth's description of Lumley's Inlet (Frobisher's Strait) and by the widely publicized tide-rip and "furious overfall" John Davis had described near the eastern end of Hudson Strait; he was determined to try the Northwest Passage in earnest.[5] On his previous expedition for the Dutch, when the crew of the *Half-Moon* mutinied off Nova Zembla, he had offered them two alternative ways west to Cathay: one by some yet to be discovered strait leading to the Sea of Verrazano just beyond Virginia as visualized by his correspondent Captain John Smith, the other the Northwest Passage. His men chose the former. Now, on the fourth voyage, he would attempt the only course left open to him.

On April 17, 1610, Hudson sailed from London in the *Discovery* with a crew of twenty-three. They sighted Greenland on the fourth of June and, sailing between Cape Wolstenholme and Digges Island on August third, headed into an open sea which Hudson felt sure was the passage he had been seeking. Continuing down the east coast of Hudson Bay, the expedition was forced to winter in the desolate and unfriendly area on the southern coast of James Bay. Hudson's compulsion to push on had led him to neglect the few opportunities they had to live off of the country, and there was constant grumbling among the men. Ten days after they left their winter quarters, on June 21, 1611, Hudson, his son John, and seven others were cast adrift in a small shallop and never heard from again. The remaining men in the *Discovery* sailed for home. En route they ran aground at Digges Island where four were killed by Eskimos. Two more died on the way home (on September 6, 1611) and only Robert Bylot, Hudson's mate for a time; Abacuck Prickett, who was later to leave an eyewitness account of the expedition; and six others reached England.[6] Bylot and Prickett lived to sail again to the Arctic, and they, along with the other survivors, were absolved of guilt in the mutiny.[7]

Although we cannot doubt that Hudson sailed into the bay that bears his name on August 3, 1610, there is a shadowy assortment of Scandinavians, Basques, Portuguese, and others whose adherents claim priority of discovery for them. But only Champlain can be given real credit for having had the gleam of Hudson Bay in his mind's eye just before Hudson actually saw it. Champlain thought seriously about the tale of the Indians he had met on his brief trip up the Saguenay in 1603 that to the north there was a sea which is salt. He says, "if this is the case, I think it is a gulf of that sea which flows from the north into the interior, and in fact it cannot be otherwise." [8] Crouse points out that Champlain "guessed the existence of Hudson Bay several years prior to its discovery." It would be of more than passing interest to know whether Champlain was thinking of the "Mare dulce" shown on the world maps of Gerardus Mercator (1569) and of his son, Rumoldus (1587).[9] This invagination of the north coast of North America was hinted at by Hakluyt in 1587 and was called "Lago de Conibas" by Corneille Wytfliet shortly thereafter.[10] Of course Karpinski assures us that this temptingly situated body of water is merely an analogue to Hudson Bay because, in actuality, the sea in the north could only be an early representation of the Great Lakes, based on rumors brought back by Cartier.[11] But did Champlain think so?

In the absence of circumstantial accounts or of charts giving evidence of an earlier penetration into Hudson Bay, one must begin to examine its exploration and mapping with the Hudson expedition of 1610–1611. The contemporary sources of information are few and yield relatively little primary data. The first announcement of the discovery by Hudson was on the back of a map included as part of a small tract entitled *Beschryvinghe vander Samoyeden Landt in Tartarien* which appeared in Amsterdam late in 1612. This tract, a compilation of miscellany directly or indirectly related to the finding of a route to the East, was edited and published by Hessel Gerritsz, a talented young cartographer, publisher, and understudy of the Reverend Peter Plancius, Holland's geographical expert.[12] It achieved great popularity, six issues of it appearing in 1612 and 1613.[13] Gerritsz also engraved the "Tabula nautica" which is the first representation of the Hudson Bay region (Figure 4). Of great interest to us because of the accuracy with which it shows the east coast of Hudson Bay and because of the strange inaccuracy of James Bay, it purports to be based on a chart sketched by Hudson, a copy of which came early and mysteriously into Gerritsz's hands.[14]

How the chart and other data reached Gerritsz and how he prepared and published them a scant year after the fatal expedition returned is not entirely clear and merits discussion here. Certainly this material flowed through clear but hidden channels — such channels as had provided Plancius with the logbooks of the Englishman, Weymouth; it was in Amsterdam that Hudson had seen these logbooks, not in England.[15] In all probability Abacuck Prickett, as the representative of Sir Dudley Digges on the *Discovery* during the fourth expedition, turned over all pertinent logs and charts to his patron upon his return. It seems unlikely that Digges would have made this firsthand information available to possible Dutch competitors. A good share of this material was undoubtedly transferred to Richard Hakluyt, the English collector and publisher of travel accounts relating to geography and navigation and an adviser of the newly formed English East India Company.[16] Hakluyt could have turned over the data about Hudson's discoveries to Emanuel van Meteren, the noted Dutch historian, who, though born in Holland, had spent his adult life in England and had many friends on both sides of the channel. He might then have passed this material on to Plancius, who ultimately gave it to Gerritsz.[17] There is even the possibility that Gerritsz acquired the information and material on a trip to London, for the traffic between Amsterdam and London was heavy. The spirit of Anglo-Dutch cooperation at this time is epitomized in the important meeting between Hudson and Plancius in 1609 when the Dutch geographer and the English captain discussed and pored over maps and other documents relating to a northerly route to the East, in preparation for a voyage to be made for the Dutch, with Dutch and English seamen, in a Dutch ship.[18]

The second source of contemporary information was the Reverend Samuel Purchas who, in the last years of Hakluyt's life, became England's foremost collector, editor, and publisher of material dealing with history, geography, and navigation.[19] The first three editions of his *Pilgrimage* (1613, 1614, 1617) contain stray notes about Hudson gathered from Gerritsz's first published announcement and from conversations with Hakluyt, Sir Dudley Digges, and others. In about 1620, four years after Hakluyt died, a considerable quantity of material from Hakluyt's collection came into Purchas's possession. Using this, he published, in 1625, a four-volume geographical work entitled *Hakluytus Posthumus, or Purchas His Pilgrimes*. Only therein did a fragment of Hudson's log appear, along with Abacuck Prickett's "Larger Discourse," and Henry Briggs's map (Figure 5), "The North Part of America." The fragment of Hudson's log is certainly authentic and must have come from Sir Dudley Digges or Sir Thomas Smith. Prickett's account, on the other hand, is that of an eyewitness — although it seems to have been set down from memory without reference to notes made during the voyage — and one hopes that he had access to Hudson's (and Bylot's) logs when he wrote it. What the sources of Briggs's map might have been is not made clear, but of definite interest is that while it deviates in many other details from the Gerritsz version it yet shares the strange inaccuracies in the James Bay area.

Supplementary material was published only long afterward: additional bits of the log of the *Discovery* taken from the *Transactions* of the Trinity House for October 26, 1611, in 1894;[20] and Baffin's and Bylot's manuscript chart of their 1615 expedition, in accurate reproduction, in 1958.[21] The original logbooks of the *Discovery* must therefore have been accessible to qualified persons in 1611, and the similarity

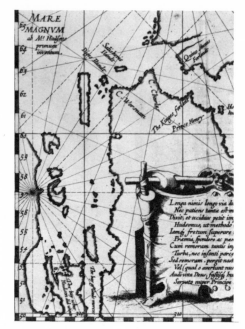 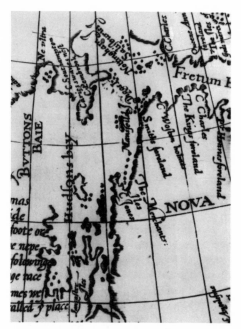

Figure 4. Hessel Gerritsz's map from his *Descriptio ac Delineatio Geographica Detectionis Freti* . . ., Amsterdam, 1612 (Bell Collection). *Figure 5.* Parts of Henry Briggs's map, "The North Part of America," from Samuel Purchas, *Purchas His Pilgrimes,* London, 1625 (Bell Collection).

between the Baffin-Bylot chart of 1615 and the Gerritsz map suggests that they had a common source.

Along with these, important data may be gleaned from other contemporary expeditions and maps. In the remaining part of this work, the total available resources will be divided and discussed in two sections, as follows:

The contemporary sources dealing directly with Hudson's fourth expedition to be discussed in detail are the following:

1611: fragments of Hudson's log and of Bylot's log as recorded in the Trinity House *Transactions.*[22]

1612–1613: Hessel Gerritsz, "Tabula nautica" (Figure 4) and the texts in the various editions of his *Beschryvinghe vander Samoyeden Landt* which deal with Hudson and his discoveries.[23]

1613, 1614, 1617: references to the Hudson expedition in the first, second, and third editions of Samuel Purchas, *Purchas His Pilgrimage.*[24]

1625: Samuel Purchas, *Purchas His Pilgrimes,* with its fragment of Hudson's log and the "Larger Discourse" of Abacuck Prickett.[25]

Other expeditions and maps of the period, less directly related to Hudson and the bay he discovered and to be briefly surveyed here, are:

1612–1613: the Sir Thomas Button expedition.[26]

[93]

1613: Samuel de Champlain's map (Figure 6) in his *Voyages du Sieur de Champlain Xaintongeois.*[27]

1615, 1616: the William Baffin–Robert Bylot expeditions and a portion of the chart resulting from one of these.[28]

1619–1620: the Jens Munk expedition and his map in *Navigatio Septentrionalis* (Figure 7).[29]

1622: Hessel Gerritsz and his "Great Chart of the South Sea."[30]

1624: Abraham Goos's map of North America (Figure 8).[31]

1625: Henry Briggs's map in Purchas's *Pilgrimes.*[32]

1631: the Captain Thomas James expedition and map (Figure 9).[33]

1631: the Captain Luke Foxe expedition and map (Figure 10), with his oblique references to Hudson's place names.[34]

An examination of these sources reveals an over-all similarity (Figure 11); yet certain discrepancies require more detailed examination. Moreover it is not unlikely that Prickett's account may permit a fairly precise delineation of the course of the *Discovery.*

The fragments of Hudson's and Bylot's logs. These are virtually useless for our purpose. It is an interesting coincidence that "An Abstract of the Journall of Master Henry Hudson . . ." in *Purchas His Pilgrimes,*[35] and the presumed abstract of the logbook of the *Discovery,* printed from the manuscript *Transactions* of the Trinity House for October 26, 1611,[36] parallel each other for the "Owteward Bound" westerly course. Purchas gives nothing more of the logbook after August 3, 1610. But the rest of the material from the *Transactions* of Trinity House continues in the form of abstracts from a logbook for both the outward and homeward bound parts of the period "In the Bay." This suggests that Abacuck Prickett had something more than simply his memory to draw on when he prepared his account of the voyage for Hakluyt; it also suggests that Bylot regularly kept a log on the way home. For our purposes, it is most unfortunate that these presumed extracts of the log include virtually nothing about the bay itself except brief comments on August 12, 13, and 22, 1610.

The "Tabula Nautica" of Gerritsz. This was published in its original state by Hessel Gerritsz in 1612 (Figure 4).[37] Presumably the map which appeared in the various printings by Gerritsz is reproduced from a single plate which was slightly altered in its second state, in the second Latin edition of 1613.[38] It was very accurately copied and presented on a smaller scale, with certain English place names and comments put into Latin, by both De Bry (1613),[39] and Hulsius (1614).[40]

The circumstantial evidence suggests that Hessel Gerritsz had Hudson's original charts at hand when he compiled the "Tabula Nautica," "noviter a H. Hudsono."[41] The use of English for a good share of the place names reinforces this impression. As Asher points out, Prickett's testimony gives evidence that the original chart was preserved by the mutineers and used on the way home.[42] Asher interprets the text accompanying the Dutch edition of Gerritsz's map to mean that he used Hudson's chart.[43] Furthermore, as has been mentioned previously, Asher thinks it very probable that Plancius, friend and adviser of Hudson, secured Hudson's original charts for Gerritsz's use.[44]

An overlooked bit of evidence may also be provided by the Baffin-Bylot manuscript chart. When the northern part of the east coast is transferred to the Gerritsz map, but offset for ease of comparison, both trend and detail show remarkable similarity. Since the Baffin-Bylot expedition of 1615 did not touch this coast, its outlines on their map must have come from an earlier source. It is most unlikely that Bylot, Hudson's mate on the expedition of 1610–1611, would have taken Gerritsz as his source, and much more likely that he would have preserved for his own use a copy of the original chart in the making of which he must have had a hand. The close correspondence, then, between the Gerritsz and the Bylot rendering of this part of the coast suggests a similar source.

Gerritsz's presentation of Hudson Bay is thus a primary source of compelling significance. It is the earliest map of the region based on firsthand exploration of the coast by experienced navigators — for Bylot must be included here with Hudson.

The map inspires confidence, especially when it is compared with a present-day map in such a way that latitudes but not longitudes are made to coincide. When this is done, the Salisbury Island–Digges Island–Cape Wolstenholme complex is fairly similar to actuality, and the "bottom of the bay" is only a degree or so too far south. A more detailed examination of the east coast shows that it bears comparison, down to about 52°, with current maps. One must make allowances for longitude, but major features, notably capes and points, seem to correspond reasonably well, suggesting that Hudson actually determined his latitude only occasionally and that the location of the rest of them was based on dead reckoning. Considering the evil weather along this coast — the fogs and the onshore winds — the observations are very satisfactory indeed.

As far as the coast of the bay between about 55° and 60° is concerned, we find it oriented almost due north and south, very nearly straight, and having three bays: a small one, subtending Cape Smith near 60°, could be interpreted as Mosquito Bay; a medium-sized one at about 57° is uncertain; and a larger one whose lower horn may be Cape Jones appears just above 55°. More or less alongshore are islands, a largish one just north of 55° and a group of smaller ones opposite the central bay; well offshore are the four large islands, three of which Flaherty, their rediscoverer in the early twentieth century, would identify as the Belcher Islands (Flaherty's hypothesis is barely tenable but difficult to disprove).[45]

The internal evidence at hand points to a careful exploration of the east coast of Hudson Bay and its onshore islands by Hudson. This is borne out in Prickett's account, which tells that the expedition followed the shore very closely much of the way on both the southward and northward trips.

In contrast with the reliable data gathered by Hudson and Bylot for the east coast of Hudson Bay, the Gargantuan distortions in James Bay west of "the bay of Goods merces" come as a shock. The large peninsula west of "the bay of Goods merces" extends over nearly 4° of latitude and the west shore runs north to nearly 60°, instead of to 55° — badly out of scale and proportion. In the light of the general reliability of the delineation of the east coast it is obvious that something has gone awry. Hudson spent an abundance of time sailing about in what is now known as James Bay — he must have become thoroughly familiar with it; it is inconceivable that this monstrous misrepresentation is without meaning. Is it possible that among Hudson's records brought back by the mutineers there were *several* original charts, each drawn to a different scale? Were these combined by Gerritsz without a knowledge of the latitudes determined by Hudson? How could this have been done if Hudson's logbooks had indeed been available to Gerritsz? Did the *original* chart, or charts, show only the details observed by Hudson, and, when he was abandoned, was that chart incomplete over more or less of the coast?

The map itself suggests that Hudson did not round Cape Henrietta Maria. Had he done so, the charts, whatever their scale, would show the pronounced change in trend of the coast to the west of the cape. Thus we must take the delineation of the west coast of James Bay as being based on some unknown source or sheer guesswork on the part of Gerritsz. Oddly enough, the feature labeled as "The bay wher Hudson did winter," if considered out of the context of the oddly shaped peninsula at the tip of which it is found, is approximately correct for Rupert Bay, Hannah Bay, and the stubby peninsula between these bays. This peninsula is but a half degree too far north, although well to the west of its proper location. What the rest of the shorelines and islands might represent is inexplicable. Even if the scale for the remainder is several times greater than it should be, there is an embarrassment of islands in places where they do not exist, and the shape and size of the tip of the peninsula enclosing "The bay wher Hudson did winter" are badly out of proportion. It could be maintained that the present shoreline is not the same as it was in 1610 — that the marked up-warping of the earth's crust here has led to marked alterations in an area of slight relief — but such a hypothesis does not take care of the extension of the west shore 5° to the north of Cape Henrietta Maria. We are left only with the conviction that fragments of records for James Bay have been added inexpertly to the very adequate representation of the east coast. After all, Hudson was very jealous of the observations he made on this trip; Abacuck Prickett suggests that Hudson forbade "any man to keepe account or reckoning, having taken from all men whatsoever served for that purpose." [46] He may well have left his charts difficult to interpret, especially those for the later part of the trip.

The thought also arises that Hudson may not have been in any way responsible for the delineation of the west side of James Bay, especially for the westernmost group of very large islands shown almost due north of "The bay wher Hudson did winter." Perhaps the mutineers sketched these features in, or Gerritsz himself may have tried to supply them from the account of his anonymous informant. It is too late to settle these questions — whatever the sources, Gerritsz's misrepresentation of James Bay long survived in the maps of his successors.

Gerritsz's texts accompanying the "Tabula Nautica." [47] These are interesting from various points of view. In the "Introduction" to the first Dutch edition, the "Prolegomena" of the Latin edition of 1612, and in accompanying texts, Gerritsz says that Hudson's winter quarters were established at 52° of latitude. This corresponds well with his "Tabula Nautica," which identifies "The bay wher Hudson did winter" as just north of 52°. Only in the second Latin edition is this locality given as at 54°.

Though Gerritsz makes a definite reference in the first Dutch edition to Hudson's maps, which he says he saw when they were in Plancius's possession,[48] we are not to assume that these are maps or charts resulting from Hudson's fourth expedition, but rather that they are maps which Hudson secured through correspondence with Captain John Smith and which he must have left with Plancius after their Amsterdam meeting between the second and third expeditions. These maps must have shown clearly that Hudson had the idea of seeking an outlet to the South Sea "West of New England, where an Englishman, as he had marked out, had passed through." [49] This is a tantalizing statement — is it merely an ambiguous reference to Captain John Smith's efforts to prove to Hudson that there probably was a passage to the Sea of Verrazano?

Gerritsz also refers in his texts to Weymouth's or "Winwood's" [50] logbooks' having fallen into the Reverend Peter Plancius's hands, which means that Hudson had a chance to consult them when he was in Amsterdam in the winter of 1608–1609. According to Gerritsz's first and second Latin editions it was these logbooks that led Hudson to conclude that Weymouth's route, pursued further, would take him to India. Plancius tried to disabuse Hudson of this idea because of "the accounts of a man who had reached the western shore of that sea." [51] With the wisdom of hindsight Gerritsz apparently believed Plancius mistaken, for he says in his second Latin edition that Hudson seemed to have purposely missed the right road to the western passage on the expedition of 1609.[52]

Gerritsz also tells us the latitude at which Hudson was cast adrift. Both in the first Dutch edition and in the Latin edition of 1612 he places this at about 63°. Prickett's account of the incident as occurring in James Bay did not see print until 1625, so Gerritsz's informant must have been badly mistaken or else this is an uncaught and persistent typographical error for 53°.

Also of considerable interest is the comment in the second Latin edition that after he left his winter quarters Hudson "ran along the western shore for forty leagues, and fell in, under 60°, with a wide sea, agitated by mighty tides from the north-west. These circumstances inspired Hudson with great hope of finding a passage." [53] This part of the account accords well with the "Tabula Nautica," but not with the actual location of Cape Henrietta Maria at 55°. Perhaps this statement in the last edition merely compounds the persistent error in the first Dutch and Latin editions that Hudson sailed up the *west* side of the bay after leaving the place where he had wintered.

In summary, it is clear that Gerritsz had seen certain of Hudson's maps in the hands of Plancius; these showed that Hudson had the idea of seeking a Northwest Passage by way of "Lumleys Inlet in Davis' Straits," basing the idea on Weymouth's logbooks which Plancius also had. These maps of Hudson's must have antedated the expedition of 1610–1611, and may have been influenced by his correspondence with Captain John Smith. The rest of Gerritsz's statements, made in the texts of his various editions, must have been based on hearsay; these include the notion that Hudson wintered at 52°, that he sailed up the western shore of the bay until he fell in with a wide sea agitated by mighty tides from the northwest, and that he was cast adrift at 63°.

The first three editions of Samuel Purchas's Pilgrimage. These lead in an orderly sequence to his *Pilgrimes,* 1625; their contents are considered individually in the following paragraphs.

In 1613 Purchas hastened to include a brief account of Henry Hudson's fourth voyage in the first edition of his *Pilgrimage.* He gives credit to Gerritsz for bringing out information about the voyage and the discovery of Hudson "this last Mart, at Amsterdam" (that is, at the last book fair), and clearly follows the first Latin edition of 1612, as is evident from his use of Gerritsz's misspelling of Weymouth ("Winwood"). That he was puzzled about Gerritsz's sources of information is evident from his statement that the latter "hath (I know not by what instructions) set forth this voyage." [54]

The next year, in the second edition of the *Pilgrimage,* Purchas shows that he has got access to the original materials finally published at full length in his *Pilgrimes.* These, he says, were communicated to him by his "painful friend Mr. Hakluyt"; he also implies great indebtedness to the "learned and industrious Gentleman, Sir Dudley Digges." [55] And Sir Thomas Smith comes in for special comment for "at his house are kept the [co]urts, cons[ult]ations etc." [56] The "Winwood" error persists, though on the page preceding it Purchas refers briefly to the *Weymouth* voyage. In spite of the availability of Hakluyt's manuscript materials, Purchas manages to avoid giving any useful geographical information in this edition.

Purchas's third edition (1617) raises "Hudsons Discoveries and Death" to the dignity of being a separate section but adds nothing to the content of the earlier editions. [57]

Abacuck Prickett's account in Purchas's Pilgrimes, *1625.* Prickett's "Larger Discourse," as published in Purchas's *Pilgrimes,* [58] provides the only circumstantial account of Hudson's fourth voyage. If, as seems reasonable, Prickett had access to Hudson's log for the trip out and to Bylot's for the trip home, then his "Discourse" deserves to be taken seriously. Even if he did not use Hudson's and Bylot's logs, his account is still a primary, eyewitness source. Under any circumstances, as pointed out by many commentators, his handling of his sources, whatever they were, is sadly clumsy and landlubberly; but for this there is no remedy.

Prickett's descriptions of the Cape Digges–Cape Wolstenholme region are substantiated by the descriptions in the *Arctic Pilot* and in Low.[59] From Digges Islands they "lose [their] way downe to the south-west," presumably to Nuvuk Point. They lost sight of the mainland "because it falleth away to the East, after some five and twenty or thirty leagues," which brought them, according to Asher, somewhat to the north of Mosquito Bay.[60] But the order of magnitude of the distance they sailed is roughly that to Kovik Bay, just north of which "the water is shallow for several miles off the coast" according to Low;[61] this accords reasonably well with Prickett's "Now we came to the shallow water, wherewith wee were not acquainted since we came from *Island*."

Prickett next says that "now we came into broken ground and Rockes, through which we passed downe to the South," which fits well with Low's description of the bouldery and broken shore as far south as Portland Promontory.[62] After rounding Portland Promontory they would have "stood to the Southeast, because the Land in this place did lie so." Immediately after, had they hugged the shore, they would have proceeded through Hopewell Sound, so that they "had Land on both sides," until they came to Hopewell Narrows, through which they could not have passed and thus "came to an anchor." The "point of the West Land," erroneously identified by Asher as "Perhaps Charlton Island, in James's Bay," [63] was presumably Harrison Island, from the other side of which they observed that "there was a large Sea," namely the main body of Hudson Bay. They "weighed from hence, and stood in for this Sea betweene the two Lands." Thereafter, once having made their way out of the Hopewell Narrows, they continued to hug the shore of the mainland. They would promptly have got into Nastapoka Sound. Presumably it is this that "is not two leagues broad downe to the South" and which they followed "for a great way in sight of the East shoare."

"In the end" they lost sight of the east shore "and saw it not till [they] came to the bottome of the Bay," from which we may justifiably assume that at the bottom of the bay they saw the east shore of either Hannah Bay or Rupert Bay. It seems to us more likely that this would have been Hannah Bay, because they then "stood up to the North by the West shoare." Had they instead been in Rupert Bay and made for the west shore they could hardly have done so without first going west and south, which Prickett does not mention doing. Furthermore, to have reached Rupert Bay would almost certainly have involved them in the intricacies of navigating the shallows of the east side of James Bay — and such a procedure would have called for comment from Prickett.

They "stood up to the North by the West shoare, till [they] came to an Iland in 53, where [they] tooke in water and ballast." If it is correct to believe that Hudson made his first landfall in James Bay on the east shore of Hannah Bay, and if the latitude cited is correct, then Akimiski would almost inevitably be the island referred to. From Akimiski they proceeded further north "til [they] raised Land," toward Cape Henrietta Maria or Bear Island — which of these can hardly now be determined. They then, Prickett tells us, went down to the south, up to the north, down again to the south, in and out of Michaelmass Bay, and then again to the north which brought them "into shoald water." The emphasis on shoal water immediately suggests that here they made their first landing on the east shore of James Bay. Hudson's Michaelmass Bay would be Rupert Bay (although tentatively identified by Asher as Hannah Bay);[64] just before this they would have zigzagged from west to east across James Bay.

From the shoal water of the east shore they "stood to the South and Southwest" and, after a presumably brief excursion eastward, were again off to the south and southwest until they "came to [their] Westermost Bay of all, and came to an anchor neerest to the North shorae." Asher identifies this as "North Bay, the south-west corner of James's Bay." Prickett, however, refers to this as the "*Westermost* [our italics] Bay of all," and furthermore describes their difficulties in getting out because of a "ledge of rockes . . . , some league of length" which may well correspond to "the shore bank [which] extends about 4 miles offshore in the approach to Albany River" described in the *Arctic Pilot*.[65] As a candidate for their "Westermost Bay" perhaps the mouth of the Albany River is more suitable than Asher's southwest corner of James Bay.

They then "stood to the East and raysed three Hills, lying North and South" and "went to the furthermost, and left it to the North of [them]" and so into a bay where they anchored and explored in a small boat "downe to the East, to the bottome of the Bay," looking for a possible wintering place. The most prominent hill on the east coast is Sherrick's Mount on the north side of the entrance to Rupert Bay — but a difficulty is the requirement that there be "*three* [our italics] Hills, lying North and South."

They found the east side of this bay unsuitable and the next day went to the south and southwest from their anchorage and presumably came to the west side of Hannah Bay, where they wintered. This corresponds, after a fashion, to the place shown on Gerritsz's map as that in which they wintered.

It is from this wintering place that Hudson, in a vain effort to get food from the natives, made a brief trip "to the South" in the shallop.

When they left their wintering place they "stood to the North-west" and promptly "fell into the Ice," where they lay for several days "in sight of Land." After casting Hudson and the others adrift in the shallop, the mutineers steered toward the east "in a cleere sea," righted the helm, and lay to for a time. Then, getting under way again, they came to the east shore, "cast about," and "stood to the West and came to an Iland" which could have been Charlton, and there anchored. Getting under way again they "stood to the North-east" upon Bylot's insistence, and had the eastern shore in sight. After another episode with the ice, they again continued to the north-east "in sight of the Easterne shoare, till [they] raised foure Ilands which lay North and South" and at last came to anchor between the two northernmost. These four islands may be the ones shown on Gerritsz's map at about 57°, but cannot be the Belchers in spite of their location, if for no other reason than that the Belchers are too far offshore to be visible from the mainland. Furthermore, had they actually seen the Belchers, they would have considered them to be many, rather than only four, islands; this is because they are so deeply invaded by a multitude of interdigitating inlets. It is much more likely that the four islands were some of the onshore islands setting off Nastapoka or one of the other sounds.

They continued on still "to the North-east and the Easter Land still in sight: [they] raysed those Ilands, that our Master called *Rumnies* Ilands," but which are identified on none of the maps of the time. Asher thinks these are "certainly near the mouth of Mosquito Bay" or that "perhaps some of the islands near Cape Smith are meant," which is as satisfactory a solution as can be expected.[66]

It is interesting that Prickett consistently speaks of a northeast course from James Bay northward. This is quite at odds with Gerritsz's "Tabula Nautica," and also with Prickett's description of the course as being southeast or south when they came down the coast. If Prickett followed Hudson's log for the trip south we may assume that Hudson had corrected his bearings for the magnetic declination. By the same token, if Bylot kept a log which Prickett was following for the trip north along the same coast, it must be assumed that Bylot recorded uncorrected compass bearings, on the assumption that in 1611 the declination became progressively more westerly as they proceeded from south to north along this coast. This latter assumption is based on the premise that the magnetic pole was in its present position in 1610–1611; but this may well be incorrect.

To return to the mutineers: They retraced the rest of their course to Cape Wolstenholme; this is described in reasonable conformity with reality by Prickett.

The expedition of Sir Thomas Button, 1612–1613. The Button expedition left London in mid-April of 1612 with two ships, the *Discovery* and the *Resolution*, and two of Hudson's old crew, Robert Bylot and Abacuck Prickett, aboard. It sailed with two generally-known objectives: to search for the lost Henry Hudson — about which little was done — and to effect a passage to Cathay. Many believed this was the expedition that would find a navigable passage — Hudson had found the way, all the next expedition had to do was to sail through it. There was a good deal of secrecy connected with the voyage — a full and official account of the expedition never did appear — and only Purchas, Henry Briggs, and Luke Foxe could discover anything about its findings. It was Foxe, finally, who printed the only account of the expedition, garnered from a number of sources, in his *North-West Fox.*[67] The discoverer of Port Nelson and the Nelson River, among other geographical points, Button was the first to cross Hudson Bay from east to west and to make known almost the entire west coast of the bay. No cartographical record showing the course of the expedition or its findings exists, but both Foxe's account and the chart in Miller Christy's 1894 edition of the Foxe and James voyages give information about Button's route and discoveries.[68]

The Champlain map of 1613.[69] We have already commented on Champlain and noted that he had more than a vague idea of the existence of Hudson Bay, based on information from various Indian tribes he encountered in his broad travels over the St. Lawrence River–Great Lakes region. It must have been rewarding to him to have his beliefs about a salt sea in the north substantiated by the appearance of the Hudson-Gerritsz chart. He now knew for certain what he had before only surmised, and he promptly incorporated the geographical data given on the "Tabula Nautica" on his map, "Carte geographique de la Novelle Franse en son vray meridien," which accompanied his *Voyages du Sieur de Champlain Xaintongeois* of 1613 (see Figure 6). The map, drawn by him but rendered by a somewhat heavy-handed engraver, was simply his 1612 map of New France included in the same work, but on a smaller scale, with the northern part of Canada added.[70] That it is based almost entirely on Gerritsz is obvious from Champlain's depiction of Hudson Bay with the distorted peninsula (though not so exaggerated as the original) jutting out from the bottom of James Bay, from place names, and from such comments as "the bay wher Hudson did winter." There are a number of differences, however, which can be attributed to careless draftsmanship or to fresh information Champlain had. Lacking in the Hudson-Gerritsz original but a part of the Champlain map is a pronounced turn to the west of the land at what is now Cape Henrietta Maria. The delineation of the entire western coastline of James Bay is, in fact, closer to reality, with its depiction of three rivers here and one just west of Cape Henrietta Maria, than is the earlier map. Another feature of the Champlain map is that the periphery of Hudson Bay is lined with deep bays, jagged capes, and numerous embouchures. One transfer of a place name is difficult to explain — the location of "C. Charles" (the modern Charles Island), which is shown on the Gerritsz chart in Hudson Strait, between "C. Worsnam" and "Quine Annes Forlandt," whereas on the Champlain map it stands for a point of land at the middle of the group of three islands in James Bay, at about 57°. The map of Nouvelle France is but a small part of Champlain's contribution to the history of the cartography of North America. Coordinating with Hudson's findings the geographical data collected during his wide travels in New France over a number of the early years of the seventeenth century, he compiled and produced a cartographic milestone which gave for the first time a reasonably accurate picture of the northeastern part of North America.

The Baffin-Bylot expeditions of 1615 and 1616 and the "Baffin" chart.[71] William Baffin was a navigator of exceptional ability and a meticulous keeper of records. With him as pilot and the experienced Bylot (who had been on both the Hudson and the Button voyages) as master, the hope of finding a passable way to Asia was high. They set sail March 15, 1615, visiting Resolution Island, the western end of Hudson

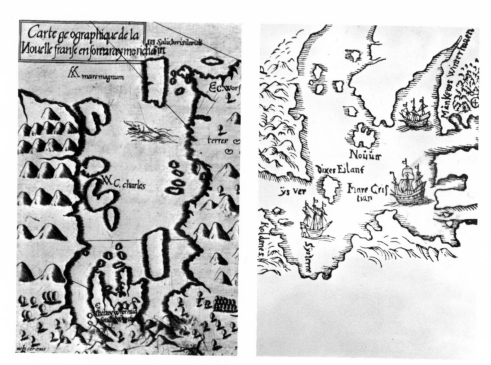

Figure 6. Samuel de Champlain's map from his *Les Voyages du sieur de Champlain*, Paris, 1613 (Bell Collection). *Figure 7.* Part of map from Jens Munk, *Navigatio Septentrionalis*, Copenhagen, 1624; north is at the bottom.

Strait, and the southern end of what later became known as Foxe's Channel. As it turned out, no passage was found and the amount of original discovery was small. But the voyage was a success in that a number of accurate surveys and important tidal studies were made. Baffin's belief that if a passage existed it was to be found through Davis Strait led to the second Baffin-Bylot expedition which departed from England, once more in the old *Discovery* (her sixth and final voyage to the Arctic), in March of 1616. Again the results, insofar as finding an outlet to the East were concerned, were disappointing and prompted Baffin to announce that the passage was a myth. But once more, in the world of science and scholarship the expeditions were noteworthy because the whole of Baffin's Bay was described with remarkable accuracy and the chart which illustrated Baffin and Bylot's findings gave a distinctive picture of the new geographical information. This chart must not be overlooked as a primary source. Attributed to Baffin, it is more than likely that Bylot is responsible for the precise draftsmanship of the northern and western coasts of the Labrador mainland. The coastline, as much of it as is shown, closely resembles that in Gerritsz's "Tabula Nautica," departing primarily in the more realistic size of Mansel Island, which has three smaller islands near it. Unfortunately the Baffin-Bylot chart does not run south of about 58°N in the reproductions of Rundall and Skelton (55°N in Markham). The reliability of the Gerritsz chart, at least in the northern part, is much strengthened by this contemporary evidence. Bylot played an important but as yet undocumented role in many of the Arctic expeditions of the time, and it is likely that he has been overlooked as a possible contributor to our knowledge of the details of Hudson's fourth voyage.

The Jens Munk voyage, 1619–1620, and his map.[72] One of the most tragic and perhaps least productive of the voyages to Hudson Bay was that of Captain Jens Munk, the courageous and energetic Danish navigator and explorer. Leaving Copenhagen in May 1619 with a crew of sixty-four in two ships, the expedition wintered at the mouth of the Churchill River where all except Munk and two others perished. The three surviving adventurers returned in the smaller vessel in September 1620. Munk's own narrative of his voyage first appeared in *Navigatio Septentrionalis*, published in Copenhagen in 1624 (see Figure 7). It was unknown or ignored outside Denmark for years, and neither Purchas nor Foxe mentions it. It is illustrated by a rough-looking woodcut map showing Greenland, Davis Strait, Hudson Strait, and Hudson Bay. That map seems to add little to our knowledge; yet though the representations of the east coast of Hudson Bay and of James Bay are based on Gerritsz (freely rendered), parts must be looked upon as entirely original. Munk's map, as far as we know, was the first published of the whole of Hudson Bay and second only to Gerritsz as a published map of Hudson Strait based on an original survey. We are apt to overlook these facts because all our knowledge of Hudson Bay has been conceived with the many English explorations in mind. Because of the many geographical features represented on it for the first time and because of its remarkable fidelity in many details, Munk's map, simple and crude as it may seem at first sight, occupies a unique place in the history of the mapping of this region.[73]

Hessel Gerritsz and his "Great Chart of the South Sea."[74] We now come to another distinctive map by Hessel Gerritsz: a manuscript map on vellum, dated 1622, of western America and the Pacific Ocean and surrounding lands. Included in the extreme northeast portion of the chart is the southwest corner of Hudson Bay. Not much is shown of this region — the distorted peninsula in James Bay is still there — but we see that Gerritsz has now separated James Bay from Hudson Bay proper by showing a stretch of land tending directly to the west at the present-day Cape Henrietta Maria along which is inscribed "Buttons Bay" and "Port Nelson." This is interesting; apparently the naming and locating of these points is another first for Gerritsz. But where did he get his information? Leading scholars, publishers, and voyagers could not find out anything about Button's voyage, and Baffin and Munk did not go that far south. Those who in all probability helped him get the materials to fashion his 1612 map of Hudson Bay — Hakluyt, van Meteren, and Plancius — were dead. He must have got it from some member of Button's expedition — Prickett, Bylot, or another — when no one else in England could, and at a time when Anglo-Dutch relations were at a breaking point over commercial rights in the Arctic and in the East

Indies. After all, he had shown great interest in the Button expedition when it was still at sea, giving varying references to it in each of the four editions of his *Beschryvinghe.*[75] Is this map of Gerritsz perhaps dated wrongly; did he take his information from Briggs's map of 1625? We think not. Three authorities give its date as 1622: Johannes Keuning, Gerritsz's chief biographer, and R. A. Skelton and Henry F. Wagner, two reputable scholars in the history of cartography.[76] One other possibility is that he took his data from the "platt" of Josiah Hubbard, no longer extant and, in fact, nowhere documented as having been seen by a contemporary.[77] Hubbard had sailed as pilot of the *Resolution* in Button's expedition.

Abraham Goos's map in the West-Indische Spieghel.[78] Chronologically the next cartographic rendering of Hudson Bay is found in a map engraved by Abraham Goos, " 't Noorder deel van West-Indien," from a descriptive work, *West-Indische Spieghel,* attributed to Athanasium Inga and published in Amsterdam in 1624. This map is a near twin of the next one, by Henry Briggs, and will be discussed with it.

Briggs's map, "The North Part of America." [79] The great Oxford mathematician, Henry Briggs, provided Purchas with this widely known and beautifully drawn map as a vehicle for his conviction that a Northwest Passage must exist (see Figure 5). Briggs wrote, while a member of the trading company interested in Virginia, "A Treatise of the North-West Passage to the South Sea, Through the Continent of Virginia, and by Fretum Hudson," which accompanies the map in Purchas and serves as a commentary on it. The "Treatise" had first appeared, in full, in 1622 appended to Edward Waterhouse's *Declaration of the State of the Colony and Affaires in Virginia* (London, 1622). Almost certainly Goos's map, included in a 1624 publication, was copied from Briggs. Such place names as "Lancaster Iles," "Smiths foreland," "C. Jones," "The Merchants Iles," and "Hudsons bay" are used on both maps for the first time and could hardly have been invented by Goos and copied by Briggs; undoubtedly the reverse is true. We can only believe, then, that Briggs's map was available before it appeared in Purchas's *Pilgrimes* of 1625. Perhaps it was ready when his "Treatise" was first published in 1622 or at least shortly after. Briggs might in fact have been Gerritsz's source for the place names "Buttons Bay" and "Port Nelson," used for the first time on Gerritsz's 1622 chart.

Briggs's map is not a simple copy of Gerritsz's 1612 version of Hudson Bay. Since Briggs was known as a reputable scholar in both the sciences and humanities and respected by men of letters, in commerce, and in government, he must have had access to all available material, including, one would think, almost anything in private hands at the time. Not only Hudson's and Bylot's logbooks for 1610–1611 could have been available to him, but their original charts as well. And the data about the tides in Hudson Bay on his map must have come from records of the Button and Baffin-Bylot expeditions. Briggs would want to use this information with the intellectual integrity produced by his background and training to produce a map that would be a valuable, original contribution to the knowledge of Hudson Bay. His "North Part

Figure 8. Abraham Goos's map of North America from Athanasius Inga,
West-Indische Spieghel, Amsterdam, 1624 (Bell Collection).

of America" is just that; it uses the original Gerritsz map, adding geographical data
from unknown sources and carefully leaving blank those areas — the coastline between Cape Henrietta Maria and Port Nelson and at "Hubbarts hope" and "C. Phil-
ips" — he lacked reliable data about. To Briggs there were still possible openings that
might be the Northwest Passage. The trend of the east coast he shows as somewhat
east of north from Cape Jones to Cape Smith and Cape Wolstenholme. This is contrary to what is given in Hudson's logbook, but is in keeping with the orientation
given in Prickett's account in Purchas's *Pilgrimes*. Cape Jones is shown as a very
pronounced peninsula, the peninsula between Rupert and Hannah bays is greatly
exaggerated, and the west shore of James Bay breaks off abruptly at about 57°. The
islands are differently handled from those in the Gerritsz version, including a series
close inshore north of Cape Jones. Briggs's was an important map-making achievement, and, through its inclusion in Purchas's *Pilgrimes*, widely circulated. It appeared,
almost without change, in the world maps of Sir Francis Drake (1628), Henricus
Hondius (1630), and Philip Eckebrecht (1630).[80]

The Thomas James expedition and map, 1631–1632.[81] Both the James and Luke
Foxe voyages were undertaken in 1631. James, who had gradually gained a reputation as an experienced seaman, sailed for the merchants of Bristol on May 3, 1631, on

an expedition fraught with many accidents; eventually his ability as a navigator was thought much less than Foxe's. It was close to mid-August when James finally reached the west coast of Hudson Bay. At Port Nelson he passed Foxe, harboring there, and separately they began surveying the southern coast of what was then called Button's Bay, between Port Nelson and Cape Henrietta Maria. They met at the latter point on September 2 and separated, Foxe sailing north and James south. Wintering in "James his Bay," which he modestly named for himself, James encountered many hardships and troubles. In the spring he began what was perhaps his single outstanding achievement in the exploration of Hudson Bay — a thorough examination of the islands in the western part of James Bay. He is responsible for the names of Weston, Danby, and Charlton islands, among other points, in this bay. It is also his name for Cape Henrietta Maria which has survived rather than Foxe's "Wolstenholme Vale." Unfortunately, when he tried to round what he considered the north end of the peninsula, named by him "Cape Monmouth" and shown by Gerritsz and Briggs as separating the east and west bays, he was foiled by contrary winds, thus barely missing the chance to disprove the existence of the east bay. He returned to Bristol on October 22, 1632.

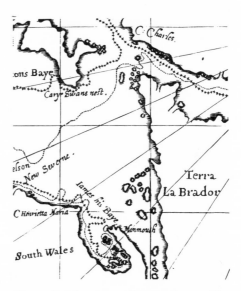

Figure 9. Map from Thomas James, *The Strange and Dangerous Voyage of Captaine Thomas Iames,* London, 1633 (Bell Collection).

If Foxe was the better navigator, James was certainly the better author. His narrative, *The Strange and Dangerous Voyage of Captaine Thomas Iames* (London, 1633), has been popular since it was first issued, and, of considerable interest simply as a tale of a sea adventure, it has often been reprinted. Foxe's volume, however, has more geographical worth. The James map, "The Platt of Sayling for the Discoverye of a Passage into the South Sea, 1631–1632," shows his route from England, and includes the bays of Hudson, Baffin, and James, and Hudson Strait (see Figure 8). For some undisclosed reason he shows the east coast, which he did not visit, as tending slightly west of north, thus departing both from Briggs and Gerritsz, but oddly enough resembling Munk and following Hudson's logbook rather than Prickett's account of sailing northward out of the James Bay area. Now James has a "C. Charles" shown on the northern coast of Hudson's Strait. Until it gradually became known that the previously mentioned "C. Charles," on the southern coast of the strait, was an island, both of these separate geographical points called by the same name were indicated on many of the maps which followed James's. The James expedition and the resulting map deserve an honorable position in the discovery and exploration of Hudson Bay. It is to be regretted that James was a not very capable mariner and therefore failed to exploit his opportunities fully. Above all, it is unfortunate that luck did not permit James to sail around Cape Monmouth and by this means discover the fallacy of Gerritsz's fictitious peninsula, a cartographical monstrosity which existed well into the eighteenth century on the maps of Hudson Bay and in the minds of men seeking the Northwest Passage.

Luke Foxe, his expedition of 1631, and map.[82] Luke Foxe came from a family long settled at Hull which had had connections with the sea for several generations. He was himself an apprentice mariner young, taking an immediate interest in mathematics and navigational instruments. He became a close friend of Henry Briggs, who was in large part responsible for Foxe's securing permission, sponsorship, and financial support from the king and London merchants for an expedition which was to be the first attempt in some twelve years to find the passage. He spent close to a year preparing himself by examining previous accounts, records, and maps; selecting a ship and crew; and outfitting them before leaving London on May 5, 1631, two days after James left Bristol. Entering Hudson Strait on June 22 and reaching the northwesterly point of "Sir Thomas Roe's Welcome Island" on about August 1, Foxe began a thorough search of the west coast to Port Nelson, where he put in for repairs. He then sailed east to Cape Henrietta Maria, meeting and visiting with Thomas James before reaching there, and from there north to discover the "Ile Sleepe" (actually one of a group now called the "Sleepers") as well as what is now known as Foxe's Channel and the western side of Fox Land. He returned home on October 31 of the same year.

In preparation for nearly three years, the complete account of Foxe's voyage, *North-West Fox*, appeared in London early in 1635. It is not known as a literary masterpiece; Foxe himself admitted he was "no Scholler." Less than half the work is Foxe's own narrative, the major part consisting of summaries of previous explorations to the area chiefly abstracted, Foxe admits, from Hakluyt and Purchas. Three narratives, those concerned with Button, Gibbons, and Hawkridge — the latter two expeditions of so little consequence as to add almost nothing of geographical importance — have a special value because they gave us almost all the information we have about the three voyages. Foxe's own narrative is hard to read and understand. His "Polar Map," found in one or two existing copies of his work, is valuable in the history of Arctic exploration (see Figure 10). Based on information taken from previous records, it includes much that is original. James Bay was undoubtedly taken from James's map; and part of the Port Nelson — Cape Henrietta Maria stretch, explored by both Foxe and James, might also have been. The minor differences in arrangement of the various islands are without significance, except that Foxe omitted some of the fictitious islands shown by Gerritsz. Baffin Bay is very nearly correctly delineated and probably

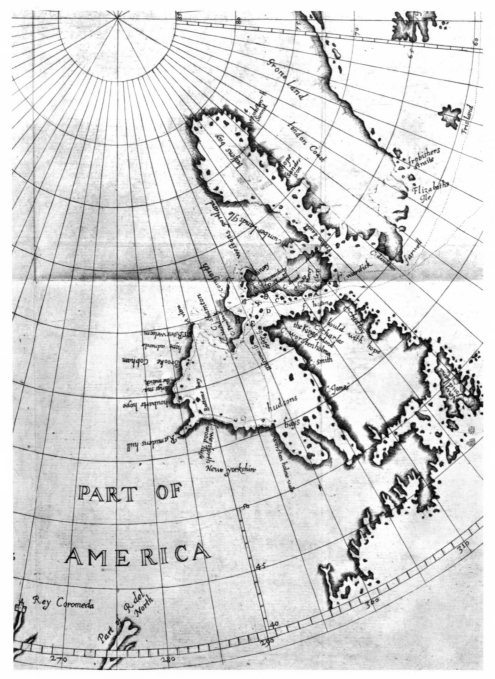

Figure 10. Part of map from Luke Foxe, *North-west Fox*, London, 1633 (used by permission of the Trustees of the British Museum).

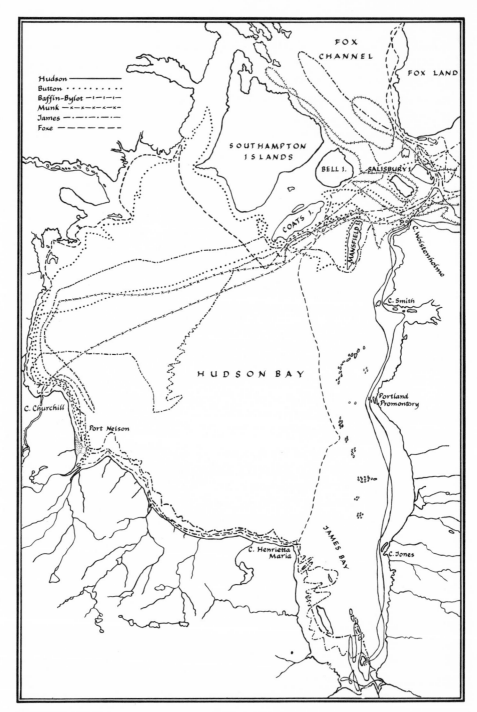

Figure 11. Major routes in Hudson Bay, 1610–1632; after Miller Christy's map in Christian Carl August Gosch, ed., *Danish Arctic Expeditions, 1605 to 1620*, 2 vols., London: Hakluyt Society, 1897. Map by Mary Nakasone.

was copied from Baffin's lost map.[83] Various islands discovered on his way north-ward and the openings at Roe's Welcome and Foxe's Channel, as well as the western side of Fox Land, are original. His source for information about the east — as well as the source of previous cartographers of this area, since only the Hudson expedition sailed north and south along this coast — is not known. Foxe helped to fix Briggs's names for Cape Jones and Cape Smith and must be credited with introducing the name of the Sleepers, though he does not show them on his map. There is some ques-tion about his use of the name "Lancaster Iles." On his homeward voyage in 1631, he describes his course from Cape Henrietta Maria; he was, he reckoned, 48 leagues from the cape in latitude 57°28'. Because of a violent storm out of the north-northwest he changed course to the west "for feare [he] might hazard [himself] in the night amongst those Ilands which Mr. *Hudson* (for good reason) calls by the name of *Lan-caster's Iles.*" [84] Christy says these islands are not in Hudson's or Prickett's narratives or on Hudson's chart and that they "seem to have been either King George Islands or one of the groups of the Sleepers," [85] according reasonably well with Foxe's account. At the same time, Foxe could be right when he says that Hudson named them. In-deed if it was one of Hudson's names, it must, along with "Cape Jones," "The Mer-chants Iles," and "Smiths foreland" (Cape Smith) have the honor of having first seen the light of day on Briggs's well-annotated map, his publicity vehicle for a Northwest Passage. Should the naming of "Lancaster's Iles," which are unidentifiable on Briggs's map, be attributable, as Foxe implies, to Hudson, then the rest of Briggs's new names may also be, although there is no mention of them in the obvious primary sources.

Foxe's contribution, by virtue of his original discoveries and through his book and map, is one of the most important in the history of the search for a Northwest Passage. In many ways his work stands as summary and synthesis of all that had been gained through earlier Arctic explorations.

Although Hudson did not himself survive to taste the fruits of his successful fourth voyage, that voyage was of utmost importance in the history of geographical explo-ration, for Hudson showed conclusively the back side, previously unknown, of the Labrador peninsula. His insistent probing of James Bay demonstrated that there was no passage out of it and thus dispelled the shadow of any suspicion that may have lin-gered in his mind that the Sea of Verrazano lay in that direction. Above all, it offered the promise of a positive solution to the great puzzle of a passage to Cathay by the Northwest. Clearly, it was so judged at the time, for, as we have seen, it triggered a whole series of expeditions through Hudson Strait. The completion of Foxe's and James's voyages of 1631 marked the beginning of a lull in the search for a Northwest Passage; their maps no longer showed the possibility of a western outlet out of Hudson Bay. John Oldmixon, summarizing this period in 1708, says, "thus we see all the Adventures made to the North West, were in Hopes of passing to China," and adds, pensively, "but that is a Discovery as latent as the Philosophers Stone, the pe[rpe]tual Motion, or the Longitude." [86]

We hear of no more such adventures until the year 1668, when Zachariah Gillam and Sieur des Groseilliers entered Hudson Bay and established the first permanent trading post there. On the return of Captain Gillam to England, and through the active interest of Prince Rupert, the organization of the Hudson's Bay Company followed, and there began a whole new cycle of events influencing exploration. The Foxe and James voyages may thus be considered to end the "Hudsonian Revolution" in the search for a Northwest Passage.

NOTES

page 89

During the preparation of this paper, the writers have become indebted to many people and institutions for their help. First, the James Ford Bell Collection has provided a large part of the basic material incorporated in this paper. Also, invaluable help has been provided by James Kingsley, Jr., Chief of the Special Collections and by John Wolter, librarian of the Map Collection of the Walter Library of the University of Minnesota. The staff of the Library of the American Geographical Society was most helpful during an all too brief study visit there. The generous loan of Miss Margaret Oldenburg's private library of Arctic literature is gratefully acknowledged. Last, but not least, are W. Kaye Lamb, Dominion Archivist and Mr. T. E. Layng, head of the Map Division, Public Archives of Canada, who together provided invaluable information.

[1] See, however, John Meredith Read, Jr., *A Historical Inquiry Concerning Henry Hudson*, Albany, 1866, and Thomas A. Janvier, *Henry Hudson*, New York, 1909, both of whom examine a wide variety of source material in presenting a brief and tentative picture of Hudson's background and early life.

[2] For a better understanding of the temper of the times and Anglo-Dutch relations as seen by a Dutch expatriate in London, see John Parker, *Van Meteren's Virginia, 1607–1612*, Minneapolis, 1961. By extrapolation one may readily visualize the immense number of covert connections between the English and the Dutch during this time of common political and religious interests but growing commercial rivalry.

[3] In 1609 Hudson was on the point of concluding arrangements with Isaac Le Maire and French government officials and merchants whereby he was to search the passage for King Henry the Fourth of France. The Dutch, with whom Hudson had previously been dickering and who were hesitating because of dissension among themselves, now hurriedly settled their differences and signed an agreement by which Hudson was to sail for them. This is fully discussed in Henry C. Murphy, *Henry Hudson in Holland*, The Hague, 1859, reprinted, with notes, documents, and a bibliography, by Wouter Nijhoff, The Hague, 1909.

page 90

[4] For more detailed accounts of Hudson's voyages, accompanied by important related documents, see the works by Read, Janvier, Murphy, and Nijhoff, as well as George M. Asher, *Henry Hudson the Navigator*, London, 1860, and Llewelyn Powys, *Henry Hudson*, New York, 1928.

[5] See Asher, *op. cit.*, pp. cxcvi, 44, where it is made clear that Hudson had the possibility in mind as early as his second voyage.

[6] This brief account of Hudson's fourth voyage, sufficient for our purposes here, is based on data given in Asher, *ibid.*, *passim* and the *Transactions* of Trinity House as published by Miller Christy in his *Voyages of Captain Luke Foxe . . . and Captain Thomas James*, London, 1894, 2 vols. (continuously paged), vol. 2, pp. 629–634. Needless to say, there are disagreements among various authors concerning some of the dates, distances, locations of geographical points, and other data connected with the expeditions. June 22 and June 23 have both been suggested as the date Hudson and the other men were abandoned.

page 91

[7] Information about the proceedings against the mutineers will be found in Janvier, *op. cit.*, pp. 119–148 and Powys, *op. cit.*, pp. 183–198.

[8] As quoted in Nellis Maynard Crouse, *Contributions of the Canadian Jesuits to the Geographical Knowledge of New France, 1632–1675*, Ithaca, N.Y., 1924, p. 140.

[9] Gerardus Mercator, "Nova et Aucta Orbis Terrae," Duisburg, 1569, reproduced in Edme François Jomard, *Les Monuments de la géographie*, Paris, 1854–1855, pl. XXI:2. Rumoldus Mercator, "Orbis Terrae . . .," Duisburg, 1587, reproduced in Nils Adolf Erik Nordenskjöld, *Facsimile-atlas to the Early History of Cartography*, translated from the Swedish by Johan Adolf Ekelöf and Clements R. Markham, Stockholm, 1889, pl. XLVII.

[10] See Hakluyt's map in his edition of Pietro Martire d'Anghiera, *De Orbe Novo . . .*, Paris, 1587, after the dedicatory epistle; the "Lago de Conibas" of Corneille Wytfliet was shown on his map which was a part of his *Descriptionis Ptolemaicae Augmentum . . .*, Louvain, 1597, following p. 82.

[11] Louis C. Karpinski, *Bibliography of the Printed Maps of Michigan*, Lansing, Mich., 1931, pp. 81–82. See also his notes to the facsimile maps of Mercator, Hakluyt, Wytfliet, and others following these pages.

[12] For a discussion of Gerritsz's life and work see Johannes Keuning, "Hessel Gerritsz," *Imago Mundi*, vol. 6, 1949, pp. 49–66.

[13] There is no complete descriptive bibliography of this work by Gerritsz. Until known copies of the various editions and issues are thoroughly examined and collated, the following, all published in Amsterdam, would seem a useful classification of them for our purposes: I. The first Dutch edition, of 1612, appearing under the title *Beschryvinghe vander Samoyeden Landt in Tartarien . . .* II. The first Latin edition, 1612, entitled *Descriptio ac Delineatio Geographica Detectionis Freti . . .*; this edition was reprinted in *Recentes Novi Orbis Historiae*, Geneva, 1612, and Hieronymous Megiser's *Septentrio Novantiquus*, Leipzig, 1613; it was used in the German translations by Theodor de Bry, *Zehender Theil der Orientalischen Indien*, Frankfort, 1613, and Levinus Hulsius, *Zwölfte Schiffahrt oder kurtze Beschreibung der newen Schiffahrt gegen Nord Osten . . .*,

Oppenheim, 1614; it was paraphrased in the English accounts by Samuel Purchas, *Purchas His Pilgrimage*, London, 1613, 1614, 1617. III. The second Dutch edition, 1612, which adds two leaves, of which the first is blank, to the first Dutch issue. IV. The second Latin printing, 1612, usually found under the title *Exemplar Libelli Supplicis . . .*, although in some copies a second title page, the *Descriptio ac Delineatio*, is also found. V. The second Latin edition, 1613, revised and augmented, with the title as in II. VI. The second Latin issue, 1613, which differs from V in having a four-page appendix. For discussions, translations, and printings of the various editions and parts of this work, see the works cited by Murphy, Asher, and Keuning, and Pieter A. Thiele, *Mémoire bibliographique sur les journeaux des navigateurs néerlandais*, Amsterdam, 1867; Samuel Muller, *Detectio Freti Hudsoni*, Amsterdam, 1878; and Samuel P. Honore Naber, *Hessel Gerritsz, Beschryvinghe vander Samoyeden Landt*, The Hague, 1924.

[14] There exist two references which state that the "Tabula Nautica" may have been drawn in England, and by one John Daniell. These are Murphy, *op. cit.*, 1909, p. 72, and Henry Raup Wagner, *The Cartography of the Northwest Coast of America to the Year 1800*, Berkeley, Calif., 1937, 2 vols. (paged continuously), vol. 2, item no. 256. Asher, *op. cit.*, pp. xlv–xlvii, also discusses this matter. Because of the rather mysterious circumstances under which the map was issued and because it is embellished with the coat of arms of England, includes English place names and comments (although some Dutch terms are used) and a verse, which appears to have been written by an Englishman, the possibility that the map was drawn in England is very strong.

page 92

[15] Asher, *op. cit.*, p. 191.

[16] E. G. R. Taylor, in her *Original Writings and Correspondence of the Two Richard Hakluyts*, London, 1935, 2 vols. (continuously paged), vol. 1, p. 63, states positively that "the reports of Hudson's last voyage . . . came into Hakluyt's hands" in 1611. She does not, however, in a work which is otherwise thoroughly documented, say from whom or by what means Hakluyt acquired these reports.

[17] Asher, *op. cit.*, p. xlvi.

[18] See the chapter "Dutch and English Voyages" in Parker, *op. cit.*, pp. 40–60.

[19] For biographical information about Purchas and a review of his work, see Sir William Foster, "Purchas and His 'Pilgrimes,'" *Geographical Journal*, vol. 68, 1926, pp. 193–195, and E. G. R. Taylor, "Samuel Purchas," *Geographical Journal*, vol. 75, 1930, pp. 536–539. See also Christy, *op. cit.*, ix*n*–xii*n*, for a discussion of the information relating to Hudson included in Purchas's works.

[20] Published in Christy, *op. cit.*, vol. 2, pp. 629–634.

[21] R. A. Skelton, *Explorers' Maps*, New York, 1958, p. 126.

page 93

[22] Published in Christy, *op. cit.*, vol. 2, pp. 629–634.

[23] See the various editions and issues, and references cited in n. 13 above.

[24] *Purchas His Pilgrimage* (hereafter cited as *Pilgrimage*), first published in London in 1613, gives information about Hudson taken from the first Latin edition (1612) of Gerritsz's *Beschryvinghe vander Samoyeden Landt*, p. 624; the second edition, revised and enlarged and published in London in 1614, expands the account of Hudson's voyage through interviews with Hakluyt and Digges and from an examination of source material Hakluyt had procured, to cover pp. 743–745; the third edition of the *Pilgrimage*, London, 1617, again revised and enlarged, contains information about Hudson differing slightly from that of the previous edition on pp. 924–926.

[25] *Hakluytus Posthumus, or Purchas His Pilgrimes* (hereafter cited as *Pilgrimes*) was published in London in 1625. Appearing in four volumes, it is distinctly different from the *Pilgrimage*. The *Pilgrimes*, Purchas's outstanding work, gives in full the material on Hudson from original documents held by Hakluyt and procured by Purchas from the executors of Hakluyt's estate on pp. 596–610 of the third volume. In the fourth edition of the *Pilgrimage*, appearing in London, 1626, still in one volume, there is a reissue, pp. 817–819, of the Hudson material taken from the third edition of 1617.

[26] See Luke Foxe, *North-West Fox*, London, 1635, pp. 117–136. This is reprinted, with copious notes, in Christy, *op. cit.*, vol. 1, pp. 162–200. See also pp. xvi–xliii in this latter work where Christy further discusses Button and his expedition.

page 94

[27] Samuel de Champlain, *Les Voyages du Sieur de Champlain Xaintongeois*, Paris, 1613, following p. 160. The map is reproduced in the Champlain Society's Publications, *The Works of Samuel de Champlain*, Toronto, 1922–1936, new series, 6 vols., vol. 2, plate 1.

[28] The Baffin-Bylot expeditions are dealt with in Purchas, *Pilgrimes*, pp. 836–848. This account is reprinted, accompanied by texts of important manuscript documents relating to the expeditions held by the British Museum and notes by the editor, in Thomas Rundall, *Narratives of Voyages Towards the North-West*, London, 1849, pp. 97–150. Virtually the same material, with a lengthy introduction and notes, appears in Clements R. Markham, *The Voyages of William Baffin, 1612–1622*, London, 1881. Through his version of the Baffin-Bylot expeditions, Foxe, *op. cit.*, pp. 137–159, adds further information which is supplemented by Christy, *op. cit.*, vol. 1, pp. 202–239, in the notes to his reprint of Foxe's account. The first chart to show Baffin's discoveries is found in but one or two of the extant copies of *North-West Fox*. Baffin's own chart of his 1615 voyage appears in Rundall, *op. cit.*, preceding p. 97, where it is shown as drawn by Rundall "from an autographed draft by Baffin" held by the British Museum. It is shown also in Markham, *op. cit.*, preceding p. 103, where it is reproduced in color "as a facsimile," and in Skelton, *op. cit.*, p. 126, where less of the chart is shown and it is smaller than the Markham copy, though in true facsimile. Baffin's chart showing the track of his 1616 voyage has not been preserved.

[29] Jens Munk, *Navigatio Septentrionalis*, Copenhagen, 1624. An excellent modern edition, with extensive notes, is C. C. A. Gosch's *Danish Arctic Expeditions*, London, 1897, 2 vols., vol. 2, *The Expedition of Captain Jens Munk to Hudson's Bay*.

[30] A facsimile reproduction is included as part of Keuning's article, *op. cit.*, following p. 58.

[31] Published in Athanasius Inga, *West-Indische Spieghel*, Amsterdam, 1624. The map is reproduced and discussed in Wagner, *op. cit.*, vol. 1, pp. 114–115, vol. 2, item no. 292.

[32] Purchas, *Pilgrimes*, vol. 3, between p. 852 and p. 853. The map is reproduced and discussed in Wagner, *op. cit.*, vol. 1, pp. 114, 117, vol. 2, item no. 295.

[33] Thomas James, *The Strange and Dangerous Voyage of Captaine Thomas Iames*, London, 1633. Reprinted, with notes and map facsimile, in Christy, *op. cit.*, vol. 2, pp. 447–611. See also Christy's introduction, pp. cxxxi–ccix.

[34] Foxe, *op. cit.* Reprinted, with notes and map facsimile, in Christy, *op. cit.*, see also Christy's introduction, pp. liv–cxxxi.

[35] Purchas, *Pilgrimes*, vol. 3, pp. 596–597.

[36] Christy, *op. cit.*, vol. 2, pp. 629–634.

[37] In Gerritsz, *op. cit.* (see n. 13 above). A facsimile copy is included in Asher, *op. cit.*, preceding the introduction. Asher, p. xliv, holds that the map was first published by itself.

[38] A reproduction of the map in its second state accompanies Naber, *op. cit.*, following p. 125.

[39] DeBry, *op. cit.*, following p. 10.

[40] Hulsius, *op. cit.*, at end of work.

[41] Asher, *op. cit.*, p. xlv. See also n. 14 above.

[42] Purchas, *Pilgrimes*, vol. 3, p. 605, p. 606.

[43] Asher, *op. cit.*, p. 192, n. 1.

page 95

[44] *Ibid.*, p. xlvi.

[45] Robert J. Flaherty, "The Belcher Islands of Hudson Bay: Their Discovery and Exploration," *Geographical Review*, vol. 5, 1918, pp. 433–458.

page 96

[46] Purchas, *Pilgrimes*, vol. 3, p. 604.

page 97

[47] See the sources cited in n. 13 above.

[48] Murphy, *op. cit.*, 1909, p. 70.

[49] *Ibid.*

[50] "Winwood" was a definite *lapsus calami*, peculiar to the first Latin edition, 1612, and is not to be interpreted as suggesting any connection with Sir Ralph Winwood, then English ambassador to the Netherlands.

[51] Asher, *op. cit,*, p. 187.

[52] *Ibid.*, pp. 191–192.

[53] *Ibid.*, pp. 192–193.

page 98

[54] Purchas, *Pilgrimage*, 1613, p. 624.

[55] Purchas, *Pilgrimage*, 1614, p. 743.

[56] *Ibid.*, p. 744.

[57] Purchas, *Pilgrimage*, 1617, pp. 924–926.

[58] Purchas, *Pilgrimes*, vol. 3, pp. 597–608. Pp. 600, 601, 603, 605 are used throughout this section in quoting from Prickett.

page 99

[59] Great Britain, Hydrographic Office, *Arctic Pilot, Vol. III*, 4th ed., London, 1947; A. P. Low, *Report on an Exploration of the East Coast of Hudson Bay from Cape Wolstenholme to the South End of James Bay*, Geological Survey of Canada, Annual Report, 1900, Ottawa, 1902, vol. 13, part D.

[60] Asher, *op. cit.*, p. 108, fn. 1.

[61] Low, *op. cit.*, p. 22D.

[62] *Ibid.*, p. 24D.

[63] Asher, *op. cit.*, p. 108, fn. 2.

page 100

[64] *Ibid.*, p. 109, fn. 1.

[65] Great Britain, Hydrographic Office, *op. cit.*, p. 242.

page 101

[66] Asher, *op. cit.*, p. 125, fn. 1.

[67] See n. 26 above.

page 102

[68] Christy, *op. cit.*, vol. 1, following p. 258.

[69] See n. 27 above.

[70] The 1612 map followed p. 320 in the original work of 1613, *op. cit.* Of peripheral interest to our survey is Champlain's 1632 map, first appearing in his *Voyages de la nouvelle France*, Paris, 1632, which shows more of the Hudson Bay region and on a larger scale than does his map of 1613. Both the 1612 and 1632 maps are reproduced and discussed in the Champlain Society Publications, *op. cit.*, vols. 1, 2, and 6, as well as in Emerson D. Fite and Archibald Freeman, *A Book of Old Maps*, Cambridge, Mass., 1926, pp. 120–123, 132–134.

[71] See n. 28 above.

page 104

[72] See n. 29, above.

[73] For a copy and discussion of the map see Gosch, *op. cit.*, pp. 146–175.

[74] See n. 30 above.

page 105

[75] The references are brought together and published in Christy, *op. cit.*, vol. 1, pp. xxi–xxii.

⁷⁶ Keuning, *op. cit.*, p. 59, states that "the date of the chart is 1622, but a later hand has superimposed the date 1634." Skelton, *op. cit.*, figs. 135 and 140 and p. 225, gives the date as 1622, as does Wagner, *op. cit.*, vol. 2, item no. 289.

⁷⁷ The "platt" is mentioned in Purchas, *Pilgrimes*, vol. 3, p. 848, and, following p. 853, on Briggs's map.

⁷⁸ See n. 31 above.

⁷⁹ In Purchas, *Pilgrimes*, vol. 3, following p. 853. It is also reproduced in Fite, *op. cit.*, p. 128, and Wagner, *op. cit.*, vol. 1, p. 117.

page 106

⁸⁰ Sir Francis Drake, *The World Encompassed*, London, 1628, preceding p. 1. Facsimiles of both the Hondius and Eckebrecht maps are to be found in Frederick Muller & Co., *Remarkable Maps of the XVth, XVIth and XVIIth Centuries*, Amsterdam, 1895–[1899], part II, maps no. 6 and 8, respectively. Eckebrecht's map, dated 1630, is often found inserted in Johann Kepler's *Tabulae Rudolphinae*, Ulm, 1627. In view of the fact that it was not until 1633 that James published the account and map of his expedition of 1631–1632, Eckebrecht's tour de force is remarkable indeed, or else the date 1630 assigned to his map is a fine example of back-dating. The place names "James His Bay" and "C. Monmouth," given on both the James map of 1633 and Eckebrecht's map dated 1630, must be attributed to James.

⁸¹ See n. 33 above.

page 108

⁸² See n. 34 above.

page 111

⁸³ Markham, *op. cit.*, p. liv.

⁸⁴ Christy, *op. cit.*, vol. 2, p. 368.

⁸⁵ *Ibid.*, fn. 3.

⁸⁶ John Oldmixon, *The British Empire in America*, London, 1708, 2 vols., vol. 1, p. 384.

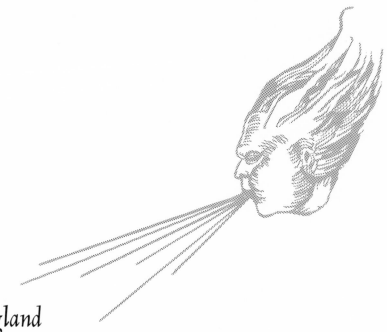

England
and the St. Lawrence, 1577 to 1602

by DAVID B. QUINN

ENGLAND'S IRRUPTION into a region which had been a reserve of French and Spanish Basque enterprise for perhaps half a century is a circumstance which requires some explanation, although it is perhaps not possible to trace all the circumstances surrounding it, even with the accession of new material which has gradually accumulated in recent years. Insofar as there is a pattern in England's concern with North America in the sixteenth century it is one of the eclectic scrutiny of one portion of coastline after another to see whether certain limited objectives could be attained by more concentrated exploitation on land or offshore. The objectives varied from the circumnavigation of the Americas to the all-embracing settlement of the eastern seaboard of North America, and from the finding of sites where Mediterranean olive trees, vines, and citrus fruits could be profitably introduced to the establishment of a walrus fishery. The only large and lasting achievement of the English in American waters in the sixteenth century was the development of a substantial hold on the cod fishery in one sector, southeast Newfoundland; the walrus fishery which was the specific reason why English expeditions were sent into the St. Lawrence in the 'nineties is best seen as an extension of the cod fishery, but it also became involved in the problem of settling Englishmen — nonconformists who could not easily be fitted into English society — outside their own country. The story of the experimental voyages to the St. Lawrence is in the end that of an unsuccessful attempt to have walrus caught by a band of congregationalist Pilgrim Fathers. It is a curious story, and the failure of the attempt may have been the principal reason why it has not hitherto been expounded at length.

The question of whether or not the English had a sufficiently acute interest in Jacques Cartier's discoveries to try to follow where he led into the St. Lawrence valley cannot usefully be discussed here, but it must be realized that the English fishermen who congregated at and off the Avalon Peninsula every summer were in intermittent touch with Breton, Norman, and French Basque seamen whose shore bases were on the south of the island, while the cod fishery shaded off into the area of mixed whale and cod fishing based on western Newfoundland under the domination of Spanish and

NOTES for *England and the St. Lawrence, 1577 to 1602* are to be found on pages 140 to 143.

French Basques. The latter in turn had their sphere of influence, extending throughout the Gulf of St. Lawrence and covering the fur trade and white-whale (*beluga*), whalebone-whale, walrus, and cod fishing. The Breton ship which Cartier found beyond the Strait of Belle Isle in 1534 and the courses plowed by the Cartier-Roberval expeditions through the gulf between 1534 and 1543 were the only and first known examples of a long run of interloping in this region. The Basques, whose claims to priority were probably good, have left few records, it appears, of their Canadian sphere of influence, but it is most likely that a good deal of information on, and speculation about, the products of the gulf which they exploited reached the English seamen in Newfoundland, even though the majority of the Englishmen seemed quite content to return each year to the same fishing stages.

Anthony Parkhurst must take pride of place among the Englishmen who had a lively interest in northeastern North America. He looked at Newfoundland in the seventies with a seeing eye, commending its potentialities for commerce and settlement, and he also saw beyond it. From 1574 onward he collected information about the gulf and river of St. Lawrence until in 1578 he declared himself willing to lead an English expedition to the river, having already advocated the seizure of Belle Isle, the occupation of Anticosti, and the consequent declaration, for this is what it amounted to, of commercial war against the Basques.[1] Just at that time Sir Humphrey Gilbert obtained a patent giving him the right to colonize or control the colonization of America by Englishmen. The two Richard Hakluyts, lawyer and clergyman, were busy collecting materials to help point the way to him and to his associates and clients. It was probably the elder Hakluyt who was responsible for Gilbert's selling off licenses "to sundry persons of mean ability . . . to plant and fortifie . . . about the river of Canada."[2] One of these was Edward Cotton, a Southampton merchant, much engaged in overseas venturing, but we know little of his companions. Their plan was to enter the gulf and imitate the Basques (and compete with them by force too, perhaps) in trading with the Indians, whaling, and making train oil. An expedition was, indeed, set out. Richard Whitbourne, who sailed on Cotton's ship, tells us only[3] that it failed "by the indiscretion of our Captain, and faint-heartedness of some gentlemen of our Company." We might suggest that the vigorous reactions of the Basques to English competition may have been the decisive factor. We cannot, on present information, tell whether this venture took place in 1579 or 1580. In the latter year, however, the younger Richard Hakluyt, taking his first independent initiative in the field of geographical publicity, arranged for John Florio to publish the Jacques Cartier material already available in print in Italian, so as to let Englishmen know clearly what the French had found, over forty years before, in the St. Lawrence basin. The Cartier narrative was prefaced[4] by an appeal for English settlement there and was probably closely linked with the anti-Basque expedition already described. Nevertheless, though Christopher Carleill paid much attention to the St. Lawrence in the colonizing tract which he published in 1583,[5] and though the younger Hakluyt carried on a vigorous campaign of economic espionage on French voyages to North America while he was attached to the English embassy in Paris (1583–1588), no evidence of English voyages to the St. Lawrence is known during these years. Gilbert had turned his attention to Newfoundland itself: after his death interest had shifted south to what is now North Carolina and Virginia, and this "Mediterranean" zone occupied the colonialists' attention until the Spanish war had blanketed off the English settlement on Roanoke Island and forced the abandonment of the southerly colonial experiment.

News about the Gulf of St. Lawrence which reached England in 1591 through the coincidences of privateering warfare restarted the long-suspended project of competing with the Basques. Sir Francis Walsingham, who, as secretary of state, had sponsored first Gilbert's and then Raleigh's colonizing projects, and had come to concentrate on the southern ventures, died in 1590: the official initiative for the more northerly ones came from Lord Burghley, the lord treasurer. He had for long been interested in the western fishery and, as far back as 1563, had pushed through parliament an act for having two "fish days" a week, in order to build up the English fishery against the competition of the five hundred ships and fifteen thousand seamen the French were thought to employ at Newfoundland. He was concerned with fish, train oil, and the naval stores which were found in northern waters and is found subscribing both to the Frobisher voyages in search of a route around North America and to the Gilbert ventures. One of Parkhurst's letters is amongst his papers, and Edward Hayes, Gilbert's associate, addressed to him lengthy pleas in 1585 and 1586 to sponsor the intensive development of Newfoundland settlement so as to monopolize control of the fishery in English hands.[6]

In the autumn of 1591 two separate pieces of information drew Burghley's attention to the Gulf of St. Lawrence (see Figures 12 and 13). The English, since the sea war against Spain had become general in 1585, had been seizing every ship they could in any way associate with Spanish ownership or with commerce to Spanish ports. Basque vessels coming from the western fisheries were especially good targets for English privateers. Even though many of the ships were in French ownership, the Spanish and French Basques were so intermingled that there were usually a few men of Spanish and a few of French nationality aboard each vessel, whereas fish brought by French and Spanish vessels alike was mainly destined for Spanish consumption. The blitz against the Basques from 1585 to 1603 has still to find its historian, but one of its fruits was the French-Basque ship the *Catherine de St Vincent* (or *Catalina de San Viçente* in its Spanish guise). She was taken on her return from America in the autumn of 1591 by the privateer *Golden Hind*, Captain Edward Lewes, and brought into Weymouth. From there it seems likely that Michel de la Ralde, captain and part-owner, made his way to London, and, through his own efforts or those of the French ambassador, induced the privy council on October 22 to order the release of the ship

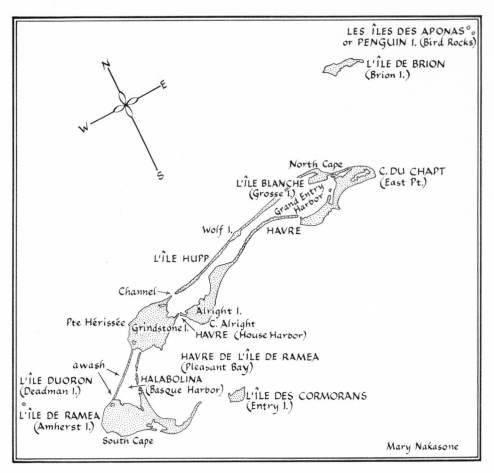

Figure 12. The Magdalen Islands (Ramea or Menquit), 1591–1597; adapted from a map by A. G. Hodgkins.

and cargo intact. It also seems likely that this was done promptly as there is no record of the sale of the ship or her cargo as prize goods, though it is not unlikely that she had suffered to some extent from pillage. Scarcely had this been achieved than a stream of correspondence reached Lord Burghley from St. Jean de Luz and Bayonne urging him to intervene to rescue the ship. Catherine, Princess of Bourbon, Henry the Fourth's sister, who administered the southern provinces for him, wrote that the ship was under her protection (its name may even have been bestowed by her) and that it was carrying merchandise for her service. M. de Chasteaumartin, who represented English interests in Bayonne, told Burghley that if the *Catherine* was not released there would be reprisals against English vessels trading to French Biscayan ports.[7] The reason for all this activity emerges only in a letter from the capable English intelligence agent at St. Jean de Luz, Edmund Palmer. Writing to Burghley on October 9/19[8] he said that the ship had been built only recently at St. Jean de Luz and was

[122]

bringing back from American waters (evidently by report of some of her consorts who returned safely) train oil, salmon and Newland fish, and, in addition, "a great stores of rich furs, as beaver, marternes, otters and many other sorts." This information explains why the French were so anxious to recover the ship and her cargo, but it also emphasized, in a dramatic form, how profitable the commerce of the St. Lawrence region had become. Palmer deliberately incited Burghley to interest himself in the *Catherine*'s cargo of furs, by saying that "sometimes they do bring black fox skins — no such things to ease a man of the pain of the gout as these black fox skins." This must have had some appeal to an aging and gouty man.

Before these letters arrived Burghley had already had his attention drawn forcibly to the Gulf of St. Lawrence through another capture and had been urged to encourage an English enterprise there. The initiative in this case came from a prominent Bristol merchant, Thomas James, who informed Burghley on September 14[9] that a ship of his had taken a Breton prize coming from the Gulf of St. Lawrence and so had uncovered a profitable branch of commerce, namely a walrus fishery on the Magdalen Islands, which it would, he implied, be most profitable for the English to exploit. He later obtained a description of the Magdalen Islands and of the Breton voyage,[10] which he probably forwarded to Burghley after he had received a favorable response to his first letter. James was also probably responsible for bringing the younger Richard Hakluyt into the affair. Now a prebendary of Bristol Cathedral, Hakluyt was frequently in the city. He is likely to have taken an active part in publishing the Magdalen Islands material, preserving for us most of the documents we have, and contributing himself, probably as part of the advertising material for the English ventures, his little essay on the walrus,[11] "A briefe note of the Morsse and the use thereof." It was on the basis of the information obtained about the French venture in 1591 that the English expeditions to the St. Lawrence were initiated two years later.

From the documents we can construct a good deal of what happened in 1591. In that year a Breton syndicate headed by M. de la Court, sieur de Pré-Ravillon et Grand Pré, who has not yet been identified in the French records,[12] sent two small vessels for a season of walrus fishing to the Magdalen Islands in the St. Lawrence. It seems clear that their knowledge of the fishery had been culled from the Basques and it is likely that they had Basque charts of the islands and possibly a Basque pilot. The two vessels left St. Malo with "the fleet that went for Canada," the Bretons having resumed their furtrading in the St. Lawrence River from 1581 onward. One of the two ships, the *Bonaventure*, passed Cape Ray on May 6 and soon sighted Bird Rocks, but was held back by a storm, and it was not until the end of the month that she was able to sail down the western shores of the Magdalens, rounding Amherst Island into Pleasant Bay and entering the inner Basque Harbor; there she evidently found her consort, in which perhaps La Court had sailed,[13] having coasted the eastern shores of the group and arrived some weeks before. The Bretons called the group, and also, it

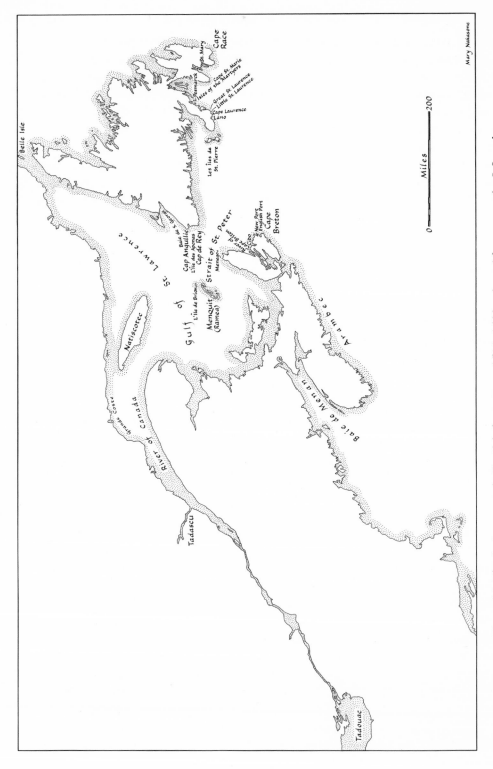

Figure 13. The St. Lawrence in English documents, 1591–1602; adapted from a map by J. Lynch.

Mary Nakisone

seems, Amherst Island in particular, Ramea (Spanish *rama, ramo*, French *rame, rameau*, branch), the form perhaps suggesting Spanish Basque influence: what are now Grindstone and Wolf islands were known collectively as Île Hupp (Spanish *rupe,* touchwood?, French *huppe*, crested?). The long beaches, with good shingle banks behind, were excellent for drying cod, and on several of them herds of walrus were thick on the ground. The Bretons set hard to work killing, flensing, and boiling. They must have had a good number of boats with them as they took cod in some quantity as well as walrus, drying it on stages on the beaches. Most of the walrus, it would seem, were hit on the head on land, though some may have had to be chased and harpooned at sea. The tusks were hammered out of their massive heads, the skin separated from the blubber and roughly salted, the blubber boiled down to oil and casked, and some of the meat from the pups used for food and barreled for provisions. By the end of the walrus season, which began in April and lasted for two months, they had taken fifteen hundred walrus, a great catch. Before all was prepared for lading, and their cod dried, it was probably mid-August. It does not seem that, this season, they had any competition from Basques or from the local Indians; at least we are told of none. Ignorance of the fact that both Spanish and French Basques normally came there in some strength was to bedevil the English enterprises.

On September 6, off the Scilly Islands, the *Bonaventure* was chased by an English privateer and taken:[14] her consort escaped and, apparently, got safely home to St. Malo. The *Pleasure*, which took the *Bonaventure*, was owned and victualed by Thomas James and Thomas Jennings of Bristol, and her captain was William Trench. She was brought to Bristol and valued there, with her cargo of "trayne oyell, feshydes and teethe,"[15] to cite the document precisely, as worth £793. The cargo was both a valuable and an unusual one, and it is not surprising that James brought it to Burghley's attention or that he took the trouble to get one of her complement, probably the master, though we do not know this for certain, to write "A relation of the first voyage and discovery of the Isle Ramea," giving the account of the Magdalens voyage already referred to which was afterward printed by Hakluyt.

The fifteen hundred walrus produced a good quantity of oil, two barrels for five carcasses, some eighty tuns in all, judging for the forty tuns and more in the *Bonaventure*. Train oil from cod, seal, and whale sold in England for from £9 to £14 a tun, though the customs valuation was only £5.[16] If we reckon the selling price of forty tuns at £12 a tun we should get £480. The walrus ivory might average five pounds a pair from the tusks of the adults among the fifteen hundred killed, perhaps seven hundred pairs in the *Bonaventure*, weighing about thirty-five hundred pounds, taking a fairly conservative weight. Elephant ivory had a customs value of 5*s.* a pound but apparently was worth retail no more than 1*s.* 6*d.* in 1591, while a prize valuation in 1590 put it at only 9*d.*[17] Nonetheless the retail price for walrus ivory was, we are told, 2*s.* 9*d.* to 3*s.* in London.[18] If we take 2*s.* a pound as the selling price we get about £350 for what the *Bonaventure* carried. As for the walrus hides, ox hides were rated for custom at 20s. each and prize valuations gave from 5s. to 8s. a hide according to quality.[19] If we reckon another seven hundred hides at 10s., giving £350, we should be safe enough. The walrus meat is not likely to have been very bulky or very valuable. Allowing £250 for her cod, we get a total sale value for the cargo of some £1,430, which probably errs on the side of caution, since the prize valuation of under £800 includes the ship and was usually about half the sale value or less.[20] It is likely that the vessel that got home to St. Malo paid the way of both ships. Nor is it surprising that Thomas James, Lord Burghley, and Richard Hakluyt became excited about the *Bonaventure's* unusual and valuable cargo.

The main value of the walrus, at first sight, was the oil. Train oil was used for lighting and lubrication, but the greatest need for oil was probably for soap, relatively large quantities of which were required for the cloth industry. Oil from cod and seal was too fishy to be freely used for soap, though whale was better: walrus oil was, miraculously, sweet — that is it did not stink of fish. The Company of Soapmakers of Bristol, a center for soap manufacture, had set itself against the use of any oil except olive oil,[21] but from 1585 this was shut off by the Spanish embargo, except for what came round from the Mediterranean or was re-exported from France, mainly from the Biscayan ports. It was thus both scarce and dear,[22] and this explains Thomas James's jubilation at the quality of the walrus oil:[23] — "if it will make soap, the king of Spain may burn some of his Olive trees." Soapmaking was thus the major incentive to the English penetration of the Gulf of St. Lawrence which the capture of the *Bonaventure* provided. Minor ones were stressed by Richard Hakluyt[24] — the comb-and-knife makers would buy the ivory at high prices; moreover, the walrus tusks were proved to his satisfaction by Dr. Alexander Woodson of Bristol to have valuable medical qualities, being "as sovereign against poison as any Unicorn's horn," a reminder to us that pharmacy was still prescientific. Finally, the hides, later much valued for their toughness in preventing rigging from chafing, were in demand. "The Leather-dressers take them to be excellent good to make light targets," said Hakluyt, noting that he had seen a piece thicker than two ox hides.

With these incentives on top of the discovery of the valuable cargo of furs on the *Catherine*, also from the St. Lawrence region, an English venture to catch walrus on the Magdalen Islands was planned. What is strange is that we have no evidence that anything was done in 1592. It may be, indeed, that there was some attempt to make a reconnaissance of the islands and that this did not succeed for lack of charts or a pilot or for other reasons, but it also may be that it was necessary for some time to be spent in convincing businessmen in London and Bristol that this was an activity which might bring profits as high as those of privateering. When a project finally emerges for a voyage in 1593 it has taken shape as a fairly professional venture. It has a backer from the London area, "Master Hill of Redrife," as Hakluyt calls him: Peter Hill (or Hills) of Rotherhithe, Surrey, as we can identify him.[25] He was born in 1535 and drew himself up the ladder from seaman to shipowner. Active in the Thames pilotage organization, he became Master of the Trinity House at Deptford in 1589. Before that his ships were ranging to Hamburg and Spain, and in 1584 his *White Hind* had been to Newfoundland to fish and had brought its cargo to sell in Spain, thus being an early starter in the triangular trade from the Banks which was later to flourish. Cut off from Spain in 1585, he may have been only too willing to employ his ship *Marigold* in the St. Lawrence in 1593.[26] Set out from the Thames in the spring, she had on her a couple of butchers for flensing walrus and three coopers to knock up the barrels in which to put their oil. Peter Hill's representative on board was Richard Fisher, who wrote a narrative of the voyage. Hill seems to have had close connections with Topsham in Devon, since Richard Strong, master of the *Marigold*, and Peter Langworth his mate both came from there. This makes it the more likely that Hill was responsible for bringing George Drake of Topsham into the venture[27] as commander of the second ship which was to be employed on the voyage. George Drake was probably a relative of Sir Bernard Drake who had seized Portuguese vessels at Newfoundland in 1585. Behind him we can see Bristol capital put up by Thomas James, by another prominent merchant, Rice Jones, and perhaps by Richard Hakluyt, but in modest quantities. Burghley may well have brought Hill into the game, but we do not know whether he ventured his own money in it.

We have not unfortunately Lord Burghley's letters to Edmund Palmer during the period from October 1591 on. It is likely, however, that he told Palmer about the *Bonaventure*'s capture when reassuring him of the *Catherine*'s release, and may have suggested then (or raised the matter later) that Palmer should find him a Basque pilot to bring walrus-fishing vessels from England to the St. Lawrence. Certainly, by the spring of 1593, a Basque pilot, Stevan de Bocall, well known to Palmer, was at Bristol, and we now know that he sailed with George Drake as pilot to the Magdalens.[28] Drake was late in preparing his ship and held back the *Marigold* so that it was almost too late for walrus-hunting when they left Falmouth on June 1. Drake sailed ahead and, with his pilot to show him the way, rapidly reached the Magdalens. Strong was tardy: the *Marigold* reached St. Francis Bay, Newfoundland, only on July 11, worked her way round and through Cabot Strait ("the Straits of St Peter"), but could not light on the islands and so turned back to Cape Breton and thence down the Nova Scotia coast, doing a little desultory cod-fishing and finally making an unsuccessful attempt to take prizes off the Azores. Peter Hill got his ship back without a cargo (except perhaps for a few cod) at the end of the year. George Drake did better. There was a single Breton ship in the harbor at Ramea (probably in Basque Harbor). Like the *Bonaventure* in 1591, she came from a Catholic League port — she is likely to have been from La Court's St. Malo syndicate. Her lading of walrus was nearly complete, three quarters so: at the rate of the *Bonaventure*'s lading she had the proceeds of between five hundred and fifty and six hundred carcasses on board, worth £800 to £900. On sight of the *Marigold* she raised anchor and took flight, getting away without difficulty. But she paid no attention to the fact that three of her boats, with twenty-three men, were out on a walrus hunt. These, with the carcasses they had, Drake and Bocall seized on their return, and then proceeded to do some hunting for themselves, taking "certain sea-oxen but nothing such numbers as they might have done, if they had come in due season." Once again we hear of no Basque or Indian competition. Drake had at least, however, begun a trade: Englishmen had got, by fair means and foul, a cargo of walrus. How much there was and how ready a sale there was for the oil, skins, and ivory in Bristol we cannot say. It seems likely, though, that we can trace the disposal of the tusks of perhaps two hundred and fifty walrus from this cargo in Russia in 1594. In May and June of that year thirteen hundred and eleven pounds of "morsse teeth" were shipped there by Thomas Pitt and Richard Merick, to be sold for £ 159 4s. (about 2s. 5d. a pound) to an English agent.[29] It may have been that London did not absorb as much walrus ivory as was expected and that it seemed best to sell it where there was already an established market for the commodity. The price realized, however, was a good one. We do not hear of any further effort to fish walrus in 1594.

Instead of that, another St. Lawrence venture was planned. Bocall had evidently returned to Bristol and put in hand an expedition to reconnoiter the Basque whale fisheries in the Gulf of St. Lawrence. Probably he wanted to get a large vessel under his control and to teach the English whaling, but he did not succeed. Though it is likely that Peter Hill and Thomas James again invested in the venture, along with Rice Jones, it proved possible for Bocall to get to sea only Jones's small ship, the *Grace*, of thirty-five tons, with Sylvester Wyet as master. Wyet informs us[30] that the *Grace* left Bristol on April 4 and sighted Newfoundland on May 19, working southward and westward round the island to the Bay of Placentia, a Basque fishing center. The two ships there were French Basques from Ciboure. Sailing on round Cape Ray to the west coast, the *Grace* was in waters not known to have been fished hitherto by English ships. Bocall piloted her to the southern end of St. George's Bay, where he had learnt, apparently from news carried by survivors to his home port, St. Jean de Luz, that two Basque whalers had been wrecked in 1593. The wrecks were badly damaged by rockfalls as well as by the sea, though there were some iron bolts considered worth salvaging, and the train oil had leaked from the barrels. Yet there remained intact "seven or eight hundred whale fins," that is, pieces of whalebone, which were all recovered and which provided them with a valuable cargo and "made" their voyage. Bocall then took the ship across the gulf to the southern shore of Anticosti, telling Wyet that whales wounded by the Basques were often cast up on the beaches. Nothing was found and after a little exploration round the north side of the island, where again the English were making the acquaintance of new territory, the ship returned toward Cape Ray, having sighted Bird Rocks on the way. In Placentia Bay they found many Basque ships, both French and Spanish, more than sixty vessels in all. They were able, no doubt with Bocall's assistance, to borrow two pinnaces with which they fished for cod, but they left the bay after some thieving by the Beothuk

Indians, completed their lading at Farillon where there were twenty-two English ships, and made an easy run home with a valuable lading to Bristol by September 24.

From the letter of Edmund Palmer's[31] which tells us all we know of Bocall's participation in the voyages of 1593–1594 — since Hakluyt suppressed all mention of him in the published narratives — it is clear that the pilot was dissatisfied with his experiences in the English service. We are told that "these two years he hath sailed from Bristow [Bristol], but he could not have that as he would have for the victualling, and when he came thither [to the Gulf of St. Lawrence] his men would do nothing, and in a bark of 35 tons." These remarks remain somewhat cryptic. He despised the *Grace* because she was too small, most probably for whaling. The men would not do something or other — perhaps they would not attempt to capture whale for themselves. It is just possible that Bocall, who as we shall see was very anti-Spanish, wanted his English associates to cut out one of the Spanish Basque whalers or fishing vessels as as prize but they would not take the risk of doing so. What he means about the victualing we cannot tell precisely. It may be, however, that he had plans to winter in Canada and that the English backers would not provide the necessary stores to enable him to attempt to do so. If this is the explanation, he may have planned to take one of the expeditions, either that of 1593 or the later expedition, up the St. Lawrence River, so as to bring this too within the range of English contacts. None of the possibilities is, it will be seen, out of the question, but none is supported by evidence. There is no doubt, though, that he considered the scale of English activity in the gulf so far as altogether too small.

In 1595 Burghley is again our link with what was planned. In the letter from Palmer to Burghley already cited, of February 24/March 6, 1595, a new project is broached. Bocall had, Palmer said, returned for the winter to St. Jean de Luz and was now going to England with a new proposition which he could commend to Burghley. He told him

there is wintered in Newfoundland in the Grand Baye [probably in western Newfoundland, though the name could apply to land anywhere round the gulf] a new ship of St Sebastyans [San Sebastian, on the Spanish side of the frontier], one of 400 tons, who went thither to kill the whale, and the ship cannot but be rich with train oil. Another small ship is preparing to get to her with victuals, and other two bound to the killing of the sea cows [the walrus on the Magdalens], out of whom they do get great store of "Balyne" [baleen, here walrus ivory] which is a rich commodity.

Bocall had discussed with Palmer a scheme for taking a ship out from England to seize the Basque whaler and "bring home these Spanishes." He has promised to "repair first to your Honour" when he reached England, and he "hath such a mind to these 'Spanyses' that he cannot be in quiet till he hath the new ship with her lading." The pilot could have reached England by the middle of March and it would have been possible for Burghley to have obtained letters of marque for an English privateer in time to make the proposed expedition, provided a ship could be found which was already equipped to make such a voyage. Peter Hill had suffered losses from the Spaniards and might be thought to have been willing to take part. A privateer officer of considerable experience, William Craston, was, we shall see, engaged for a St. Lawrence expedition in 1597 and showed on it a substantial knowledge of the gulf which might suggest he had been there before with Bocall in 1595. There is not, however, any evidence yet known which points directly to a voyage of the kind Bocall contemplated having been undertaken in 1595. All we can say is that it might have taken place, though had it been successful it is surprising that something should not have been heard of it.

Bocall was clearly an exceptional man who had a wide range of experience in North America, to which Palmer paid generous tribute in the letter already quoted. He was "called here at St Jean de Luz the Prince of Conde," we are told, which implied he was a Huguenot, and this would explain his hatred of the Spaniards and his difficulties in working in the mixed French-Spanish Basque fishing trade manned by Roman Catholics, while it might also point to arrogance on his part and a capacity for giving himself airs. Yet he was too, says Palmer, "the oneliest pilot in this land," the best they had, going on — "he knows where the copper mines be in the Newfoundland, whereof I have show, but I never saw better in my life." These mines, again, could have been on the island of Newfoundland, but they could also have been anywhere else in the Maritimes or in the St. Lawrence Basin he had penetrated. There is, indeed, circumstantial evidence that they were on the Bay of Fundy, since Bocall may well be the source of the evidence for such mines which Edward Hayes, who like Palmer had seen specimens of ore, displayed in several of his writings. Bocall had also had much contact with the Indians — "this man hath had great traffic with the savages and will warrant any man to pass that way over a point of land to the South Sea." We can only guess where Bocall thought the portage to the Pacific was, perhaps over the *saults* to Lake Ontario, but Palmer considered he knew his way: "for that country and these passages I think he has not his fellow in the world." Finally, he was an expert trader: "I have known him," said Palmer, "bring out of the Canada [thus giving proof of Basque furtrading well up the St. Lawrence] in a paltry barque three thousand pound worth in furs besides other things of rich value." This reconstruction of an otherwise unknown personality is of considerable interest for this early period of European contact with Canada.

Just as our sources leave a tantalizing gap for the events of the Atlantic voyaging season in 1595 so too they are almost empty for 1596. There is one further reference to Bocall. Palmer had said in the letter already quoted several times, "all the best men of this country as pilots are against him and have 'wrotte' [wrought] all the means they can to keep him at home," since, doubtless, they did not wish to see their hard-won knowledge of the west transmitted to the English. Bocall had nonetheless gone to England in March 1595, but he was back in St. Jean de Luz in the spring of 1596. This time he was subject to other pressures, namely, from Spanish agents. They had been maneuvering since 1594 to get him to enter their naval service because of his knowledge of the coasts of England and Ireland and had renewed their offers in 1596, desiring him especially to give them detailed information, and charts no doubt as well, of the approaches to the Bristol Channel, Barnstaple, Dublin, and Limerick. Palmer, by this time on leave in England, wrote on May 1, 1596, apparently to Sir Robert Cecil,[32] about this latest development, adding: "Which Stephen Bocall serveth here in England for merchants voyages and, being of late on a voyage there [to St. Jean de Luz], they procured all that ever might be, by money and other promotion, to have him to serve their said purpose, but he would not consent to serve them in any manner of means." It would seem from this letter that Bocall had returned to England, perhaps accompanying Palmer, but it is not certain that he had done so. We cannot, however, presume that he or his English associates made a voyage to the St. Lawrence in this year. At the same time it is clear that the walrus-fishery project had not been abandoned. It was revived in a new guise and with new personnel in 1597.

The novelty of the 1597 venture to the Magdalen Islands lay in two things. In the first place the project was planned as a colonizing rather than as a commercial one only. Since the Bretons and the Basques were known to frequent the islands and to dominate the walrus fishery, it seemed desirable that the English should attempt, if they were to gain a major share at least in the fishery, to overreach their competitors. The walrus season was short and the English ships were not accustomed to attempt the Atlantic crossing so early in the year as their rivals. If, therefore, an English settlement could be left on the islands, the colonists would be able to kill a large number of walrus as soon as they appeared and also secure good stages for drying their cod and so start the fishery in good time. The islands were known to contain some land which was promising for agriculture and there was also some timber. It is unlikely that, at this time, there was any serious idea of holding off the other cod fishermen and walrus-hunters by force. It seems to have been thought that the mere presence of the English settlement, and the priority its members would gain in harvesting the sea, would ensure the forbearance of the Basques and Bretons, and allow the settlement to be reinforced annually by vessels coming from England for which the colony would provide a base. The second new feature was the proposal to take from England a group of settlers who were willing and eager to leave the country and who could be thought likely to apply themselves conscientiously to the hard pioneering life which would be demanded of them on the islands.

The plan[33] was to send out two vessels in good time in 1597, the *Hopewell*,[34] Captain Charles Leigh, and the *Chancewell*, Captain Stephen van Harwick, which would attempt to carry through a season's walrus- and cod-fishing, while at the same time a small party of settlers, four in number would be carried in order to examine the islands, choose a site for a settlement, and assess the supplies it would be necessary to bring out for the larger party which was to come in 1598. It was expected that the four planters would stay over the winter, along with one of the ships, apparently the *Chancewell*, and her company. The spring might then be spent in fishing and in hunting walrus. This would provide, it was thought, all the necessary experience required for the establishing of a secure colony and a steady trade, the prosperity of the settlers being assured by the sale of their products each year in England. The project shows signs of Bocall's influence; the plan for the ship to winter in the gulf could have been borrowed from his experience of Basque whaling practice; his hostility to the Spanish Basques would have led him to advocate an English settlement to deny them access to the islands. It may be that he had already advocated some such measure in 1593 or 1594, the failure of the English to attempt which had been a main cause of his earlier discouragement. But whatever his influence, Bocall was not intended to accompany the expedition. Indeed, since he is not heard of after May 1596, we can not usefully speculate on the reasons for his failure to appear on the scene in 1597.

A number of men appear in the picture in 1597 who are somewhat difficult to identify and associate effectively. We cannot say definitely that Peter Hill was concerned in the venture, but, as other persons linked to it in some way had associations with Rotherhithe, and as Peter Hill had been in the walrus project as early as 1593, there is good reason to suspect that he was again one of the promoters and that Ralph Hill, who took part in it, was his representative. Abraham van Harwick certainly was a sponsor. He was a Dutch merchant, not naturalized, who had been settled in London for some years and was active at various times importing wine, purchasing prize goods, and establishing "mineral battery works" (stamp-mills), powered by water, for working copper or brass, at Rotherhithe.[35] Stephen van Harwick, also a merchant, is likely to have been his brother, but he has not otherwise been met with than as a sponsor and captain of the *Chancewell*. Ralph Hill we can trace as the second son of Edmond Hill, originally of Shere, Surrey. Born about 1573, he was apprenticed to a London goldsmith in 1585 and became free of the Goldsmiths' Company in 1594. He raised some money in February 1597, probably to invest in the voyage, and was later accused by his elder brother, Richard, of leaving him in financial difficulties in 1597 when he "departed England upon strange and desperate adventures."[36] If he was a relative of Peter Hill, which is not yet established, he could have been a nephew. The fact that William Craston[37] was only master of Captain Leigh's ship, the *Hopewell*, should not lead to his significance being minimized. He had himself been captain of the *Hopewell*, a vessel of a hundred and twenty tons, as far back as 1590, when she made a privateering voyage to the West Indies and had called at Roanoke Island in search of the Lost Colonists. He too was a Rotherhithe man, born in 1561, who undoubtedly knew Peter Hill, but who is not known to have sailed on his ships. Craston had sailed for John Watts in 1590 and had undertaken other privateering voyages for him subsequently, gaining a reputation for sharp practice on the way. If John Watts, one of the important London merchants of his time and an especially large investor in privateering ventures, still owned the *Hopewell*, as is likely, he may have invested her in the Magdalens venture, or else hired her to the other promoters. It has already been suggested that Craston was just the sort of man Bocall needed for his cutting out project in 1595. His presence on the 1597 expedition indicates that resistance was expected, since the *Hopewell* carried twenty to twenty-four guns, and that it was hoped to take some Spanish Basque prizes to pay part of the expenses of the voyage.

Captain Charles Leigh was the leading personality in the expedition, yet very little is known of his early life.[38] Born in 1572, at Addington, Surrey, the third son of John Leigh and Joan Oliph, he is described in 1597 as a merchant, and it is probable that besides serving an apprenticeship in London he had already had some experience at sea (or conceivably as a soldier). It is at least possible that he had sailed for Peter Hill. He was sufficiently well known as a responsible man by 1597 to be entrusted by the privy council, along with the Van Harwicks, with the execution of the Magdalens venture. Leigh is also the only link between the two sides of the project. He was known to and sympathized with the puritans who were designated to found the colony, while his commercial and maritime interests may have joined him with Peter Hill and John Watts, if they were indeed concerned, as well as with the Van Harwicks, in the business enterprise.

Since 1583 Archbishop Whitgift had been busy harrying puritans, if they would not conform fully, out of the Church of England. Indeed, some of them were glad to go, since various groups had developed, more or less strongly, separatist (congregationalist) tendencies. Among them the followers of Robert Browne gave their name to all the rest, though they often claimed they were "falsely called Brownists." From 1589 onward more and more of the separatists found their way to prison, and Barrow, Penry, and Greenwood were executed in 1593. A Brownist congregation, under its pastor, Francis Johnson, had been scooped up wholesale early in the year. An act of parliament which came into force on April 10, 1593, imposed involuntary exile on sectaries who would not conform if they did not wish to stand trial for their lives.[39] During the years following, some members of Francis Johnson's church chose to go into exile in Holland, but the remainder were left in prison, being unwilling to leave their native country. Now, through whose means we do not know—Burghley is a probability, Sir Walter Raleigh a possibility—they were to be given the chance to remain within the queen's dominions, but only if they created a new one for her in the Gulf of St. Lawrence. They petitioned Queen Elizabeth[40] to be allowed to go to a "foreign and far country which lieth in the West from hence in the Province of Canada," where they might worship as they wished and do their queen and country service, expecting in time to "annoy that bloody and persecuting Spaniard about the Bay of Mexico." The request was granted, and on March 25, 1597, the privy council[41] laid down the terms under which "divers artificers and other persons that are noted to be sectaries" were to be permitted to settle on "an Island called Ramea" in "the Bay of Canyda." Four of them were to go out at once under the auspices of the Van

Harwicks and Charles Leigh, and the customs officials were to let them take freely "such household stuff and other instruments as may serve for their necessary use . . . they having intention to reside [in] and inhabit these parts." They must swear an oath of allegiance and must enter into bond not to return to England under pain of death unless they were willing to conform. They were to stay with one vessel over the winter of 1597–1598, and it was clearly agreed that if things went well they should be joined by their friends and families in the spring.

Two of the four pioneers could be described as artisans. John Clarke was a husbandman of Wallsoken, Norfolk, who had been in prison since 1590, but who would be a good judge of how much agriculture was possible on the Magdalens. Though Daniel Studley was a girdler by trade, we do not know how long it had been since he had practiced it. Sentenced to death in 1593, he had been reprieved, and was a vigorous if unbalanced controversialist. George Johnson had been at Cambridge and was a schoolmaster before his arrest: he, too, was an erratic and violent pamphleteer and in one of his works, *A discourse of some troubles and excommunications in the banished English church at Amsterdam* (1603), has left us an account of the voyage and of his own reactions to America. The leading figure amongst the four was his brother Francis Johnson, a former Fellow of Christ's College, Cambridge, and a clergyman in the established church who had broken away to found an independent congregation — one he had tended carefully through its long ordeal in prison. He was clearly a man of some judgment and with some capacity for leadership. He, with Studley, was to sail with Leigh and Craston in the *Hopewell*; George Johnson and Clarke with Stephen van Harwick in the *Chancewell*.[42]

The walrus-fishery project had now taken on the guise — almost — of a state enterprise. The privy council had referred to the venture as "a voyage of fishing and discovery," whose sponsors "intend to bring divers very necessary commodities of special use for this Realm and to establish a trade of fishing there." The ships left Gravesend on April 28 or later. The *Hopewell* reached Conception Bay, Newfoundland, on May 20, after a good crossing, and was soon joined by the *Chancewell*. The ships spent some time trying to buy boats at Farillon and Renewse, succeeding only in picking up a damaged "great boat" which they repaired. After rounding Cape Race the vessels parted in fog near Placentia Bay, the *Chancewell*, through lack of an effective pilot, missing her course through Cabot Strait and going aground well to the west of Cape Breton, perhaps at St. Anne's Bay (Cibo as the local Indians called it). The *Hopewell*, well navigated by Craston, made good progress, and walrus were sighted on Bird Rocks — they put out to sea and pursued the ship. Like the *Bonaventure* six years before, the *Hopewell* worked down to the west of the Magdalens and turned successfully into Pleasant Bay on June 18, though failing to find her consort there. The "great boat" was sent to search the inner harbor and discovered two Basque fishing vessels — from Ciboure on the French side, they said — and two Bretons from St. Malo, which was by this time a friendly port. Leigh decided to bring the *Hopewell* into

Halabolina (Basque Harbor) and take the chance that the first-comers would remain friendly or at least passive. This was a tactical mistake, for which he was to pay, since without the *Chancewell* he had deprived himself of the mobility which would enable him to withstand attack by a number of ships, while it is likely that he found the Basques at least as well gunned as himself. The islands certainly did not appear to need colonists: other ships lay in the northern harbor and hundreds of Micmac Indians had come over from the mainland for the summer fishing. There were probably many drying stages above the beaches and fires going near the woods, boiling out the walrus oil from the blubber. But Leigh had no time for shore-going, or for building a settlement. He had to concentrate, in his own way, on the problem of survival.

The Breton skippers, invited to the *Hopewell* for refreshments, were polite, and volunteered the information that the other two vessels were French, not Spanish, Basques, but neither Basque ship responded to Leigh's first invitation to visit him. To his second, the master from one and a master's mate and pilot from the other appeared, with evidences (charter party and such), to stand inquisition. They, too, were polite, but reticent: both ships came, they said, from Ciboure. Leigh was not convinced about one of them. He demanded of her master that she surrender her arms to the *Hopewell*: not unnaturally, after twelve years of the plundering of Basque ships by English privateers, he refused. A boarding party under Craston then went into action; the ship was overpowered, but, as might be expected, the men began to seize more than arms. Leigh says he went on board and stopped the pillaging — a remarkable tribute to his force of character (did he succeed because he put across the fact that the *Hopewell* was outnumbered if a general action began against her?). The arms were taken to the *Hopewell*, but half his men, with Craston at their head, were ready for mutiny.

These preliminaries had occupied June 18 and 19: on the morning of the 20th the French brought matters to a head. From the ships in both harbors, Basque and Breton, two hundred men had been drawn, three guns had been mounted on land, and three hundred Indians assembled to add to the show of force. Leigh was told, in unqualified terms, to leave the harbor. It has now only eleven feet of water at the most, but even with more water and less sand, there was little chance for the *Hopewell* to maneuver. A fusillade of small arms fire poured over the ship. The *Hopewell* replied, but neither side appears to have done any damage. Ralph Hill, who was probably acting as cape merchant, along with the bosun's mate, was allowed to go ashore to discuss terms, but they were held prisoners against the return of the Basque ship's arms. Leigh had sent the guns to shore, when a Captain Charles, from a large ship of St. Malo in the other harbor, came on board to dictate further terms. Seeing their "great boat," he claimed it as one he had lost at Newfoundland: the hostages would not be released until it too (Leigh's last chance of maintaining a little freedom of movement by using it as a pinnace) was given up. In the meantime, a Breton ship had been creeping closer and, when she was partly alongside ("athwart our hawse"), her men tried to board. Leigh held them back by threatening to fire their ship's sails, Captain Charles slipping away in the confusion, and the St. Malo ship moving clear. From the shore, Charles hailed Leigh to say he would give up Hill and his companion only when the "great boat" was surrendered and the *Hopewell* ready to leave the harbor. The boat was despatched, but the hostages were still held. An anchor had been fixed on shore and Leigh was helpless to get it clear while the French refused even to cut his cable at the anchor stock: this he had to do himself at the ship's side and then he began to move the *Hopewell* slowly out of the harbor. Seeing he was at last under way, the hostages were left where he could pick them up and this he did. It was still morning as the *Hopewell* entered Pleasant Bay, but there she stuck, having gone aground on the bar. The eight hours that followed must have been hard on the nerves of all on board, though it soon became clear that the French were not eager to attack. The removal of the *Hopewell* from the inner harbor had been enough. When the tide rose Leigh got her off. A fresh wind took her up the eastern shores of the group, but off Île Blanche (Grosse Island) an approach to the fishing stages they saw there was met with a warning shot from a gun mounted on shore. The French were in possession: there was nothing now but to move elsewhere.

Anchored off Cape East, Craston discussed with Leigh and the two passengers what they should do. The settlement could not, clearly, be made on the Magdalens, but the separatists were bound only to settle there "or thereabouts." Here Craston showed his knowledge of the gulf, whether from the charts or from a previous voyage, by pointing to a possible site at "Grand Coste," eighty leagues to the westward. On the southern shore of modern Quebec, behind the northwestern shoulder of Anticosti, De Vaulx in 1584 had marked "R. des Chevaux" and Hakluyt, in all probability, was to add "R. of Sea Horses" to the English world map in 1599,[43] so that something was known of another walrus landing in this area: again, we might think, through information gained from Bocall. The name itself may, however, be a corruption of "Anticosti." Leigh was for going on, so Francis Johnson and Studley must have agreed also. Craston objected: contrary winds, and a lee shore when he got there, would make it hard for him to work the ship to Grand Coste: he preferred to sail eastward to Cape Breton. Leigh found that sailing forty leagues to Cape Breton would give them a hundred and twenty leagues to recover Grand Coste when the wind improved, so he tried to enforce orders that they would sail westward at once. Craston went through the form of complying, but the crew had had enough and threatened mutiny, so that Leigh had to give way and the ship duly set course for Cape Breton Island. The walrus-hunting venture and separatist colony were both at an end.

The epilogue to the tale is a simple sea story. As the *Hopewell* sailed southeast from St. Paul's Island, when they were probably in the vicinity of St. Anne's Bay, a ship's boat put out to meet her. In it were some members of the crew of the *Chancewell* who had thus, surprisingly, made contact with their fellows. Their ship broken and robbed by Basque fishermen, they had had a miserable time, not helped by the friction between Stephen van Harwick and his prickly passenger, George Johnson. The latter was, he tells us, trying to persuade the captain that he should not try the desperate remedy of piracy against the French; while he, in turn, was being threatened he would be marooned with the savage Indians. However, the miracle he wished for happened; the ship which they saw from the cliff where they were arguing turned out to be the *Hopewell* and they were saved.[44] Leigh recovered some of the *Chancewell's* goods from French Basque fishing vessels in the neighborhood, by some means preventing his men from seizing them, but they were now determined to take a prize, Spanish Basque or Leaguer Breton, at all costs. Failing to find one at Cape Breton, the *Hopewell* sailed to Newfoundland where, in Little St. Lawrence Harbor on July 18, Craston boarded the *Catalina* of Orio (near San Sebastian — or was she the *Catalina* taken and released in 1591 when she was identified as a French-owned ship?). Once again the Basques and Bretons showed their solidarity by mobilizing against the English, luckily intercepting Craston, and forcing the surrender of the ship.[45] Disgusted, Leigh, when he got his men back, turned to St. Mary's Bay and there a large Breton fishing vessel from Belle Isle, which was still in Leaguer hands and so lawful prize, was taken. Leigh refused to take part in further prize-taking but Craston was at last free to sail the *Hopewell* to the Azores to see what he could find, while Leigh took his prize crew, and the separatists, on board the Breton ship, and sailed for England on August 5. By September 5 Leigh, who had released his charges from their obligation not to return when their Canadian venture was seen to fail, was able to put them ashore on the Isle of Wight. They had spent the voyage in theological disputes and were on poor terms with each other.[46] Their fellow churchmembers had evidently been released on parole, and, when Francis Johnson had reunited them in London, a decision was taken at once to withdraw to Holland, where in due course they helped to foster a Pilgrim settlement in America nearly a generation later.

Leigh had brought no walrus and had founded no settlement, although the prize he had taken, with her lading of cod and, probably, train oil, is likely to have paid most of the costs of the voyage (no appraisement has been found). He had been emotionally involved with the separatists and may well have been deeply disappointed at the anticlimax which had occurred when the settlement was frustrated, yet he did not despair of returning to the St. Lawrence. On October 4, indeed, he submitted a further plan for a settlement on the Magdalens.[47] Since it is to be found among the papers of Dr. Julius Caesar, it may be that that astute lawyer and judge was one of his friends, and possible supporters: it was intended in the end to reach the queen. Leigh stated he had received promises of support from his friends (the Van Harwicks presumably, and possibly Peter Hill and John Watts) who were willing to put three ships under his charge in 1598. His plan was influenced by what he had seen: the French must be expelled from the islands by force. A small garrison strongly installed in Entry Island would hold the southern harbors and another manned post those further north. The

English must be there thirty days before the French and must have authority to seize French Basque as well as Spanish ships. The island was fertile enough for agricultural settlement which could be built up by some of the settlers while the rest concentrated on fishing. The emphasis now is wholly on cod-fishing (walrus are not mentioned), the cod coming earlier there and allowing the ships early on the scene to complete their lading at the end of the season off Newfoundland. The colony should, in time, take the trade of "all the inland countries," the fur trade of the St. Lawrence River, we may assume, being chiefly in his mind. In November, Leigh and Stephen van Harwick got a Spanish Basque hostage they had brought from Newfoundland to register a statement on their behalf in the High Court of Admiralty about the taking and loss of the *Catalina* in case they should be accused of assaulting a French Basque vessel.[48]

No record has yet been found of how Leigh fared with his latest scheme. Sir Robert Cecil, now in control of external affairs, would not have favored an assault on Henry the Fourth's Basque subjects, but the notion of transporting the crown's incompatible subjects overseas was still in the air. The Hakluyts, years before, had advocated compulsory colonization by criminals and vagrants. Now, in parliament, in November and December, a drastic bill for dealing with the unemployed, the "sturdy beggars," was on the stocks. One of its provisions, inserted at what stage is not clear from the surviving proceedings on the bill, was for the banishment of rogues, vagabonds, and sturdy beggars at the cost of the counties afflicted with them. The act, as it finally received the queen's approval on February 9, 1598, stated that they were to be conveyed into such parts beyond the seas as shall be at any time hereafter for the purpose assigned by the privy council.[49] If the Magdalens could be so designated, the act would provide a more dependable source for settlers, with the costs of their transport already provided for. But the act came into force too late to help a 1598 expedition, whether or not the proposers of the transportation clause had Leigh in mind when they put it forward. He had argued that an expedition to forestall Basques and Bretons must leave in January to reach the islands early in March. There is no evidence that Leigh got away on a venture of his own that year, and this was final. Certainly the idea of shipping the poor across the ocean was in the air that year. Joseph Hall, the satirist, attacked the landlord who was clearing his land of unwanted poor tenants "And ships them to the new nam'd Virgin-land."[50] A proclamation for the enforcement of the act was published on November 9, but it did not specify locations to which deportees should be sent,[51] though a subsequent proclamation of 1603 did include "Newfoundland" (which could have covered the Magdalens) among the places to which "rogues . . . shall be banished and conveyed."[52] The English were to do without their walrus and cod fishery, whether manned by pilgrims or paupers, in the Gulf of St. Lawrence.

There was still some residue of interest in the affair. Edward Hayes, who had served with Sir Humphrey Gilbert, and was an old advocate of settling Newfoundland with the aid of convicts, wrote a long treatise on American colonization, probably in association with Christopher Carleill, in 1592 or 1593.[53] It urged the settlement of what are now the Maritimes as containing good land for agriculture and as bases for fisheries, and it also emphasized the advantages of the St. Lawrence Basin as providing access to the interior (and to the Pacific). The general tone of the references to the St. Lawrence suggests the influence of Stevan de Bocall, while mention of mines discovered by the French on the Bay of Menan (Bay of Fundy) and of Lake Tadoac (Lake Ontario) far into the interior, suggests more specifically the use of the knowledge which Bocall brought to England between 1593 and 1595. Hakluyt also passed material to Hayes, and in 1596 Thomas Hariot put down a note "*Master* Hackluit / of Canada some mappes of it," [54] which sounds like a Hakluyt treatise which has been lost and suggests a collection of maps known to him which are most likely to have been, at least in part, connected with the Magdalen Island voyages. Hakluyt clearly remained longer than Leigh an active supporter of the project. He collected all the material he could get about the experiences of the years 1591–1597, omitting, however, for reasons we do not know, any mention of Bocall's part, and Charles Leigh contributed not only the narrative of the 1597 voyage which is our main authority (though it, in turn, suppresses the part played by the separatists), but also a short account of the natural resources of the Magdalen Islands [55] which helps to make them one of the better-documented parts of Canada in the sixteenth century. Hakluyt inserted in this collection, which may originally have been put together at the end of 1597 or in 1598, for propaganda purposes, an appeal for the continuation of English enterprise, [56] alleging that the English had allowed the French and Spaniards to take advantage of the resources of the islands, "while we this long time have stood still and have been idle lookers on, making courtesy who should give the first adventure, or once being given, who should continue or prosecute the same." This appeared in print in 1600 in the third volume of *The Principal Navigations*, but did not incite any particular response. An obscurely-worded document, which can be dated within the years 1598–1600, [57] it proves to be commentary on a scheme such as that which Hayes had advocated and which Leigh had attempted, in his own way, to put into effect. Since the French are said to carry on a secret trade to the place thought of as the location for an English settlement, the Magdalen Islands may well be intended. That puritans of some sort were meant to take part is indicated by a reference to "the precise," but they were not to be the only colonists. The author emphasized the special problems of getting enough capital together to allow settlers to accommodate themselves to novel conditions. He reached the conclusion that royal aid was necessary to bring such a colony to fruition, and urged that a commission be given to "a worthy general" to bring out settlers. The atmosphere of the tract is not, however, optimistic, and there was little chance that Queen Elizabeth, as her life drew toward its end, would subscribe to a state colonizing enterprise. Edward Hayes and Hakluyt had something to do with an English venture in 1602 which explored New England and proposed a trading post on Elizabeth's Isle, off the southern shore of Massachusetts. Hayes refurbished his old treatise for the published pamphlet which followed the return of the voyagers:[58] he added a few details about the mines in the Maritimes, culled, it is suggested, from Bocall, but he trimmed out of his analysis all reference to the availability of the St. Lawrence to English enterprise. The English concern with the gulf and river, which dated at least from 1578, and which had brought about some limited penetration and an abortive colonial enterprise in the 'nineties, had at length fizzled out. Or perhaps it is best to say that English attention had been redirected to the New England shores on which Gilbert had counted so much twenty years before, and which were, after still further failures, to provide a major site for English separatists and nonseparating puritans alike a generation later.

There is a curious parallelism between the decline of English enterprise in Canada and the revival of French activity.[59] Even before peace came to France in 1598 La Roche had re-emerged as the titular governor of New France, and in the very year the vagrants act came into force in England he set French criminals seal-hunting on Sable Island. If this project had a limited success it ended in tragedy and horror a few years later. Tadoussac, the first fur-trading post since Cartier, had a grim winter in 1600–1601 and folded up, except as a summer trading mart. But in 1602 new blood was coming into French enterprise; Champlain and de Monts were about to demonstrate that the future of Canada for a long time was to lie in French hands.

NOTES

page 120

[1] E. G. R. Taylor, *The Writings and Correspondence of the Two Richard Hakluyts*, Hakluyt Society, 1935, 2 vols., vol. 1, pp. 123–134 (especially pp. 133–134).

[2] Richard Hakluyt, *The Principal Navigations*, Glasgow, 1903–1905, 12 vols., vol. 8, 1904, p. 40. See David B. Quinn, ed., *The Voyages and Colonising Enterprises of Sir Humphrey Gilbert*, Hakluyt Society, 1940, 2 vols., vol. 1, pp. 49–50.

[3] *Discourse and discovery of New-foundland*, F. Kyngston for W. Barret, 1620 (S.T.C. 25372), sig. C5r. (See Quinn, *op. cit.*, vol. 2, pp. 426–427.)

[4] *A shorte and briefe narration of the two navigations to New France*, H. Bynneman, 1580 (S.T.C. 4699, entered June 7, 1580). The introduction is reprinted in Taylor, *op. cit.*, vol. 1, pp. 164–166.

[5] *A discourse upon the intended voyage to the hethermoste partes of America.* Not in S.T.C. Copies in John Carter Brown Library, Dulwich College, Westminster Abbey. For the

passages in question see Quinn, *op. cit.*, vol. 2, pp. 362–364.

page 121

[6] See Conyers Read, *Mr. Secretary Cecil and Queen Elizabeth*, London, 1955, pp. 271–274; B.M. Lansdowne MS 100; Taylor, *op. cit.*, vol. 1, pp. 123–127; Quinn, *op. cit.*, vol. 2, p. 329.

page 122

[7] *Acts of the privy council*, 1591–1592, p. 35; Madame to Burghley (undated), Public Record Office, State Papers, Foreign, France, S.P. 78/26, fol. 95; Chasteaumartin to Burghley, October 28, 1591, S.P. 78/26, fols. 62–63.

[8] Public Record Office, State Papers, Foreign, Spain, S.P. 94/4, fols. 64–66.

page 124

[9] For James, see Hakluyt, *op. cit.*, vol. 8, p. 155; K. R. Andrews, *English Privateering Voyages, 1588–95*, Hakluyt Society, 1959, p. 185.

[10] Hakluyt, *op. cit.*, vol. 8, pp. 150–154.

[11] *Ibid.*, pp. 166–167.

[12] I am indebted for this valuable negative

information to M. Robert Le Blant, who has searched the St. Malo records for La Court in vain. It is possible that the narrator invented a false name for the promoter.

[13] The author refers to "my Masters" as being on board the other ship, of whom La Court could well have been one (Hakluyt, *op. cit.*, vol. 8, p. 152).

page 125

[14] *Ibid.*, p. 155.

[15] *Sic* in MS, B.M., Harleian MS 598, fol. 15*v*. (prize brought in October 1); note by Burghley on list of prizes that Thomas James's prize belonged to Frenchmen of St. Malo, B.M. Lansdowne MS 67, fols. 146–147; the prize noted on another list, *ibid.*, fol. 190*r*. (See K. R. Andrews, "The Economic Aspects of Elizabethan Privateering," University of London Ph.D. thesis, 1951, p. 330.)

[16] T. S. Willan, *A Tudor Book of Rates*, Manchester, 1962, pp. xxxi, xli, 43, 79.

[17] *Ibid.*, p. 36; Hakluyt, *op. cit.*, vol. 8, p. 156; D. B. Quinn, *The Roanoke Voyages, 1584–90*, Hakluyt Society, 1955, 2 vols., vol. 2, pp. 692–694.

[18] Hakluyt, *op. cit.*, vol. 8, pp. 156–157.

page 126

[19] Willan, *op. cit.*, p. 11; Andrews, *op. cit.*, pp. 118–119; Quinn, *Roanoke*, vol. 2, pp. 692–694.

[20] For official appraisements see Andrews, *op. cit.*, pp. 20, 56–58.

[21] *The Company of Soapmakers, 1563–1642*, ed. H. E. Mathews, Bristol Record Society Publications, vol. 10, 1940, pp. 4–5, 26. A fine was levied in 1572 for using fish oil in soapmaking: the editor doubts, however, whether the prohibition was rigidly maintained.

[22] Rated at £8 to £12 a ton, its sale value was something more like £20 (Willan, *op. cit.*, pp. iii, 42).

[23] Hakluyt, *op. cit.*, vol. 8, p. 155.

[24] *Ibid.*, pp. 156–157.

[25] Brass in St. Mary's, Rotherhithe, *Surrey Archaeological Collections*, vol. 32, pp. 80–81; his trading activities can be followed in Public Record Office, High Court of Admiralty, H.C.A. 3/19, January 14 and 20, 1586; H.C.A. 13/25, October 19, 1585, January 15, 17, 21, 1586, February 18, 1586; H.C.A. 13/28, fols. 39*v*., 75*r*; Hakluyt, *op. cit.*, vol. 8, pp. 157, 161;

bounty for shipbuilding, Public Record Office, S.P. 38/4, April 6, 1594; contracting to carry troops for France to Ireland, 1598, *Calendar of Cecil* MSS, vol. 8, p. 28.

page 127

[26] Hakluyt, *op. cit.*, vol. 8, pp. 157–161.

[27] Hakluyt wrote a brief note on this voyage (pp. 161–162) after George Drake had failed to supply a promised narrative; Fisher (pp. 157–158) tells us most of what we know.

[28] [Edmund Palmer to Lord Burghley], March 6, 1595, S.P. 94–95, fols. 9–10*v*.

page 128

[29] T. S. Willan, *The Early History of the Russia Company, 1553–1603*, Manchester, 1956, pp. 363–364.

[30] Hakluyt, *op. cit.*, vol. 8, pp. 162–165.

page 129

[31] See n. 28 above.

page 131

[32] Edmund Palmer to [Sir Robert Cecil], May 1, 1596, Public Record Office, State Papers, Domestic, S.P. 12/257, 64.

[33] Charles Leigh's narrative (Hakluyt, *op. cit.*, vol. 8, pp. 166–180) is the main authority, except for George Johnson, *A discourse of some troubles and excommunications in the banished English church at Amsterdam*, Amsterdam, 1603 (S.T.C. 14664, copies in Trinity College, Cambridge, and Sion College, London).

[34] For the *Hopewell*, see Quinn, *Roanoke*, vol. 2, pp. 580–598, 662–663 (armament); Andrews, *op. cit.*, pp. 95–104.

page 132

[35] *Calendar of Cecil* MSS, vol. 14, p. 318; *Acts of the Privy Council, 1596–1597*, p. 141; B.M. Additional MS 12505, fol. 450; *Acts of the Privy Council, 1597–1598*, pp. 491–492; M. B. Donald, *Elizabethan Monopolies*, London, 1961, p. 191 (who says Van Harwick had a license from the Mineral and Battery Company). On February 7, 1601, Edward and Thomas Hayes were authorized to erect "an Engine at Redreth [Rotherhithe]," which was either a rolling or a stamp mill for preparing metal for coinage or for coining money (Public Record Office, Privy Seal Indexes, Ind.

6744). The topographical association of Edward Hayes, Van Harwick (and a similarity in his to that of Hayes's business), Peter Hill, and William Craston with Rotherhithe suggests that they were all acquainted.

[36] Public Record Office, Chancery Proceedings, Bill and Answer, C.2, Eliz. I/Hh. 24/31.

[37] For Craston, see Andrews, *op. cit.*, pp. 97, 157–158, 172.

page 133

[38] In 1602 he described himself as aged 30 years or thereabouts (H.C.A. 14/35, 127–128); the date is confirmed by the best genealogical study of his family, G. Leveson-Gower, "Notices of the Family of Leigh of Addington," *Survey Archaeological Collections*, vol. 7, 1880, pp. 77–123. The owners of the *Marigold*, which he commanded in his 1601 Mediterranean voyage (*Calendar of Cecil MSS*, vol. 11, p. 408), probably included Peter Hill, as she is likely to have been the same ship that Strong commanded in 1593. If this is so, the continuity of association with Hill would suggest that Leigh had been employed by him before as well as after 1597.

[39] Eliz. I, c.1 (see G. R. Elton, *The Tudor Constitution*, Cambridge, England, 1960, pp. 477–480). For the religious situation see M. Knappen, *Tudor Puritanism*, Chicago, 1939; F. J. Powicke, *Henry Barrow*, London, 1900; Champlin Burrage, *The Early English Dissenters*, Cambridge, England, 1913, 2 vols.

[40] S.P. 12/246, 46 (see Burrage, *op. cit.*, vol. 1, pp. 125–126). Johnson had already begged the queen in 1593 to allow him and his followers to depart to some place within her allegiance where they could worship freely. He may have been thinking of Ireland. (See B.M. Harleian MS 6849, fol. 143; John Waddington, *Congregational History, 1567–1700*, 2nd ed., London, 1880, pp. 31–32.)

[41] *Acts of the Privy Council, 1597*, pp. 5–6.

page 134

[42] The names of the four men and their disposition between the ships are from G. Johnson, *A discourse*, 1603. Biographical details are given in Burrage, *op. cit.*; H. M. and M. Dexter, *The England and Holland of the Pilgrims*, Boston and New York, 1906; and in the valuable biography, by Alexander Gordon, of Francis Johnson in *Dictionary of National Biography*.

Charles Leigh (Hakluyt, *op. cit.*, vol. 8, pp. 166–180) omits all mention of the Pilgrims. Whether the deletion was done by Leigh or by Hakluyt we do not know, most likely by the latter; Hakluyt was still, in 1599–1600, eager to encourage Englishmen to go to the St. Lawrence for commercial reasons and would not care, as a clergyman of the established church, to be associated with puritan sectaries or their disposal.

page 136

[43] Chart (1584) by Jacques de Vaulx, Bibliothèque Nationale, Cartes, Réserve Géographie C.4052; world map by Edward Wright in Hakluyt, *op. cit.*, 2nd ed., 1598–1600, 3 vols., reproduced in vol. 1, 1903.

page 137

[44] Compare Hakluyt, *op. cit.*, vol. 8, pp. 172–173, and G. Johnson, *op. cit.*, pp. 109–110.

[45] Hakluyt, *op. cit.*, vol. 8, pp. 176–178, and deposition of Francisco de Cazanova, on the part of Charles Leigh and Stephen van Harwick, November 7, 1597, H.C.A. 13/32.

[46] G. Johnson, *op. cit.*, pp. 111–112.

[47] Dated October 4, 1597, B.M. Additional MS 12505, fols. 77–77v. See J. D. Rogers, *The History and Geography of Newfoundland*, Oxford, 1911, pp. 249–250.

page 138

[48] Cazanova's deposition (see n. 44 above).

[49] 39 and 40 Eliz. I, c.4 (see G. W. Prothero, *Select Statutes and Other Constitutional Documents Illustrative of the Reign of Elizabeth and James I*, 3rd ed., Cambridge, England, 1906, pp. 100–102). For the course of the bill through parliament see J. E. Neale, *Elizabeth and Her Parliaments, 1584–1601*, London, 1957, pp. 349, 348, 347; E. P. Cheyney, *History of England from the Defeat of the Armada to the Death of Elizabeth*, vol. 2, New York, 1926, p. 69.

[50] *Virgidemiarum*, V. I. 113, *Poems*, ed. A. Davenport, Liverpool, 1949, p. 78. The satires were entered on March 30, 1598, and published soon after (*ibid.*, p. lxv).

[51] *Tudor and Stuart Proclamations*, ed. R. R. Steele, vol. 1, Oxford, 1910, no. 899; B.M. G.6413 (356).

[52] Proclamation of September 17, 1603, with

"Order" attached, the latter specifying "The New-found Land, the East and West Indies, France, Germanie, Spaine and the Low-countries or any of them," as possible destinations for the deported poor. Reprinted in C. S. Brigham, ed., *British Royal Proclamations Relating to America, 1603–1783*, Worcester, Mass., 1911, pp. 1–3.

[53] Cambridge University Library, MS Dd. 3, 38.

page 139

[54] B.M. Sloane MS 2292, fol. 41.

[55] Hakluyt, *op. cit.*, vol. 8, pp. 166–180, with his "Certaine observations touching the countreys and places where we travelled."

[56] Hakluyt, *op. cit.*, vol. 8, p. 162.

[57] Public Record Office, State Papers, Colonial, C.O. 1/1,9, endorsed "Plantacion in America," without date or indication of authorship.

page 140

[58] John Brereton, *A briefe and true relation of the discoverie of the north part of Virginia*, London, 1602 (S.T.C. 3610–3611).

[59] Charles de la Roncière, *Histoire de la marine française*, vol. 4, 3rd ed., Paris, 1923; G. Lanctot, "L'établissement du marquis de La Roche à l'Île de Sable," *Annual Report of the Canadian Historical Association for 1933*, Ottawa, 1933, pp. 33–42.

Caribbean Sugar-Production Standards in the Seventeenth and Eighteenth Centuries

by WARD BARRETT

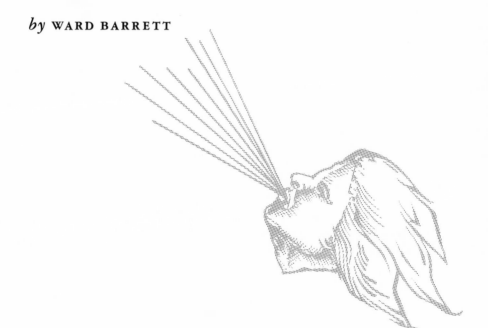

L ARGE-SCALE and intensive agricultural occupation of tropical areas
by Europeans came first as the result of their interest in the growing
and processing of sugar cane. Developing vigorously during the sixteenth century in
Portuguese Brazil and in the Spanish possessions of Hispaniola and New Spain, the
industry experienced similarly rapid growth in the latter part of the seventeenth century in the French and British West Indies and in Dutch Surinam. The rapid development resulted finally in an industry whose value of production and scale of operations
remained unequaled among agricultural enterprises throughout the colonial period;
probably only the mining industry in the Spanish possessions surpassed the sugar industry as a source of individual and national wealth.

New World sugar production, except for the output of the important Mexican
industry, was intended primarily for export to Europe. Until the late seventeenth
century, European demand was met principally by Brazilian exports of relatively
high-priced sugar, but with the entry of northern European nations into the industry
through their Caribbean possessions, there occurred a striking increase in the volume
of production and a fall in the price of sugar that helped to stimulate its consumption
in Europe.

The effects of the growth of the industry were felt in numerous ways. The participation by northern European nations in the sugar industry extended the area of their
potential conflict, led to spirited discussions of national tariff policies, encouraged the
development of national merchant marines, and forced recurrent evaluation of the relations of mid-latitude colonies and mother countries — both sources of staples — to
the African factories, the source of labor, and to the sugar colonies.

Both French and English writers recognized the importance of sugar colonies to
imperial strategy. English writers took careful note of the tendency of the French to
promote settlement in large and relatively easily defended clusters of population, such
as French Hispaniola, in preference to the unplanned English pattern of development
on small, scattered islands and in continental positions less easily defended, and suggested revision of English policy in the light of the French pattern. Even as late as

NOTES for *Caribbean Sugar-Production Standards in the Seventeenth and Eighteenth Centuries*
are to be found on pages 168 to 170.

1841, Daubrée[1] wrote that sugar colonies must be the basis of a successful imperial structure, supplementing the well-known axiom, "Without colonies, no navy," with another of his own invention, "Without sugar, no colonies."

Numerous English writers examined the English colonial system with the aim of determining the advantages offered to England by her three kinds of colony, emphasizing particularly the contrast between the amount of benefits accruing to England from the sugar colonies on the one hand and from the New England colonies on the other.[2] Ashley[3] went beyond simple contrasts to forecast in the 1730's the separation of New England from England because of the competitiveness of their production with the products of English farming and industry, underscoring the unlikelihood that the sugar colonies would ever defect from the English system because they were, from a military point of view, in a highly vulnerable position, hence necessarily dependent. Indirect benefits associated with shipping requirements that led to expansion of the merchant marine and with inter-regional trade, best typified by the Triangular Trade, were also evaluated, often in the form of elaborate balance sheets.[4]

Technical development of the Caribbean sugar industry. In addition to the political and economic features of the industry, the technical aspects, with which this paper is concerned, received continued and close attention in a great many books and pamphlets. In 1657, only fifteen years after the beginning of the industry in Barbados, Ligon[5] published the first detailed description of a Caribbean sugar plantation that might serve as a planter's guide, including an outline of a series of speculative trading ventures which, combined with a program of reinvestment of the profits in cane land, would enable a man with a capital of £3,000 to establish a plantation whose sale price would allow him to realize the perennial West Indian dream of retirement to a less productive but safer country estate in England. In 1724 Labat,[6] drawing on a decade of experience as manager of a sugar plantation in Martinique in the late seventeenth century, published a lengthy work that filled the gaps in Ligon's treatment of plantation management and sugarmaking techniques with a remarkably detailed description of his own methods and their results, leaving besides no doubt that imitation of his procedures would lead to certain and ample profits. After the middle of the eighteenth century, still more detailed works on management and technology appeared, with Belgrove's manual of 1755 the first notable work in a long series that included Edwards' widely distributed volumes on Jamaica, Martin's and Baker's shorter works, and Dutrône's and Avalle's handbooks of practice in St. Domingue.[7] From these descriptions and from nineteenth-century works critical of the older but nonetheless persistent practices it is possible to abstract a set of standards that may be used to judge performance on individual plantations that operated between about 1650 and 1800. These standards vary little from place to place or from 1650 to 1800, reflecting not only widespread adoption of a uniform body of techniques but also a lack of technical progress in a century and a half of practice. The similarities among areas, existing from the beginning, express the common origin of the practices in the fifteenth-century Mediterranean sugar industry, followed by movement to the British and French islands via Brazil, whence the first detailed technological knowledge was carried to Barbados about 1642.[8] The lack of subsequent technical improvement suggests that until the application of steam power to sugarmaking little improvement could have been expected in the best mid-seventeenth-century procedures.

This examination of performance standards will focus on figures of production of muscovado sugar per worker, per acre, and per unit of time, set against the background of eighteenth-century technical knowledge. It is organized according to the two important segments of plantation operations, each with special problems: field management and factory work, the latter consisting of milling, boiling, and distillation. These two major segments differed so widely as to demand of a plantation owner or manager a wide range of ability and knowledge. Field operations, generally simplified below the optimum, required the largest labor inputs and the most capital, whereas the factory gave the most trouble because of its technical and supervisory demands, the likelihood of process failure, the high rate of mechanical breakdown, and the ease with which the operations might be sabotaged. Thus, although most plantation owners may have preferred to think of themselves as sugar planters because planting was associated in their minds with aristocratic status, in fact the most difficult part of their work was concerned with an industrial process differing sufficiently from other known industrial processes to require local and independent experimentation without much hope of benefiting from advances made in other industries.

Field practice. The ideal layout of a sugar plantation is given in the work of Avalle,[9] here reproduced as Figure 14. The site conditions permitting such a compact and orderly arrangement must have been restricted to alluvial plans and fans such as the relatively small ones found in St. Domingue, of which Avalle was writing, to coastal plains such as the large ones of Cuba and Spanish Hispaniola, far too large in total area to be occupied by even the entire world industry of the seventeenth and eighteenth centuries, or to plane surfaces such as were typical of the island of Barbados. On such flat surfaces soil conditions might be more or less uniform within an area the size of Avalle's model, some 4,600 by 2,700 feet, permitting the application of uniform farming practices to the relatively homogeneous unit. In fact, however, the location of a plantation was governed by many factors, some following national lines; for example, in Spanish Hispaniola, the cradle of the New World industry, the large fan surrounding Azua and some small river plains nearer Santo Domingo were selected as the sites of the early industry, perhaps because the Spanish preferred dry areas with opportunities for irrigation — areas that offered more complete control over growth than did those depending on rainfall. Edwards wrote that the lightly occupied part of Jamaica was so broken and diverse that it was difficult by the late eighteenth century to find a block of only three hundred uncleared acres that were more or less uniform in soil and terrain; he emphasized instead the importance of easy transport

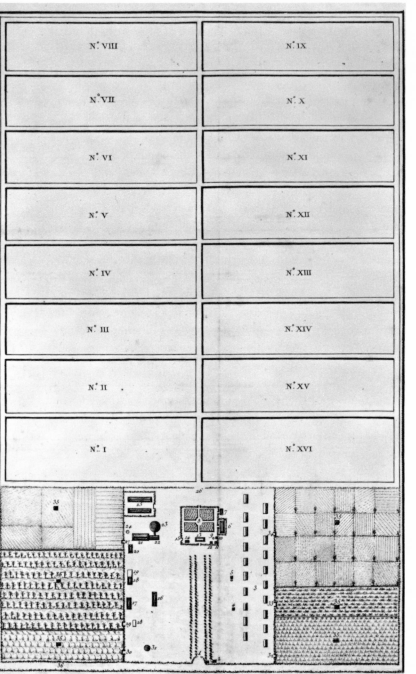

Figure 14. Ideal layout of a sugar plantation from Avalle, *Tableau comparatif*, Paris, 1799 (reproduced from the collections of the Library of Congress).

The upper part consists of canefields (I–XVI) with fixed boundaries and service roads; their planting and harvesting dates varied from year to year in a complex 5-year cycle governed by the differing maturation rates of plant and ratoon cane. The lower part of the plan contains the following: 1) entrance gate; 2) garden house; 3) slave quarters (20 buildings); 4) master clock and bell; 5) infant bathing pool; 6) hospital; 7) chicken house; 8) garden; 9) wells; 10) privy; 11) pigeon house; 12) kitchen; 13) main residence; 14) food storage; 15) gates; 16) corral; 17) coachhouse; 18) stable for sick animals; 19) corral for mill mules; 20) storehouse; 21) purging house, molasses storage; 22) boiling house, furnaces; 23) mill; 24) wells for processing; 25) bagasse storage; 26) entrance to canefields; 27) entrance to vegetable garden; 28) corral for oxen; 29) entrance to banana garden; 30) entrance to manioc garden; 31) stock pond; 32) entrance to Guinea grass pasture; 33) entrance to potato garden; 34) entrance to slave gardens; 35) garden watch posts; 36) public road.

to the sea.[10] Planters in St. Kitts had early become accustomed to wide ecological variations within a single plantation, accepting correspondingly wide variations in yields and quality of sugar from fields very near each other.[11] Perhaps everywhere an original nucleus of settlement that attracted shipping spurred further settlement, and nearby sites physically more advantageous were left untouched because of shipping difficulties. Of course, the striking underpopulation of the Spanish Antilles before 1800 led to total neglect of very attractive areas that later became extremely important producers.

Figure 15, a reproduction of a plate in Du Tertre's work of 1667,[12] shows how well the early settlers recognized the advantages of the wide diversity of terrain found within small areas in many of the Antilles. The mill and processing works are set upon a slope as recommended by Ligon,[13] to permit gravity flow during processing. The canefields occupy a small flat area, perhaps an alluvial plain, and an oceangoing vessel floats in the small cove adjacent to the plantation.[14] The widespread distribution of springs and small streams permanently fed by heavy rainfall in the mountainous interiors made numerous sites on the Antilles attractive, offering water power, irrigation, and domestic water supplies; but in fact Barbados, with little diversity of terrain and hardly any hydrologic advantages, enjoyed nearly full occupation.

The compact arrangement of Avalle's plantation allowed quick and easy transport to the mill, reduced transport time to fields and subsistence gardens, and permitted maximum ease of supervision. The plan contains no unused space; aiming for

Figure 15. Mill in the Antilles from Jean Baptiste Du Tertre, *Histoire Generale des Antilles*, Paris, 1667–1671 (Bell Collection).

[151]

nearly complete self-sufficiency, he included provision grounds ample in his view for two hundred slaves as well as acreage in cane sufficient to employ labor fully through the year. Fields were uniform in size and shape (though fields I and XVI were slightly larger than the rest) to provide an easy check on the production of individual fields. The routine of checking yields must have been as old as the industry, since Ligon recommended uniformly sized fields of approximately ten or twelve acres, about the same size as Avalle's; Labat was even more explicit about their proper size and shape; and Belgrove recommended ten-acre squares.[15] Avalle insisted as well on the need for maintenance of permanent ditches, fences, hedges, and roads, calculating that this labor, including that of keeping up the public road, amounted to about four per cent of the total annual labor spent on the plantation; the large initial investment in fences and ditches would discourage changes in field size and pattern.[16]

Besides keeping account of the production of individual fields, it was probably customary also to plan in some detail the distribution of plant and ratoon cane within the field system.[17] The latter was necessary where ratooning was practiced if annual production was to be kept steady, both because yields fell off with ratoons and because ratoons required less time to mature than did plant cane. In an effort to maintain a steady annual production and daily work load, Avalle presented in his Table XII an elaborate schedule of planting and cutting; the operations run over a five-year period, giving planting and cutting dates as well as expected yields for each of the sixteen plots. Even distribution of the work through the year was achieved at the cost of ignoring the marked seasonal pattern of rainfall that had long since come to be accepted as the prime regulator of plantation operations in the British islands, Avalle allowing instead both planting and sugarmaking in every month of the year.

The most useful way of dealing with yields per acre is by comparing revenue per acre at current prices with the minimum yield necessary to cover costs, because yields of sugar per acre varied within a wide range according to site conditions and the level of management.[18]

The accompanying tabulation shows the yields per acre of muscovado necessary to meet costs in a plantation where molasses, an inevitable by-product of the muscovado process whose collection required little labor, was sold for a price covering the costs of its collection,[19] a simplifying assumption made necessary by lack of information concerning the price of molasses. It should be remembered, however, that these plantations produced very large amounts of molasses, whose price was extremely important to their owners. All these authors except Edwards included replacement of stock in their total of annual charges, but none included an interest charge on the capital investment. The interest rate on borrowed capital was generally high, at a minimum between eight and ten per cent, and often higher than the returns on capital invested in plantations; where the current rate was not given by the author, a rate of eight per cent has been selected for purposes of calculation and added to the depreciation costs in order to give a clearer picture of the yields per acre required to cover all costs. In every case except that described by Ashley in a pamphlet written at a time when the industry was in a very bad way, the expected or actual average yield resulted in a profit if one ignored the interest charge on the capital; but if actual interest charge on a mortgaged plantation had been considered, the expected yields could not have met the costs except in the earliest years of the industry. The planters would thus depend heavily on the sale of molasses for their profits.

ANNUAL CHARGES AS PERCENTAGE OF CAPITAL	PRICE OF MUSCOVADO (PER LB.)	YIELDS PER ACRE REQUIRED TO COVER COSTS	AUTHOR'S EXPECTED YIELD
		1657, Ligon	
10*	3.0d.	560	3,000
18†		1,008	
		1690, Thomas	
3*	1.2d.	850	2,000
11†		3,095	
		1727, Anon.	
8.6*	1.5d.	940	1,500
17.6†		1,922	
		1733, Ashley	
10.6*	1.8d.	2,115	2,100
18.6†		3,710	
		1793, Edwards	
7.2*	2.2d.	781	1,066
15.2†		1,653	

The difficulties of speaking generally about yields are illustrated by comparing various figures in the tabulation on page 166. Ligon, for example, expected 1.5 tons per acre and so was able to obtain an annual yield of 300 tons from 200 acres using 200 slaves; at Worthy Park, about 560 acres produced only 250 tons with 400 slaves. Beckford believed that Jamaican yields were mostly lower than those in Barbados, and presented with succinct descriptions as to frequency of occurrence the following information about classes of yields of muscovado: for *plant cane* — 3,200 pounds per acre, "uncommonly great"; 2,400 pounds per acre, "10% of all estates"; 1,600 pounds per acre, "may be a saving average"; for *ratoons* — 1,600 pounds per acre, "very few"; 1,200 pounds per acre, "good"; 800 pounds per acre, "above the common medium." [20]

Not all writers were convinced that it was necessary to allow the seasonal distribution of rainfall to regulate plantation work, but most insisted that better results were achieved by doing so. The growth cycle of sugar cane fits Caribbean seasons very well: wet weather is required to induce sprouting from the nodes of two- or three-foot sections of cane stalks and most growth takes place during the six or seven

* Author's charges expressed as a percentage of capital invested.
† Author's charges plus interest (usually 8 per cent) on capital expressed as a percentage of capital invested.

months of the year in which the rainfall is concentrated. During the following dry months the sugar content of the canes increases to a maximum, then decreases, a change requiring adjustment of planting schedules to mill capacity for optimum results. The schedule in the English islands involved planting canes between August and November for harvest about sixteen months later; Edwards thought that these months were the "properest season," while Belgrove preferred even narrower limits, trying to plant at least three fifths of the area in plant canes in October and leaving the rest to be planted in November and the first two weeks in December.[21] The harvesting and grinding period was similarly clearly defined by dry weather, extending from January into May or June. Ligon, writing in the early years of the industry, described the harvesting period as forty weeks long, less than the full year because heavy rains made the access roads impassable; had these roads been constructed to allow easy movement in the rainy season, the grinding period, he believed, could have been extended over the entire year.[22] Thomas, writing about thirty years later, described a seasonal distribution of labor nearly like Edwards's; Labat cut the grinding period to thirty weeks; Belgrove, writing in 1755, said that March and April were the best months for making sugar and would not allow much variation from a twenty-week period centered on April 1 — he warned that one must expect a lot of variety in sugar in February, whereas at the end of May there were usually rapid decreases in yields and a weak dark sugar was produced.[23] Avalle, however, allowed both planting and harvesting in every month of the year.[24]

Pest-control measures were probably absent from the repertory of skills of most planters, with the exception of burning the fields to kill the dense population of rats supported by the cane. There was little opportunity for varietal experimentation because the range of varieties available was limited, hence little opportunity to increase by this means yields or resistance to lodging, pests, and diseases until the introduction of Otaheite cane at the end of the eighteenth century; its superior milling qualities and yields led to wide acceptance.[25]

The cane mill. From the beginning of sugar-cane culture in the British and French Antilles the three-roller vertical mill, a Sicilian invention of 1449,[26] was considered best, no well-equipped plantation having either a two-roller mill or one with horizontally placed rollers. The mill shown in Du Tertre's plate (Figure 15) is typical of the early three-roller mills. In this most widely recommended and probably most common arrangement, the motive power was applied to the center roller of three placed with their centers on a single axis; as the center roller was turned, teeth on both its upper and lower ends [27] engaged teeth on the outer rollers, causing them to turn in opposing senses, hence permitting cane to be passed twice between the rollers; one operator passed cut canes between one set of rollers to another operator who returned them between the other. Double crushing with a single power source was the most important feature of this mill; an appreciation of its great advantage over other types available for use in the sixteenth century may readily be gained by comparing it with plates in Deerr's *History of Sugar* that show late sixteenth-century Brazilian and Sicilian mills.[28] Dutrône [29] notes that the invention about 1755 of the *doubleuse*, a shield that guided once-crushed cane into position for a second crushing, eliminated the need for one of the two workers, but this improvement seems to have been the only important addition to the parts of the three-roller vertical mill from the time of its invention in 1449 until its supercession about 1800 by an English innovation better suited for use with the new steam power. This innovation consisted in placing the rollers parallel and horizontally to form a triangle. Before the rollers were arranged in a triangle, horizontal placement of three rollers in the same vertical plane resulted in losing part of the cane juice extracted between the upper rollers through absorption by cane passing between the lower set; eliminating one of the rollers to prevent this loss would have reduced the extraction rate. Although these considerations favored the adoption of the upright three-roller arrangement, in fact some juice was lost through reabsorption even with the vertical arrangement when more than one stalk was passed through at the same time until the adoption of shallow vertical fluting in the late eighteenth century provided easier flow of juice down the rollers.[30] Besides the invention of the *doubleuse*, the only important change in the mill that was widely adopted before 1800 was the substitution of wood for iron in its construction, a change leading to greater dependability and length of life.

Edwards considered the substitution of a lantern wheel for the cogs in universal use on the center roller to be the principal advantage of Woollery's improved design for a mill of 1794, pointing out that the reduction in friction achieved by substituting the trundles (in effect, bearings) of a lantern wheel for cogs resulted in a large increase in the hourly capacity of the mill; whereas without a lantern wheel an animal-powered mill did well to produce 300 to 350 gallons of juice an hour, 400 to 500 gallons an hour might be expected upon substitution of a lantern wheel, bringing the rate of milling by animal-powered mills within the range of some water-driven mills.[31] Since a gallon of juice was commonly reckoned to yield a pound of muscovado sugar, with a mill supplying 500 gallons per hour and an adequate boiling house a planter might reasonably expect five tons of sugar per work day of twenty-four hours. No other single improvement of the vertical three-roller mill since its invention could so markedly have increased the milling rate as did this one, but because the improvement was introduced in the same year that Collinge offered the horizontal triangular arrangement of rollers which rapidly became standard, it does not seem likely that the use of the lantern wheel became widespread. For example, Porter, after discussing the advantages of this device and noting that the vertical three-roller arrangement was "still very generally adhered to," says merely that the rollers are furnished with cogwheels.[32]

In the nineteenth century, when a large number of milling arrangements more efficient than the three-roller vertical mill had become available, numerous investigations were undertaken to show the deficiencies of this nevertheless extremely persistent fifteenth-century device. These experimental data, discussed below, contain information on extraction and milling rates not directly available before the nineteenth century.

The extraction rate of the three-roller vertical mill. The amount of juice expressed from the cane by the mill may be compared with the total weight of juice present in the cane or the total weight of the cane, and the ratio is the extraction rate. Even when Edwards was writing, only qualitative statements were available concerning the efficiency of the mill: Edwards himself writes that the mill "squeezes [the canes] completely dry, and sometimes reduces them even to powder," while Leslie notes that after milling in a horse-driven mill with iron-covered rollers, the bagasse is dry enough to burn after an hour in the sun.[33]

The accompanying tabulation shows some nineteenth- and early twentieth-century observations of the extraction rates of three-roller vertical mills with various kinds of drive in comparison with the extraction rates of the new horizontal mills.[34] There is very little difference in extraction rate between the animal- and water-driven vertical mills studied by Daubrée and the wind-driven vertical mill described by Reed; the intermittent high speeds of the windmill led to losses through spilling, accounting for its relatively poor showing. Leon[35] reported a series of experiments carried on in the period 1830–1844 by Urrutia, a well-known Cuban planter, who showed that the old type of cattle-driven vertical mill was superior in the amount extracted to new horizontal steam mills due to its extreme slowness, an advantage cattle held as well over the faster mules.

Probably few planters achieved an extraction rate of sixty-five per cent with the old cattle mills, and to the planters of St. Domingue the slow milling rate associated with cattle-driven mills was a disadvantage that accounted for the scarcity of cattle there.[36] The combination of higher extraction and milling rates in the new steam-

PLACE AND KIND OF MILL	PERCENTAGE OF WEIGHT OF CANE EXTRACTED
c.1840, Daubrée	
Martinique, Guadeloupe, 3-roller vertical mill	50
Cayenne, 3-roller vertical mill	36–40
Steam-driven horizontal mills, Martinique, Guadeloupe	
Maximum rate	60
Potential rate	70–75
1830–1837, Leon	
Matanzas cattle mill	65
Matanzas horizontal steam mill	46.8
Matanzas horizontal steam mill with double crushing	62
1866, Reed	
Antigua windmill	49.5
1910, Walker	
Negros, Philippines, 8–10 horsepower steam mill	64.5

driven horizontal mill gave it great competitive advantage. Urrutia found, however, that the double crushing ruptured the cane so much as to lower the quality of sugar produced, and prevented the *bagasse* from being used for fuel.[37]

It seems reasonable to accept an extraction rate of fifty per cent for the vertical mill, irrespective of the nature of the drive; this means that a ton of cane might be expected to produce approximately half a ton, or about a hundred gallons, of juice.

The milling rate of the three-roller vertical mill. The figures given in the accompanying tabulation were arrived at in two ways: some writers give the maximum milling rate, whereas other writers, particularly earlier ones, offer figures for only the hourly production of muscovado, which may be employed to estimate the milling rate if one uses the rule of thumb: one gallon of juice yields one pound of muscovado.[38] The maximum milling rate of a four- or five-team cattle mill was probably about four hundred gallons of juice an hour in the eighteenth century, but the actual rate achieved was determined by the hourly capacity of the boiling house because juice could not be stored for longer than an hour without fermenting. In fact, the milling rate must have been rather low, with canes being fed only singly or at most by threes between the rollers, since the rollers of an animal-driven mill usually wore out in one spot.[39] Because of the slow feed and low milling rate, a large boiling house might require two animal- or wind-driven mills. The mill shown in Du Tertre's illustration, driven by only two teams of oxen, might have produced about a hundred gallons of juice an hour to yield at most sixty tons of muscovado sugar in a ten-week grinding season.

The rates at which cane had to be cut and supplied to the mill are given in the tabulation below. These are based on the assumption of a fifty per cent extraction rate and on the use of the respective authors' expected yields per acre. The advantages of a long grinding season are immediately apparent: Ligon with forty weeks and La-

MOTIVE FORCE	GALLONS OF JUICE PER HOUR	TONS OF CANE PER HOUR	ACRES HARVESTED PER HOUR
1657, Ligon			
5 oxen or horses	125	1¼	1/12
c.1700, Labat			
water wheel	95–110	1	1/14
c.1785, Avalle			
6 mules	180	1¾	1/7
c.1790, Edwards			
1 water wheel or 2 cattle mills	900–1,200	10	
c.1820, Bell			
cattle	400	4	
1842, Ure			
steam	100 per hp.	1 per hp.	

bat with thirty required not only a much smaller investment in processing works, but also a much smaller harvesting crew, because they needed to cut only about an acre of cane each day, whereas Edwards's planter required much more stock and a very large field gang, as well as a larger processing works, to meet the more rapid pace set by a shorter season.

The mill did not demand a great deal of labor. Du Tertre's mill probably needed five workers — two men assigned to the teams, two to the mill, and one to carry away the *bagasse*. The same number were employed in Labat's larger mill, which employed women to feed the mill and carry the *bagasse*.[40] More teams required more men, one per team being standard.

The mills did not represent a large part of the plantation cost. Edwards, for example, allows about three per cent of the capital for the mill, Long only two per cent.[41]

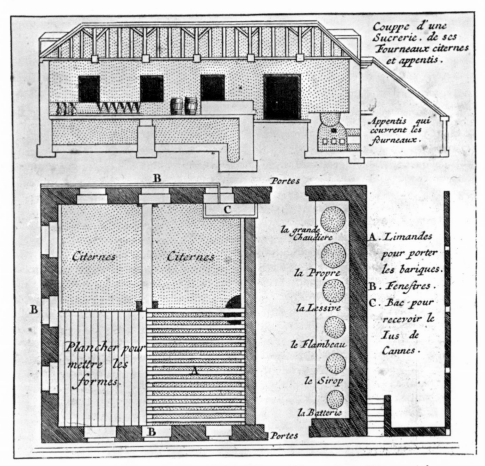

Figure 16. Curing house from Richard Ligon, *A True & Exact History of the Island of Barbados*, London, 1657 (Bell Collection).

The boiling house. Figure 16 illustrates with extreme clarity and simplicity all the essential features of the boiling house as well as does Figure 17, Labat's much more sophisticated version of the same thing; excellent plates of the boiling house as well as the other buildings of a sugar plantation also appear in Diderot's *Encyclopédie.*[42]

Not only the plan and elements of the boiling house, but also the techniques used in it changed so little in many boiling houses from about 1650 until the latter part of the nineteenth century as to give substance to Ligon's prophecy of 1657: "The right and best way of sugar making used in Barbados will admit of no greater or farther improvement."[43] Indeed, so few changes of importance in boiling-house practice occurred after Edwards wrote that Porter was content in 1831 merely to paraphrase slightly Edwards's pages on boiling practice in his own chapter called "Making the Juice into Sugar," and he offers without apology as an improvement over current practice Dutrône's innovations of 1785.[44]

Two principal processes, both requiring application of heat to cane juice, were conducted within these works: clarification and evaporation. Clarification, also known as defecation or purging, had as its aim the removal of nonsaccharine materials from the juice, while the process of evaporation aimed simply at reducing the water content of the liquid to the point where granulation would take place. Both processes were necessary to achieve granulation, and were conducted simultaneously (except that partial clarification was achieved in a separate first step) by treating the juice in a series of kettles, usually arranged in a row of four or five, decreasing in size as the volume of liquid decreased. (See Figures 16 and 17.)

Traditionally, the juice from the mill was conducted into a large vessel called the receiver (on the righthand side of the boiling shed in Figure 16; c in Figure 17), whose function was to collect juice that shortly was to be transferred to the first and usually largest vessel subjected to heat; some set the upper limit of time spent in the receiver at one hour, after which fermentation would occur that prevented crystallization of sugar, but Ligon allowed one day.[45] The receiver was necessary to allow the mill to continue to work while the first vessel in the battery contained juice being clarified, and usually these two vessels were the same size.

Only partial clarification was achieved in the vessel called the clarifier by the English, the *grande* by Labat. Ligon distinguished the first vessel of the battery as the clarifier in early recognition of the need for at least some clarification before boiling. Impurities were mechanically separated from the juice by heating it to a temperature below its boiling point; boiling had the effect of setting up currents within the juice that prevented complete mechanical separation. Reduction in the volume of the liquid sufficient to enable it to be contained within the next smaller kettle was the signal to transfer or skip the contents, usually by ladle (in Figure 15, held by the man on the right in the boiling house), and this rule held for each successive skipping[46] until the last and smallest vessel, the teache (Labat's *batterie*), was reached. Reduction in volume was caused largely by evaporation of water, which most writers believed

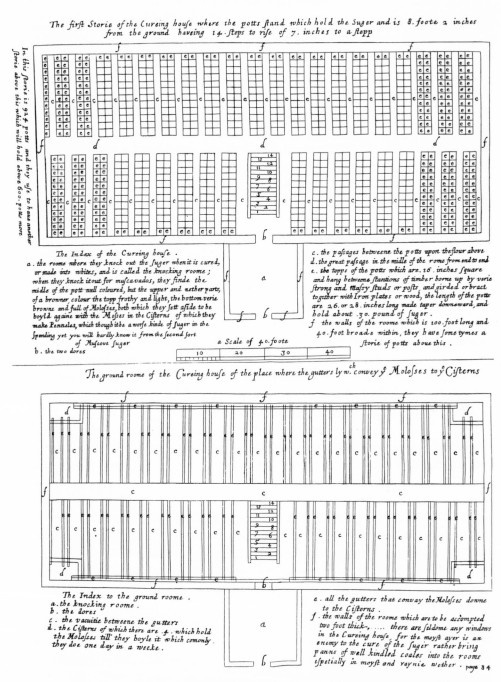

Figure 17. Boiling house from Jean Baptiste Labat, *Nouveau voyage aux isles de l'Amerique*, Paris, 1724 (Bell Collection).

to make up about eighty per cent of the original juice, and the remainder was lost through the skimming off of impurities and a small part of the sugar. After treatment below the boiling point in the clarifier itself, further clarification was wrought by the addition of alkali — usually lye or milk of lime — to the boiling liquid and skimming off the resulting froth or scum; this process achieved a minor reduction in volume (impurities were usually assumed to make up ten per cent of the cane juice) and was necessary for crystallization. Although filtering the juice to remove impurities both as it came from the mill and during skippings was recommended by some writers in addition to clarification, it was opposed by others and does not seem to have been a necessary part of sugarmaking.[47]

In the last vessel, the teache, the liquid was subjected to the strongest heat in the battery[48] until it was considered ready for striking or removal and cooling. There were many rules for determining this point, perhaps the subject of more speculation than any other of the boiling-house processes. As Baker remarked, "The Negro-Boilers have no Rule at all, and guess by the Appearance of the Liquor; and indeed it is wonderful, what Long Experience will do."[49] Even Dutrône, who introduced the use of the hydrometer about 1785 to determine the proper time of striking, agreed with most other eighteenth- and even many nineteenth-century observers that an experienced sugar master had a high rate of success in the matter of striking.[50]

When one considers the major outlines of the sugarmaking process and the major features of the equipment used, the differences between English and French practice and the innovations made before the use of steam appear minor. For example, both Ligon and Labat describe kettles hung to separate fires (cf. Figure 15), whereas most later writers show a single fire under the teache and a long flue used to heat the remaining vessels of the battery or Jamaica train, the name often applied to this arrangement. The principal value of the Jamaica train seems to have been a reduction in the amount of fuel required, but until separate fires with dampers were added for an increased number of clarifying kettles[51] an undesirably large amount of control was also lost through this arrangement. Apparently the saving in fuel that made the Jamaica train necessary in other places did not become important in Cuba until rather late, since Leon states that the Jamaica train was not introduced there until 1828, before which time numerous émigrés from St. Domingue, where it was standard, had entered the Cuban sugar business.[52] Another change that had the effect of introducing a minor alteration in the basic layout of the boiling house was the increasing use of more than one clarifier, in contrast to the single one recommended by Ligon and Labat. If several were used, mechanical separation was improved because of a longer stay in the clarifier, which allowed settling as well as rising of impurities to take place after the initial heating, the now purer juice appearing as a layer between a heavier and a lighter layer of impurities. Discussion continued through the eighteenth century as to whether boiling should go on at night, when failure was more common because of inadequate supervision, and as to the best alkali for clarification; but without engaging in these controversies, the owner of a boiling works built in 1700 according to a plan similar to Labat's could make acceptable sugar at a profit in 1800 without having introduced important changes in practice or equipment.

The labor requirements of the boiling house were small. The two men shown in the boiling house in Figure 15 were capable of doing all the work in a house of such small size, although probably another was needed to tend the furnaces, gathering *bagasse* if it was dry enough, cane leaves for the large kettles, and wood for the smaller.[53] If the boilers worked at night, two or at most three crews were needed. Labat assigned nine men from his force of a hundred and twenty slaves to the mill, six to the boiling house (one per kettle was the common rule), and three to the furnaces; six more men cut wood for the boiling house and the distillery.[54]

Edwards estimated the cost of a boiling house to be about equal to that of a water mill or two cattle mills, and Long's estimates show similar relative values.[55]

The curing house. After the formation of grain in the cooler, where the mass remained for about twelve hours, two different procedures might be followed, depending on whether muscovado or white (clayed, refined, or Lisbon) sugar was to be made. The muscovado process was far simpler, requiring less labor and equipment than did the manufacture of white; the choice of which to manufacture followed national lines: the British islands generally, except Barbados, made muscovado and the French made clayed.

In the manufacture of muscovado, the warm mass from the cooler was placed in hogsheads with pierced bottoms ranged upon an open framework of joists. (In Figure 16 these barrels are shown in vertical section, and in Figure 15 the stick — probably a plantain stalk — inserted in the forms filled with cooling sugar assists drainage of molasses into a trough behind the boilers.) Most of the molasses drained through the pierced bottoms of the hogsheads into a cistern, whence it was removed for reboiling to extract more sugar, or for distillation. After three or four weeks the mass had dried sufficiently through evaporation and especially drainage to allow shipment, although in fact drainage continued during shipment and ten per cent or more of the weight of the shipment might be lost in this way. A large part of the muscovado was then refined in England.

In the manufacture of clayed sugar, the standard practice was to move sugar from the coolers into pots, made of wood in the early years of the industry but later of clay, and of capacity that varied from place to place within the range of twenty-five to sixty pounds uncured or green. The pots were inverted cones with a hole at the apex through which the molasses drained. The earlier pyramidal wooden type is shown in Figure 15 in a rack in the boiling house; these could have been used in the manufacture of muscovado as well. In the first stage of the process a stopper was left in the hole for about twelve hours, then removed to allow the molasses to drain into a jar, the conical pot resting on the rim of this vessel. After twelve to twenty-four hours of free drainage, further removal of molasses, the source of the characteristic yellow-brown color of raw sugar, from the crystals was assisted by placing a layer of moist clay over the top of the sugar; at the same time the pot was changed, since a different quality of molasses was obtained during this stage. Water moved slowly downward from the clay, dissolving a great part of the molasses that remained in the pot, thus making the sugar nearly white and rather soft, as well as dissolving and carrying off part of it with the molasses. Some standard of allowable loss through unavoidable solution of sugar by the percolating water was necessary; Porter estimated an average loss of approximately a sixth of the weight of sugar in the pot, Labat a third (some of this amount was recovered in subsequent boiling of the molasses). This loss and the economic advantage of claying formed a frequent topic of discussion in the English islands in the eighteenth century.[56] The two sorts of molasses were reboiled separately to get two kinds of sugar, and the molasses remaining after this second round of curing was used in the distillery.

The curing house shown in Figure 16 was apparently the plan of the house on the Modiford plantation in Barbados, very well known to Ligon. Here the claying process took about sixteen weeks, the time becoming shorter later when stoves were more commonly used to hasten drying. Very little labor was required in the curing house, Labat allowing for a plantation with about eighty-five acres of cane only three people, but its cost, equipped, might be about the same as that of the boiling house.[57]

The manufacture of rum. Molasses was an important byproduct of the muscovado process, produced at the rate of about a hundred and thirty gallons of molasses per ton of muscovado,[58] but the rate of production was much less on plantations making clayed rather than raw sugar. Although some of the molasses was fed to the slaves and stock, a considerable amount remained unconsumed and could only be made into rum or thrown away. The distillery was widely used in the British islands, less widely used in the French, where at least in the eighteenth century much molasses was sold to Americans for shipment to distilleries on the east coast of North America.[59] Rum seems to have been made from the earliest times in the Caribbean, since the process is described by Ligon and Labat,[60] and a simple distilling apparatus is shown in Du Tertre's plate (Figure 15).

Although the most expensive ingredient in rum-making was molasses, the skimmings from the boiling house and the lees or dunder of other distillations, as well as water, were also necessary. A solution or wash of these four materials was allowed to ferment for about a week and then subjected to a double distillation to produce what was known as oil-proof rum (from the fact that olive oil sank in it).[61] Rum of this proof was produced at the rate of one gallon per twenty-two to twenty-five pounds of muscovado; it was also thought possible to get a gallon of rum for every gallon of molasses used.[62]

A distillery cost about as much as a boiling house or curing works, but required very little labor: Labat, for example, assigned one woman to this work.[63]

[163]

The labor force. Far more labor was expended on field operations than on processing. Also, the processing went on for less than half the year, whereas field operations went on all the time with land preparation, manuring, planting, and weeding in the wet season and harvesting in the dry committing most of the labor force to relatively unskilled and repetitive agricultural work much different from the more skilled and specialized, though still repetitive, work in the boiling house.

Probably the most detailed breakdown of labor requirements available is in the work of Avalle,[64] published in 1799 and based on conditions in French Hispaniola. Although this is a planter's guide rather than a description of an operating plantation, its agreement in numerous details and gross features with other works published in the eighteenth century gives the appearance of practicability to its elaborate schedules. Of the two hundred slaves on the model plantation — a number Avalle regarded as a minimum necessary for successful operation — eighty-two of both sexes were in the *grand atelier* that performed the heavy field operations, and about forty-three in the *petit atelier* assigned to less heavy work.[65] Both groups worked six hours in the morning and four in the afternoon for three hundred days a year, giving an annual total of thirty-seven thousand five hundred workdays devoted to tending the canefields and manufacturing sugar — about two thirds of the total labor expended on the plantation. The remaining third of the labor was not directly concerned with canefields or factory. The details of the two kinds of work are given in the tabulation at the bottom of this page.[66]

Avalle's and Dutrône's figures for workdays per acre harvested are as follows: plant canes, Avalle, 179, Dutrône, 87; ratoons, Avalle, 77, Dutrône, 47; harvest, grind, and boil, Avalle, 63, Dutrône, 42; all field work, Avalle, 162, Dutrône, 102. The large discrepancies between Dutrône's and Avalle's figures are difficult to explain; Dutrône's are based on experience, but Avalle's are supported by the estimate of Beckford[67] as well as others (see the tabulation on page 166) that an estate with two hundred Negroes could not harvest more than a hundred and eighty acres of cane per year, with sixty acres each of plant cane and first and second ratoons. Dutrône carried on for at least a year a far more efficient operation than others believed possible without overworking the slaves,[68] but even with respect to workload his efficiency was remarkable, since he allowed only two hundred eighty workdays per year

	WORKDAYS			WORKDAYS
Field and mill work			Transport of sugar . . 289	(0.5%)
Plant canes 11,989	(20%)		Total 37,500	(62.5%)
Ratoons 10,345	(17%)			
Harvest, grind, boil . . 10,715	(18%)		*Other work and losses*	
Ditches, hedges, roads . 2,072	(3.5%)		Lost days 11,000	(18.5%)
Loss due to bad weather 1,375	(2.3%)		Pasture 5,100	(8.5%)
Repairs on buildings			Guarding crops 3,000	(5.0%)
and public roads . . 720	(1.2%)		Domestic 3,300	(5.5%)
			Total 22,500	(37.5%)

in contrast to Avalle's three hundred. The difference remains striking no matter how productivity is expressed; for example, there is a wide gap between Dutrône's production of 18 pounds of muscovado per workday and Avalle's 13.6 pounds. The level of management skill was obviously a factor of extreme importance in these industrial enterprises.

Avalle says that it was common in St. Domingue to replant a third of the land in cane each year, an operation requiring 20 per cent of the annual labor expenditure; caring for the other two thirds of the cane land required slightly less time, only about 17 per cent of the total, because the weeding of ratoons was lighter and no other field operations of importance were required in ratoon fields. In Avalle's scheme, approximately 170 acres — 85 per cent of the total cane area of 203 acres — were harvested each year, but in contrast to the high labor requirement of other field operations the work of harvesting (together with the manufacture of sugar) required only about a fifth of the total labor expended. The principal labor requirements were as follows: work in the canefields, pasture, and on food crops occupied 50.5 per cent of all workdays; harvesting, sugarmaking, and transport, 18.5 per cent; time lost for sickness and owing to bad weather, 20.8 per cent; miscellaneous work, 10.2 per cent. Thus, the major field operations except harvesting occupied about half the time, and work more directly connected with the manufacture of sugar took only about a fifth — nearly the same as the large amount of time lost for various reasons.

It does not seem likely that a large increase in the labor force would cause significant changes in this allocation of the work force, nor would the addition of such work as the manufacture of clayed sugar or rum, omitted from Avalle's highly specialized operation that produced only muscovado and molasses, because these operations did not consume large amounts of labor. Labat,[69] for example, assigned one woman from his work force of a hundred and twenty to the distillery operation (a woman, he believed, would drink less rum than a man) and three men to the curing house, where they performed a wide variety of jobs.

The accompanying tabulation shows (column 13) that from the beginning of the Caribbean industry the ratio of slaves to acres of cane harvested was very near 1:1, the chief exceptions being Barbados with ratios near 2:1 and Louisiana,[70] where the ratio was approximately 1:3. Barbados was long distinguished for intensive cultivation dependent on heavy manuring, but it is interesting to see that in the case of an actual Barbadian plantation described by Ashley [71] in 1733 its very high ratio (column 13) was associated with the lowest yields per slave (column 11). By contrast, Leon reported the highest annual yield per slave (5,000 pounds) about a century later and the lowest ratio of slaves to acres harvested (1:3). Leon's figures were included in order to illustrate the effects of two innovations not present in the Caribbean before 1800, the plow and steam power. Partial mechanization of field operations through the use of the plow greatly reduced labor requirements per acre, and the great difference between Leon's figure and those of earlier times in the Caribbean

1	2	3	4	5	6	7	8	9	10	11	12	13	14	15
1649	Barbados	Ligon	500	200	600	3.0d.	3,000	200	2,240	3,000	134	c.1.0	73	10
1690	Barbados	Thomas	100	40h	80	1.2d.	2,000	50	5,000	1,600	32	1.2	14	m
1727	St. Kitts	Anon.*	200	150h	225	1.5d.	1,500	150	4,000	1,500	37	1.0	...	4
1733	Barbados	Ashley	1,000	200h	420	1.8d.	2,100	500	4,000	840	21	2.5	240	...
1755	Barbados	Belgrove	500	140h	340c	...	2,430c	300	...	1,133c	...	2.1	175	...
1774	Jamaica	Long	900	300h	480	2.2d.	1,600	300	5,454	1,600	29	1.0	130	16
1777?	Jamaica	Beckford	...	180h	240	2.4d.	1,333	200	5,000	1,200	24	1.1	140	9
1785	St. Domingue	Dutrône	...	240h	402	...	1,677	150?	...	2,680	...	0.6	...	m
1788	St. Domingue	Avalle	304	170h	450	...	2,640	200	...	2,250	...	1.2	121	m
1791	Jamaica	Edwards	600	300	320	2.2d.	1,066	250	5,454	1,280	23	c.0.7	140	14
1792	Jamaica	Phillips†	...	560h	497	2.2d.	888	400	...	1,244	...	0.7	...	15
1822	Barbados	Porter	314	72h	186	4.0d.	2,583	150	4,248	1,809	43	2.0	122	5
1840	Louisiana	Leon	840	560h	1,000	4¢	1,786	200	13,750	5,000	36	0.3	...	...

1: Date
2: Place
3: Author
4: Plantation size, acres
5: Acres in cane (h: acres harvested)
6: Production of muscovado in 1,000 pounds (c: clayed sugar)
7: Price or value of a pound of muscovado
8: Production of muscovado per acre, in pounds
9: Number of slaves
10: Value of each slave in pounds of muscovado
11: Production of muscovado per slave in pounds

12: Production per slave as a percentage of value as slave
13: Slaves per acre harvested
14: Numbers in livestock
15: Rum produced, in 1,000 gallons (m: molasses sold)

* Anonymous, *A Detection of the State and Situation of the Present Sugar Planters, of Barbadoes and the Leeward Islands*, London, 1732, p. 41.
† U. B. Phillips, "A Jamaica Slave Plantation," *American Historical Review*, 1914, pp. 543–547.

suggests that the plow was never widely used there, contrary to the claims of several Jamaican writers.[72]

Annual production of muscovado per slave (column 11 of the accompanying tabulation), counting all slaves of all ages on the plantation, varied somewhat, with earlier writers showing more optimism than later writers, and the French in general being more demanding than the English. Ligon suggested 3,000 pounds per slave as reasonable, Labat 2,812 pounds, and most of the later English manuals give figures within the relatively narrow range of 1,200 to 1,600 pounds of muscovado. Just before the insurrection of the slaves in Haiti Dutrône obtained yields per slave twice as high as the English thought possible, and Avalle expected half a ton more than Beckford [73] emphatically said was desirable from the point of view of the morale and physical well-being of the slaves.

There is no indication in these figures that economies of scale were practiced, although Ligon was able to write in 1657, "I believe, when the small plantations in poor men's hands, of 10, 20, 30, acres, which are too small to lay to that work, be bought up by great men, and put together, into Plantations of 500, 600, and 700 acres [conditions will greatly improve]." [74] Long [75] gave simple linear relations among size, costs, and production in his examples, and it is worth noting that the two largest plantations with the most slaves (Ashley and Phillips, column 9, both descriptions of operating enterprises) had the lowest production per slave; Phillips's Worthy Park was supposed to be barely paying its way. Adequate supervision by the owner, emphasized as a prime necessity by such careful and skilled managers as Labat and Dutrône, may have been difficult with more than two hundred slaves; Labat, for example, used only a hundred and twenty slaves in his model, and Dutrône probably had no more than a hundred and fifty, whereas the Ashley and the Phillips plantations had, respectively, five hundred and four hundred.

A considerable amount of labor was contributed by animals; where the need for manure was high the numbers of stock had to be large. Most experts set the required number of draft animals at about half the number of slaves. In Barbados, where windmills were common, many animals were needed to supply manure as well as auxiliary power if the wind failed. In Jamaica and St. Domingue, where manuring was apparently less heavy and windmills uncommon, large numbers were kept for use in the mills as well as to supply manure.

Slaves and livestock represented a large part of the capital invested in a plantation and their high mortality rates were a heavy annual charge on the plantation as well as a never-failing source of anxiety to the planters. Ligon estimated that 37 per cent of the annual costs were for replenishing the work stock, while Edwards allocated nearly 50 per cent of the capital to stock and slaves, Belgrove 43 per cent, and Thomas, at a much earlier date, 29 per cent.[76] The value of slaves in pounds of muscovado sugar (column 10 of the table on page 166) remained fairly stable between 1690 and 1822, except in times of crisis, and annual production per slave expressed as a percentage of the value of each slave (column 12) was within the range of 25 to 35 per cent.

Summary. The data in this tabulation and an analysis of plantation equipment and field practice suggest no important changes in efficiency or in contemporary views of optimum or desirable size from the beginning of the industry in the French and British islands to the year 1800. Some marketing changes took place: for example, changes in the demand for rum or for molasses used in rum manufacture affected the abilities of planters to cover costs by changing the profits from these low-cost commodities. The range of variations in efficiency attributable to variations in the level of management was fairly large, with contemporary criticism of average practice suggesting that average practice led to unnecessarily poor results. Given these characteristics of technological stability and managerial variability tending toward inefficiency, it is not surprising that external crises such as wars, the normal variation of climate, changes in government tariff policy, plant diseases, and pests led to instability of ownership and heavy debts in an industry that began with great promise.

The relation of the suggested optimum size of operating units to actual plantations requires separate analysis, but it may be worthwhile to mention some examples of differences between them. Ligon described a plantation operating in the 1650's whose annual production of about two hundred tons remained large for about a hundred and fifty years. Blome [77] wrote in 1687 that there were approximately a hundred sugar works in Jamaica whose total average annual production was only a hundred tons. As capital flowed into the island and population increased the average size increased, reaching an average annual production of about eighty tons in the last quarter of the eighteenth century.[78] Even as late as 1866 the average annual production of some twenty-five hundred Cuban mills was probably only about a hundred and fifty tons,[79] midway in the optimum range of one hundred to two hundred tons suggested long before the adoption of steam power.

NOTES

page 148

[1] Paul Daubrée, *La Question coloniale au point de vue industriel*, Paris, 1841, p. 6.

[2] An early example of comparisons among Dutch colonies is found in Otto Keye, *Otto Keyens kurtzer Entwurff von New Niederland und Guajana*, Leipzig, 1672. See the anonymous *The Present State of the Sugar Plantations Considered*, London, 1713, for an English example.

[3] John Ashley, *The Present State of the British Sugar Colonies Considered*, London, 1731, p. 20.

[4] *Ibid.*, pp. 22–24. Cf. J. Bennett, *Two Let-*

ters and Several Calculations on the Sugar Colonies and Trade, London, 1738.

[5] Richard Ligon, *A True and Exact History of the Island of Barbados*, London, 1657.

[6] Jean Baptiste Labat, *Nouveau voyage aux isles de l'Amerique*, Paris, 1724, 2 vols.

[7] Bryan Edwards, *The History . . . of the British Colonies in the West Indies*, 3rd ed., London, 1801, 3 vols.; William Belgrove, *A Treatise upon Husbandry or Planting*, Boston, 1755; Samuel Martin, *An Essay upon Plantership*, 5th ed., London, 1773; John P. Baker, *An Essay on the Art of Making Muscovado Sugar*, Jamaica, 1775; Dutrône la Couture, *Précis sur*

la canne et sur les moyens d'en extraire le sel essentiel, Paris, 1790; Avalle, *Tableau comparatif des productions des colonies françaises aux Antilles, avec celles des colonies anglaises, espagnoles et hollandaises de l'année 1787 à 1788*, Paris, An VII, 27 Fructidor.

page 149

[8] In spite of the fact that the much older sugar industry of New Spain was both highly developed and technologically sophisticated, it seems not to have served as a model for the later Caribbean industry. Although no manual appears to have been published in New Spain, data concerning the productivity of the mills that operated there in the sixteenth and seventeenth centuries may be found in Felipe Ruiz de Velasco, *Historia y evoluciones del cultivo de la caña y de la industria azucarera en México, hasta el año 1910*, Mexico City, 1937.

[9] Avalle, *op. cit.*

page 151

[10] Edwards, *op. cit.*, p. 290.

[11] Richard Pares, *A West-India Fortune*, London, 1950, pp. 104–105.

[12] Jean Baptiste Du Tertre, *Histoire naturelle des Antilles habitées par les francois*, Paris, 1667, vol. 2.

[13] Ligon, *op. cit.*, p. 87.

[14] A cargo of 50 tons was common at the end of the seventeenth century. "A Merchant," *A Discourse of the Duties on Merchandize, More Particularly of That on Sugar*, London, 1695, p. 18.

page 152

[15] Ligon, *op. cit.*, p. 88; Labat, *op. cit.*, p. 231; Belgrove, *op. cit.*, p. 31.

[16] Avalle, *op. cit.*, p. 41.

[17] Belgrove, *op. cit.*, p. 32.

[18] Noel Deerr, *The History of Sugar*, London, 1949, 2 vols. Price data are in vol. 2, ch. 32. Sales prices in England are contained in William Beveridge, *Prices and Wages in England*, London, 1939, pp. 75, 170, 263, 383, 557. The price of muscovado in the islands remained generally high in the first few decades of the industry, fell sharply to a relatively low level in the 1680's, rose irregularly to a high level in 1700, from which it fell irregularly to another low in the 1730's and rose from the end of this decade for most of the eighteenth century.

[19] Anonymous, *Remarks upon a Book, Entituled, the Present State of the Sugar Colonies Considered*, London, 1731. This work contains the notice (p. 14) that in the early years of the industry in Jamaica all the molasses was thrown away until the planters learned to make rum. In later years it was all sold or consumed on the estates or made into rum; several choices were available to planters.

page 153

[20] *Ibid.*, p. 86.

page 154

[21] Edwards, *op. cit.*, p. 250; Belgrove, *op. cit.*, pp. 17–18.

[22] Ligon, *op. cit.*, p. 55.

[23] Belgrove, *op. cit.*, pp. 16–17.

[24] Avalle, *op. cit.*, Table XII.

[25] Deerr, *op. cit.*, pp. 20–21.

[26] *Ibid.*, p. 536.

[27] In Du Tertre's plate the teeth are slightly above the center of rollers, as they are in an illustration in Guilherme Piso, *Historia natural do Brasil ilustrada*, São Paulo, 1948, p. 58.

page 155

[28] Deerr, *op. cit.*, pp. 78, 104.

[29] Dutrône, *op. cit.*, p. 104.

[30] Plate in Edwards, *op. cit.*, facing p. 262.

[31] *Ibid.*

[32] George R. Porter, *The Nature and Properties of the Sugar Cane*, Philadelphia, 1831, pp. 182–183.

page 156

[33] Charles Leslie, *A New History of Jamaica*, London, 1740, p. 319.

[34] The tabulated data were obtained from the following sources: Daubrée, *op. cit.*, p. 21; John A. Leon, *On Sugar Cultivation in Louisiana, Cuba, . . . and the British Possessions*, London, 1848; William Reed, *The History of Sugar and Sugar Yielding Plants . . .*, London, 1866, p. 97; Herbert S. Walker, *The Sugar Industry of the Island of Negros*, Manila, 1910, p. 93.

[35] Leon, *op. cit.*, pp. 21–22.

[36] Dutrône, *op. cit.*, p. 105.

page 157

[37] Leon, *op. cit.*, pp. 21–22.

[38] In addition to the sources previously identified, the following were also used as sources of data for this table: John Bell, *A Practical

Treatise on the Culture of Sugar Cane and Distillation of Rum, Calcutta, 1831, p. 22; Andrew Ure, *A Dictionary of Arts, Manufactures, and Mines*, New York, 1842, article on sugar.

[39] Daubrée, *op. cit.*, p. 21.

page 158

[40] *Ibid.*, p. 231.

[41] Edwards, *op. cit.*, p. 292; Edward Long, *The History of Jamaica*, London, 1774, 3 vols., vol. 1, pp. 459ff.

page 159

[42] Denis Diderot, *Encyclopédie, ou dictionnaire raisonné des sciences . . .*, Neufchâtel, 1765, vol. 1, *Oeconomie rustique*, Sucrerie; the plate of the mill is nearly identical with Labat, *op. cit.*, p. 258.

[43] Ligon, *op. cit.*, 2nd ed., 1673, p. 86.

[44] Porter, *op. cit.*, preface, ch. 7, 10, and 11.

[45] Ligon, *op. cit.*, p. 89.

[46] John P. Baker, *An Essay on the Art of Making Muscovado Sugar*, Jamaica, 1775, p. 41.

page 161

[47] *Ibid.*, p. 30.

[48] Baker guesses 400°F to be the temperature of the liquid in the teache as contrasted with a temperature of 230°F in the clarifier; *ibid.*, p. 32.

[49] *Ibid.*, p. 34.

[50] Use had already been made of the hydrometer in making potash, an operation somewhat similar to sugarmaking. W. Lewis, *Experiments and Observations on American Potashes . . .*, London, 1767, pp. 18–27.

[51] An improvement claimed by Edwards, *op. cit.*, p. 273, to have been due to Baker in his work of 1775.

[52] Edwards, *op. cit.*, p. 17.

page 162

[53] By use of different fuels flames of different temperatures were obtained.

[54] Labat, *op. cit.*, p. 323.

[55] Edwards, *op. cit.*, p. 293; Long, *op. cit.*, p. 459.

page 163

[56] Ashley, *op. cit.*, p. 26; Porter, *op. cit.*, p. 98; Samuel Martin, *An Essay upon Plantership*, 5th ed., London, 1773, pp. 48–50, where Martin suggests the decision about making clayed or muscovado should be made after inspection of the boil.

[57] Labat, *op. cit.*, p. 323.

[58] Martin, *op. cit.*, p. 58.

[59] Anonymous, *The Present State of the Sugar Plantations Considered . . .*, London 1713, p. 21.

[60] Ligon, *op. cit.*, p. 94; Labat, *op. cit.*, p. 323.

[61] Edwards, *op. cit.*, p. 284.

[62] *Ibid.*, p. 285; Beckford, *op. cit.*, p. 207; Martin, *op. cit.*, p. 58.

[63] Long, *op. cit.*; Labat, *op. cit.*, p. 323.

page 164

[64] Avalle, *op. cit.*, see Tables.

[65] *Ibid.*, p. 15.

[66] Dutrône, *op. cit.*, p. 225.

[67] William Beckford, *A Descriptive Account of the Island of Jamaica*, London, 1790, 2 vols., vol. 2, pp. 206–207.

[68] *Ibid.*

page 165

[69] Labat, *op. cit.*, p. 323.

[70] Leon, *op. cit.*, p. 9.

[71] John Ashley, *Proposals Offered for the Sugar Planters Redress . . .*, London, 1733, p. 23.

page 167

[72] Beckford, *op. cit.*, vol. 2, pp. 198ff.

[73] *Ibid.*, p. 88.

[74] Ligon, *op. cit.*, p. 86.

[75] Long, *op. cit.*, vol. 1, pp. 459ff.

[76] Ligon, *op. cit.*, p. 113; Edwards, *op. cit.*, pp. 295–296; Belgrove, *op. cit.*, p. 36; Dalby Thomas, *An Historical Account of the Rise and Growth of the West India Colonies*, London, 1690, p. 14.

page 168

[77] Richard Blome, *The Present State of His Majesties Isles and Territories in America*, London, 1687, p. 13. Deerr, *op. cit.*, p. 198, shows that the production in Jamaica between 1697 and 1711 was between 4,000 and 6,000 tons, so that the average size was nearer that described by Thomas, *op. cit.*, p. 14, in his model, rather than the total production of 10,000 tons suggested by Blome.

[78] Beckford, *op. cit.*, vol. 1, p. xxx.

[79] Reed, *op. cit.*, p. 24.

Slaves
for the Galleys of France, 1665 to 1700

by PAUL W. BAMFORD

ON THE GALLEYS of France, a third of the rowing force was composed of slaves, a proportion considered ideal. Greater numbers of slaves than that, it was thought, were difficult to control, and became a threat to the "free" part of the crew and to the security of the galley itself. Conversely, smaller numbers of slaves made the rowing force too weak, because oarsmen of all other kinds were believed inferior to slaves. The criminals, conscripts, and condamnés who worked with the slaves at the oars were a miscellaneous lot, and even if they were not the dregs of society some believed them to be, condamnés were hardly selected with their physical qualities and their suitability for the oar as the prime objects in view. More select and uniform in quality, perhaps, were the volunteer oarsmen known as *bonnevoglies*. But after volunteer oarsmen were required to accept the chain, the lash, and certain other disadvantageous conditions of employment, there were very few volunteers. Conscription and force were the methods of recruitment from then on. Louis the Fourteenth's minister of marine after 1669, Jean Baptiste Colbert, believed that force was indispensable to make men fully effective at the oars; oarsmen, he thought, worked best under threat of the lash.[1]

The slaves on French galleys were usually non-Christian captives or prisoners of war, mostly Moslems bought in the slave marts of Europe. Frequently the slaves acquired by the French had been sailors or passengers on Moslem vessels captured at sea; a few had been soldiers taken on some battlefield and afterward sold. Naturally not every seagoing man or prisoner of war was fit; many were weeded out before they reached the prime markets for slaves. Buyers were interested only in younger men for the oar — those between twenty and thirty-five, sound and strong in body and build. When slaves arrived at the base at Marseille they were examined by naval inspectors, who rejected the unfit. Such careful selection offered the best guarantee that slaves would be, at least at the start, physically fit for their lives on the galleys. Since they were carefully selected, there was good reason why Moslem slaves were considered, on French galleys and others, the elite of the oar; thus there was reason to say that the "Turks," as they were called, were "tall, extremely vigorous, very resistant to fatigue" and much better suited than condamnés or others for the work.[2]

NOTES for *Slaves for the Galleys of France, 1665 to 1700* are to be found on pages 188 to 191.

Only part of the "Turks" on the galleys came from the eastern Mediterranean Empire of the Ottoman Turks, but "Turk" passed as a virtual synonym for slave. Until 1682 most of the slaves were from the coastal city states of western North Africa — Algiers, Tunis, Tripoli, and Salé in particular. The name, age, and place of origin or residence of each slave arriving at Marseille was recorded in a register kept by the navy. Fragments of one register survive, and suggest that more slaves came from Algiers than from any other place in the western Mediterranean, just about equaling the men from Tunisia, Tripoli, and Salé together. Constantinople accounted for more than any other regular source in the Levant, but fewer than half as many as Algiers; significant numbers also came from Smyrna, Alexandria, Cairo, Cyprus, and Rhodes, with scores of other localities, coastal and inland as well, being represented among the slaves on French galleys. Large numbers of the men included in the extraordinary "windfall" shipments of 1690–1692 gave various Balkan localities as their points of origin.[3]

There were never enough of these elite Moslem slaves to go around, the reason, reduced to essentials, being simply excessive demand for the usual number of slaves that the Mediterranean market could supply. Moslem slaves had many users and buyers: the most regular Mediterranean users were the Christian navies and the Knights of St. John (of Malta);[4] the Italian city states and Spain used them, and the most active of buyers in the 1660's and 1670's was the French galley corps. As a result, the price of slaves was frequently high, and the pressure relieved only by occasional shipments from sources outside the Mediterranean — Africa or the Balkans, for example.

Some of the slaves on French galleys were captured in campaigns aimed at stamping out pirates. Moslems, renegades, and Christians alike sailed the waters of the Mediterranean in the seventeenth century as seagoing thieves; neither Moslem nor Christian had a monopoly on maritime theft. Men guilty of such crime found haven in the ports of both Christendom and Islam, and both Moslem and Christian states had reason to try to eliminate piratical dangers to shipping and trade. Each made prey of corsairs and pirates based at the ports of the other, and both enjoyed successes in running down such prey. Each identified its prey either by place of origin or religious belief, often without regard for the activities the particular prey was engaged in. Campaigns against so-called pirates and corsairs produced a good many of the captives put to the oar as slaves by Moslem and Christian powers. But certainly only a minority of the captives taken and held by Moslems and Christians had actually been corsairs or pirates before they were imprisoned or put to the oar.

Even as late as the end of the seventeenth century, religious war was the principal means by which slaves were acquired for Mediterranean galley oars. When Christian states warred against each other in that theater, their struggles did not produce slaves, for the simple reason that they did not class or treat Christian prisoners as slaves. They occasionally used a few Christian prisoners in the galleys, but such prisoners were not held and worked at the oar for indefinite lengths of time as a matter of regular policy as the slaves were. A very different code of behavior, however, was applied by Christian states in treating prisoners taken in war with infidel enemies. Infidel prisoners of war were classed and treated as slaves by Catholic and Protestant powers alike, and an abundance of slaves was apt to result from wars of that sort. The western European Protestant powers, the English and the Dutch, not having galleys themselves, commonly sold such prisoners at one of the Mediterranean markets for slaves. The Roman Catholic powers of the Mediterranean, those having galleys of their own to maintain, kept the Moslem prisoners they took and bought others, usually holding and working them as long as they were physically able to pull an oar. In short, religious distinctions were the basis for the classification of prisoners of war as slaves, and wars against the Moslem produced most of the slaves used by Christian states in their galleys.

Some Christian princes and powers considered all Moslems as enemies, and attacked them whenever and wherever they could, not because every Moslem they met broke the laws of the sea, but because Moslems were infidels in Christian eyes. The Knights of Malta and the papacy held this view, as did the kings of Spain, and less consistently the kings of France. In the seventeenth century all these Christian princes, with varying frequency, sent expeditions against the states of North Africa and the Ottoman Turks. With or without the banner of religion (some kept it furled), expeditions against the Moslems were by nature crusades, having the blessing and sanction, and the financial and naval collaboration of the Church of Rome. Crusades of that sort produced a great many slaves for the galleys.

But until the 1680's the most regular and prolific suppliers of Moslem slaves were the Knights of St. John of Jerusalem, established at Malta. The Knights of that order were certainly the most active and tenacious of Islam's Mediterranean enemies. They were crusaders in the medieval tradition; indeed they preserved, cherished, and epitomized the crusading tradition. For them, the objects of campaigns at sea were the protection of Christian trade and the elimination or capture or conversion of infidels by means of the sword.[5] "When a man becomes a Knight of Malta," one of them observed, "he has the apparent intention of performing the principal duties of a Knight, or at least he should have that intention whether he has it or not. And what duties are these? To defend the Faith against the Infidels, to destroy the pirates and Mohammedans."[6] Other Christian powers made treaties with Moslems, but not the Knights of St. John.[7] Knights from the Order of Malta campaigned against Moslems year after year under oar and sail in the name of their faith. They encouraged privateers to use their flag and their islands as a base for operations against Moslem shipping and trade, and levied a ten per cent tax on the value of the prizes those privateers were able to take. The Moslem prisoners captured in this unceasing war were encouraged to become converts to Christian faith; Moslem prisoners refusing Christianity were apt to be used as slaves on the galleys of the order, worked in the labor force on the island, used as domestics or personal servants, exchanged against Christians held by the Moslems, or held for ransom; many were sold as slaves to the Catholic Christian powers needing oarsmen for galleys. The sales of booty and slaves and the exchanges of slaves, plus the ten per cent tax on the privateers, helped to maintain the order and finance its campaigns. By their traffic in slaves, by the perennial war for religion they engaged in, and by providing a base for the use of privateers that preyed on Moslem shipping, the Knights made a major contribution to maintaining the stock of Moslem slaves available for use at the oar.

The last third of the seventeenth century saw a sharp increase in the demand for such slaves. The most important reason for this growth was the increase in the number of galleys being put into service, especially by France. In numerical terms, the French galley fleet grew from half a dozen vessels in the 1660's to more than half a hundred in the 1690's. Concurrently, the Spanish and the Venetian fleets were reported being enlarged. In building their enormous fleet of galleys the French faced far fewer problems in getting materials to construct the vessels themselves than in getting men for their oars. The cost of the slaves alone, for an ordinary galley, could exceed the cost of building the vessel.

Only two slave markets of any consequence were open to the French in the western Mediterranean: Leghorn and Malta. All the rest were monopolized or controlled by other Christian powers having galleys of their own. Spanish or Habsburg influence unfriendly to France dominated most Italian markets. The north Italian port of Leghorn was open to the French only because the dukes of Tuscany chose to create and persist in maintaining at that place a "free port."

Leghorn attracted many of the corsairs and privateers that scoured the Mediterranean, offering an open market for the sale of their loot, and a market where premium prices were paid for slaves. Leghorn's status as a free port in the western Mediterranean also attracted the shipping of non-Mediterranean powers, notably the English and Dutch, without ports of their own in the inland sea. Their convoys regularly touched at Leghorn voyaging both to and from the Levant. Any Moslem (or other) prizes and crews taken by the men-of-war escorting the convoys could be brought into Leghorn for sale. An important part of the slaves on the Leghorn market were brought in by the English and the Dutch.

In the period from 1660 to the middle 'eighties, the Leghorn consuls of France were exceedingly active, and successful, as buyers of Moslem slaves for the galleys of France.[8] But they were far from satisfying the needs of the French, even in the 'seventies. In the 'eighties, French requirements were greater than ever. The Leghorn market was then less able to supply slaves than before, having fewer because treaties of peace had been concluded with the Barbary states by some of the European powers,[9] and in consequence, privateers and convoy escorts brought fewer slaves to the Leghorn market for sale.

Malta was an even better market than Leghorn for French buyers of slaves, at least from 1665 to 1675.[10] Many slaves were sold by knights to the French in those years, and the order had the appearance of being very amicably disposed toward the French. A sizable number of French-born knights took commissions, and many accepted commands in the new French Corps des Galères.[11] Indeed, some of them earned their commands in the new French Corps des Galères by securing large numbers of slaves for purchase by the French. But relations between the order and France underwent some deterioration in the later 'seventies, and still more in the 'eighties. That change was accompanied by a notable reduction of the number of slaves made available at Malta for sale to the French.

Sales of slaves to the French were reduced to a trickle after 1682. The French consul who served at Malta in 1682–1697 was able to supply fewer than two hundred slaves from that market in fifteen years.[12] That was poor performance, considering that in the decade and a half before his tenure as consul, many times that number had been supplied.[13] Why Malta ceased to be a rich and regular source of slaves for France remains obscure. The plague of 1677 there may have had some temporary effects; a new grand master, Gregory Caraffa, elected in 1680, may have instituted some changes of policy covering the sale of slaves.[14] For a variety of reasons, probably, Malta ceased to be a rich market for the French.

In the last two decades of the century, at the very time when French needs were especially great, the two markets on which they relied most heavily for supplies of Moslem slaves — Leghorn and Malta — became relatively unproductive. Yet the decade 1680–1690 was the period when the French need and demand for slaves rose to an all-time high. Just when demand was greatest, slave supplies from Leghorn and especially from Malta were shorter than ever before. Nor was that all.

The effects of this shortage were worsened for the French by the fact that certain eastern Mediterranean sources of slaves — sources scattered and irregular but productive of Russians and Greeks for the oar were entirely closed to the French by the end of the 'seventies.

Since religious differences allowed the employment of non-Christian prisoners of war as galley slaves, religious differences might also allow Eastern Orthodox Christians to be enchained on French galleys alongside Moslems, renegades, and the occasional Jews that were used. That was apparently the point of view of Colbert, *de facto* minister of marine after 1665 (officially from 1669). Colbert was heartily in favor of buying as slaves such nonconformist Christians as Russians and Greeks, as long as they were abundant and less in demand and hence substantially cheaper than Turks. There is some doubt as to whether or not Louis the Fourteenth himself ever openly sanctioned their use; he may have approved without letting his sanction be publicly known. With or without his explicit permission, the use of Russians and Greeks offered a step toward solution of the problem of procuring larger numbers of men for the oar.

In Colbert's view, the needs of the navy were too great to allow qualms of conscience about the enslavement of Christians to interfere with the acquisition of supplies of men. Russians, presumably Eastern Orthodox Christians, were regularly offered for sale by the Turks at the Constantinople market, and Colbert ordered them bought.[15] Apparently this program was given less than enthusiastic support by one of his subordinates, the Intendant des Galères at Marseille, Nicolas Arnoul. Voicing the hope that the Constantinople market could satisfy their needs, the intendant expressed his own preference: "It would be a great advantage for me if they would agree to serve as volunteers, and thus heal the scruples I have about holding Christians on the galleys in chains." [16] No such scruple bothered Colbert; he issued orders to purchase the Russians. "It is certain that we must profit from all possible opportunities that present themselves for strengthening the rowing force of the galleys; that is why, if you find you can get Russians from Constantinople, you must buy as many as you can. I will instruct M. de la Haye [French ambassador at Constantinople] to give you all the help he can." [17]

Opportunities to acquire and use "schismatic" (Orthodox) Greeks also presented themselves. As late as 1673 there was some uncertainty in the ministry as to whether or not certain Greeks on hand, captured by the king's vessels, should be used at the oar;[18] but by the summer of 1674 the doubts seem to have been resolved. The Chevalier de Piancourt, a Knight of Malta then serving as consul for France at Malta, made a contract with a corsair who sailed under the flag of Savoy whereby the corsair agreed to deliver "schismatic Greeks" to Marseille for sixty piastres a head, a very low price compared with the prevailing prices of Turks; the minister (probably Seignelay)[19] quickly approved the proposition with the endorsement: "Good, he can purchase the Greeks." [20]

Encouraged by this easy approval, the Chevalier de Piancourt told a good number of French corsairs who made Malta their base of operations that the king of France would willingly buy "all Greeks found on Turkish ships that fell into their hands." [21] The corsairs must have been pleased at that, since a large percentage of the shipping under the Ottoman flag was manned by Christian Greeks and other non-Moslem subjects of the Ottoman Turks. The opportunity to sell such Christians as slaves could mean windfall profits for them. But some of them, said the consul at Malta, found it hard to believe that they were really free to capture and sell such Christians as slaves. According to the consul, the corsairs were ready to deliver Orthodox Greeks to Marseille as slaves, assuming the king would pay the usual delivery costs, but they insisted "that His Majesty obtain assurances that they would not be oppressed or troubled in their traffic either by the Pope or by his Inquisitor at Malta." [22] Perhaps the consul was expressing his own sentiments and qualms, and probably those of brothers in the order and the Grand Master Cottoner, a Spaniard, when he pointed to the need to get this authorization from the Inquisitor or the Pope; at Malta, they may have suspected that the purchase policy of the French ministry of marine was not that of Louis. Louis himself could not give, nor was he likely to ask for or get such guarantees from either the Inquisitor or the pope. He was aware, as were they, where the limits of his power actually lay.

The minister eventually learned, if he was not already aware, that the purchase and use of Christian Greeks for French galley oars was no longer desired. Indeed the Intendant Brodart at Marseille was warned by the minister in late 1676 that in buying Russians from Constantinople he must not allow his buyers "to mix any schismatic Greeks with the Russians"; the Russians were wanted, but the Greeks were not.[23]

The limitations imposed by religious policy apparently also affected the use of prisoners already in hand. Thus in 1680, when Admiral Duquesne captured about fifty Greeks aboard Turkish vessels, he wrote to inquire how they should be disposed of. Navy officials must have been tempted to put them to the oar, where they were certainly needed; but instead orders were speedily issued for their release.[24]

In the later 'seventies the policy of buying Russian slaves was also questioned and changed. A few months after the purchase of Greeks was stopped, the Intendant Brodart was unequivocally told that the king did not want to buy any more Russians: "in case you have given any orders in this regard, revoke them."[25] Those instructions constituted a definite decision, one that may have been hastened by the rumor that circulated in the navy that year, 1678, that some of the "Russians" then serving on French galleys were not Russians at all; an investigation proved there were about twenty Poles on the galleys, Roman Catholics one would guess — probably purchased in the eastern Mediterranean market from Turks. By April 1679, when it was proved beyond doubt that the "Russians" were actually Poles, orders were issued for their release.[26] At least as late as 1687 Russians were reported to be among the oarsmen on the galleys of Louis the Fourteenth,[27] but no purchases appear to have been made after 1679.

Many causes must have helped to produce this definite and notable change of policy concerning the purchase of Christian Russians and Greeks for the oar. Perhaps the king of France, up to then, had never been wholly sympathetic to the use of Christians as slaves; perhaps he had not even known they were being bought for his galleys; or perhaps he had known and had not cared, up to then. But the fact that they were used as much as they were must have been more the result of the zeal of suppliers and ministers than of any enthusiasm, or permission, of the king's.

Through this affair, it became apparent that the Roman Catholic Church could exercise decisive influence on naval administration, an influence extending even to changing the navy's purchase policy and determining that certain types of men would not be put to the oar as slaves. Friction was notable when the corsair captains were reported as refusing to deliver the slaves needed by the navy unless Louis secured what amounted to papal permission for their use. The Inquisitor at Malta, according to the French consuls on that island, was strongly opposed to the sale of Christians, including Christianized Turks, to the French for galley use. The Inquisitor went to the extremity of excommunicating one French consul, a Knight of Malta, the Chevalier de Tincourt, for selling Christians to the French as slaves.[28] At least once, when two baptized Turks were being sent by Tincourt to Marseille for the galleys, the Inquisitor at Malta had one of the slaves removed, brought back, and for safekeeping put into prison. This action was apparently a warning. Tincourt admitted that though the slave in question belonged to the king of France, "once inside these prisons, I can not get them out except by means whose consequences are not to be desired." There was, he added, no hope that the Grand Master might openly intercede: "He is an Italian, and you know in what respect Italians hold the Inquisition," said this Knight of Malta.[29]

All this — the decline of the Leghorn and Malta markets and the renunciation of the practice of buying Russians and Greeks — had serious effects. It reduced the number of slaves that France could buy for her galleys, aggravating a shortage that had long existed, with demand almost always exceeding supply. The minister of marine was evidently led to conclude that the king had little or no chance of getting, within the confusion of the Mediterranean, the elite oarsmen he needed to enlarge his galley corps.

But outside the Mediterranean there was one important, promising source of supply as yet untried. Indeed, even as the purchase of Orthodox Christians was being abandoned in 1679, steps were being taken to tap this new source. Africa could provide Negroes for the oar, brought from Cape Verd on the West African coast. The French minister of marine was enthusiastic about the potentialities of Negro slaves; neither high prices nor religion seemed likely to hinder their use. Furthermore, they could be bought from the Senegal Company in almost any quantity desired: the company was eager to provide them. As for the capacities of the Negroes, the enthusiasm of the minister led him to say that "these *naturels*," as he called them, "do unbelievable labor in all American colonies; there is reason to believe they would be very suitable for the galleys, if treated well." [30]

Not all officials of the navy shared the minister's enthusiasm for Negroes and his confidence in their capacities; not all shared his hopes for their success. Some outright opposition to the use of Negroes was expressed, part of it the customary conservative response to change, the deep-rooted tendency to continue as before. Opposition could be expected from persons and groups whose economic interests were tied up with the procurement or use of galley slaves of conventional sorts. Even the experimental use of Negro slaves threatened their vested interests. The consuls, the merchants and shippers of Marseille who transported or dealt in slaves, and any of the many persons connected with the trade in slaves, would have had an interest in continuing the use of the Turks, for they could not expect to share in the new traffic in Negroes as they had in the traditional trade in Turks. The Senegal Company held a monopoly on the African trade.

There may also have been opposition on religious grounds to the use of Negroes. Knights of Malta could be expected to oppose them as replacements for Moslems.

Mediterranean Moslems were religious enemies but pagan Negroes from Senegal were not. Having vowed "to defend the Faith against Infidels" and "destroy pirates and Mohammedans," the Knights might understandably prefer to see Moslem enemies rather than innocent Negro *"naturels"* at the oars of their commands. The hallowed aura of sanctity accompanying the use of infidel Moslems may have been dissipated for the Knights when African heathens were substituted for Moslems. Considering that the captains of most French galleys, and many of the other officers in the corps were Knights of Malta, the influence of such religiously-inspired opinion could have been strong.

But one must conclude that there were many reasons why the systematic use of Negro slaves might have been opposed, and many reasons why the officers and the captains of galleys in particular were at the outset skeptical, unpersuaded of the utility of the Negro slaves. The minister of marine was moved in 1679 to tell the Intendant Brodart that one of his principal duties must be "to persuade the Captains of the value of the Negroes." [31]

Other persons, including some very influential ones, profited by allowing unauthorized releases and escapes. The use of dark-skinned slaves would seriously hamper some of their illicit machinations, and such persons could be expected to use whatever influence they could contrive to oppose the use of Negroes. Conversely, the high visibility of the Negro slaves would seem to make dependence upon them an incomparable help in preventing escapes, and recognition of that advantage along with the ease of acquisition must have underlain the favorable attitude of the ministry. [32]

The primary spokesman for this varied opposition to Negroes was the Intendant Brodart, chief of the galley base at Marseille. Adamant, he expressed opposition even to the idea of using Negroes experimentally. His determined, uncompromising opposition led the minister to say to him in November of 1677 that "His Majesty has been surprised at His Intendant. Without ever having tried to see whether or not Negroes can work the oar, he decided absolutely that they are not fit to serve." [33]

The minister was determined to give the Negroes a try. Brodart continued to resist and was so uncooperative as to refuse comment on the plans that were being made, though the minister explicitly and repeatedly pressed him to explain his point of view. The minister chided Brodart in January, and again in February 1678, saying "You have written me nothing on this subject; you could not have forgotten an affair of such importance as this"; but there was no response from Brodart, at least for a long time. [34]

The Senegal Company agreed to deliver to Marseille two to three hundred Negroes of premium quality at 130 livres a head — an attractive price, because the usual cost of a prime Turk was 350 livres or more. [35] An early shipment of seventy-seven Negroes, made in April 1679, included thirty-eight who were judged too young to serve. But the quality of those accepted left little to be desired. According to Colbert, "The king has never had stronger or better-built men for his galleys." [36] At least three more shipments were delivered in 1679–1680. Of the three hundred–odd men delivered in all, the inspectors at Marseille accepted only two hundred seventy-three.[37]

The minister ordered that special care be given to any of the new arrivals who appeared to be sick or debilitated after the voyage on the slaver. Indeed, the minister, always attentive to detail, seemed to do everything possible to enable the Negroes to "succeed on the galleys." Since they had little or no knowledge of French, he saw to the appointment of a certain Monsieur Mariage to teach them and to serve in the meanwhile as translator and overseer. He ordered that Negroes should be kept from contact with *forçats* and Turks when the galleys were in port; a bad example would be set for the Negro newcomers by the veterans of the oar, he said, and as soon as possible they should be put at work that would minimize their association with the Moslems. On the positive side, the minister wrote in November 1680 to the Superior of the Congrégation de la Mission at Marseille[38] asking that a member of the order be appointed "to instruct them on the lights of our Religion, and make them fit to be Christians." [39]

The minister urged Brodart to send him reports on the condition of the Negroes and their performance at the oar and otherwise, because "that is at present one of the most important matters of concern to the galleys." [40] The shortage of oarsmen, as he very well knew, was the bottleneck that then held back the growth of the fleet; the minister went so far as to say that "the ease with which we can get these Negroes will enable us to put thirty galleys to sea." Perhaps in the future, he said, they could equip some galleasses (large galleys mounting heavy guns) as well.[41]

The minister's solicitude stemmed not only from the apparent importance of the newcomers as possible substitutes for Turks but also from other causes. There were grounds for anxiety: from the start it seemed possible that the Negroes might be receiving improper care. As early as 1679 the minister learned that eighteen of them had died in the hospital for slaves.[42] That was hardly an encouraging start; but there was reason to believe that those who died, newly arrived, had simply failed to survive the aftereffects of their voyage on the slaver.

In December of 1680, the minister was pleased to learn from the Superior of the Congrégation de la Mission at Marseille that during that winter (1680–1681) he would have the Negroes instructed in "the Truth of our Religion," as he had been asked to do; that program proved successful. It had the minister's hearty support: "There is nothing," he wrote to Brodart, "more important for the Glory of God and the service of the King than to make them all Christians. Do not fail to contribute as much as you can to the success of that good work." [43] The following August the minister expressed satisfaction that a "very considerable number of the Negroes are now capable of being baptized," and he urged "continued application in this important work to complete the instruction of those that remain at Marseille." At that date fifty were considered converted to Roman Catholic Christianity, and the Marèchal de Vivonne, it was said, had them baptized.[44]

In contrast to their spiritual condition in 1681, the Negroes' physical health went from bad to worse. In spite of the minister's cares, the treatment they received at Marseille was obviously unsuited to the needs of debilitated men. Diet on the galleys was notoriously poor. Until the fall of 1681 the Negroes were given the same diet that was ordinarily given to condamnés, and that diet was kept purposely scant, ostensibly to encourage the men to work.[45] The king allowed a modest "sea-ration" supplement while the galleys were out on campaign, but in port all sorts of oarsmen were expected to work at the docks, in the arsenal, in the city of Marseille, or at some handicraft if they possessed a skill. By such work they could earn the extra food they needed to live. From the standpoint of modern penology the system had positive merit; in the seventeenth century it had the notable virtue of saving the king a tidy sum on the cost of food for the eleven or twelve thousand men he had on his galleys (during most of the 1690's).[46] But the Negroes necessarily required some time to learn the peculiar ways of this strange and complicated workhouse-prison in which they were held. Pulled out of their own society and lacking the experience, skills, and even the language needed for many types of work in their new environment, and kept apart from the experienced oarsmen, they were certain to have real difficulty getting supplements to their basic, insufficient ration. As early as February 1681 the Negroes were reported "suffering and dying from the winter and cold."[47] But the winter weather alone was not responsible. The following August they were reported to be "dying every day."[48]

To put a stop to this, and in the hope of improving their condition, their translator and overseer Monsieur Mariage, at his own request, was made responsible for feeding and maintaining them.[49] Three months after he assumed that responsibility, however, in mid-November of 1681, the minister had ample grounds for doubts about Monsieur Mariage and for reprimanding him. It was then disclosed that the Negroes were still being grossly neglected and abused: "His Majesty has often ordered special care for the Negroes at Marseille; yet now he learns that they are barefoot. It is very important to protect them from the cold, to clothe them fully, and to give them shoes, even though that man Mariage pretends that for what it would cost the King [to do that] he could give them eight ounces of *ris de febres* [a day?]."[50] Certainly there was good evidence for doubting the value of Monsieur Mariage's services, and still more reason for doubt when it later came to light that Mariage, instead of caring for the Negroes and discharging his responsibility for bettering their condition, in the minister's own words, "abuses the trust confided to him by converting part of their subsistence to profit for himself."[51] The minister asked Brodart "to see if he can be discharged without prejudice to the Negroes. If so, let me know, and the King will discharge him forthwith. But in case he still must be retained, he must be watched."[52]

As of that date, early December 1682, during the three years the experiment had been under way, a total of two hundred seventy-three Negroes had been brought to Marseille and accepted for service as galley slaves. The following February only ninety-eight remained alive; at about that time Monsieur Mariage was discharged.[53] Several years later, since the eighty-six survivors were considered "useless and at His Majesty's charge," the minister approved their shipment to the West Indies for sale.[54]

This attempt to use Negro slaves obviously did not justify the conclusion that Negro slaves were physically unfit for the oar, or less suited to the oar than Turks. Yet one commentator expressed the prevailing view, or excuse, when he remarked in 1682 that "the purchase of blacks is an expenditure from which one gets almost no return because these men, being unable to endure the fatigues, are unsuited to the galleys." [55] Apparently the officers and administrators of the navy did not discern any inconsistency between their opinion that Negroes were "unsuited" to the fatigues of the oar and the fact that the labor of Negro slaves was the basis for plantation and mining economies in all the Americas. No effort was afterward made, on a significant scale, to secure such slaves for the oar, though isolated individuals did serve.

Louis and his ministers of marine also tried to tap North America as a source of supply for galley slaves. The Iroquois were a serious problem for the settlers of the struggling French colony in Canada; both the colony and France might reap benefits if some of the troublesome Indians could be shipped to France. If thousands of Negroes could be sent from east to west, it may have seemed reasonable that American Indians could be shipped from west to east; the principal difficulty, as could be expected, would consist in getting them together to send.

Some such thought must have been in the mind of the king himself in 1684 when he gave orders to the governor general of New France "to do everything possible to capture [in the forthcoming war] the greatest possible number of prisoners from the Iroquois Indian tribes; ship them to France for the galleys at every opportunity," he urged.[56]

So small was the hope of capturing Iroquois in war that the French Canadians were reduced to preying upon some friendly Iroquois who sometimes brought fish and game to Fort Frontenac for sale, Indians who probably felt secure because the French had Recollet missionaries working among them. But as Louis's letter of 1684 had made clear, he and his colonial governors were secretly planning war against the Iroquois, hoping to take many prisoners; the friendly Iroquois certainly did not foresee that.

In 1685 the governor general of Canada, the Marquis de Denonville, was not only planning war with the Iroquois in accord with instructions from France, but asserting to the minister of marine that the Iroquois tribes had to be "exterminated." [57] The governor general and the intendant used trickery as their method of declaring war on the Iroquois; by that means, they hoped, a sizable group of prisoners could be taken at the very start.

The friendly Indians of several Iroquois tribes were invited to take part in a powwow and feast. "They knew nothing of the impending war with their Iroquois kinsmen and came trustingly, with their wives and children, in a party of about two hundred." [58] The Intendant Champigny gave them a feast and then, in an act of betrayal that neither the Indians nor the French were soon to forget, French troops suddenly moved in and arrested the Iroquois. About forty braves, including several chiefs, were soon afterward shipped as prisoners to France and put to the oar.

It was an act of clemency for the minister of marine in France to decree that the Iroquois need not to be shaved as slaves usually were, and that they need not be chained "provided you are certain they are thus secure, and will not escape." [59] At first the Iroquois were fed the standard rations given to Frenchmen condemned to the galleys, but later, because of a belief that they needed more than the usual fare, the minister ordered that their rations be increased.[60] It was reported in 1688 that the Indians were docile, getting along well with their religious instruction, and taking the sacraments.[61]

Meanwhile, in Canada, the governor general was instructed to continue fighting the Indians and sending prisoners to France. "It is [now] certain," wrote the minister, "that these men, vigorous and accustomed to hardship as they are, can be of service on His Majesty's galleys." [62] But able-bodied Iroquois braves were seldom taken prisoner by any means: they were unlikely to be taken by treachery twice. Thus the Denonville expedition against the Seneca (Iroquois) tribes in 1687 encountered deserted villages and ambush, and took only a few stragglers as prisoners; many of those merely served as feed for the governor general's cannibalistic Indian allies.[63]

The avenging Iroquois, for their part, ravaged the country far and wide and massacred the French at Lachine, in the very environs of Montreal. Denonville admitted that sending Iroquois braves to France for service in the galleys had "very much contributed to irritate the Iroquois against the French." [64] But he could justifiably blame that blunder on others, as he did in writing to the minister in 1687, saying that he had no choice but to send Indians to France, for he was obliged to obey blindly the orders of the king.

At Denonville's request and that of his successor, the returning governor general Frontenac, the king consented to return the captive Iroquois to Canada. "His Majesty is pleased to use these savages to make peace with their nation it being inconvenient in present circumstances to continue this war." [65] Only twenty-one of the Iroquois remained alive; they set out again across the south of France, on the road to La Rochelle, and thirteen (some sources say three) survived to return to New France in the fall of 1689.[66]

Since the Iroquois nation had proved an illusory source of supply, and Negroes were thought not fit for the oar, the navy was thrown back on Mediterranean sources for slaves. Of the two sorts of slave commonly available there, only Moslems, on religious grounds, could be used and they, for the reasons described, were in extremely short supply in the early and middle 'eighties, with the Leghorn and Malta supply reduced to a trickle.

An extraordinary further aggravation of the shortage resulted when an agreement was signed in 1681 between France and Algiers, providing for reciprocal restitution of the captives held. Since more of the men on French galleys came from Algiers than from any other place,[67] this agreement promised to remove hundreds of slaves from the benches of the galleys themselves. Colbert declared that he would rather have war with the Barbary states than return the men from that city who rowed on the galleys.[68] The force of such opinion was probably strengthened by the disclosure that the number of Algerians on French galleys exceeded the number of Frenchmen held at Algiers. The agreement of 1681, when it came to be executed, failed. It required embassies to Algiers and bombardments of that city in 1682, 1683, and 1684 to reach another accord. The expedition of 1683, without producing a treaty, brought about the release of five hundred seventy Frenchmen at Algiers. A new French expedition the following year, commanded by Admiral Tourville, obtained a treaty Louis was disposed to accept, one including reciprocal exchange provisions and also a promise that henceforth all Frenchmen captured by Algiers, whatever the flag of their ship, would be released.[69]

Problems arose in carrying out the provisions of this treaty. All, or nearly all, the French held at Algiers had already been released. Louis and the ministry of marine, as the Algerians could have known from experience, were very slow in releasing able-bodied slaves. That reluctance was notably apparent in March of 1682 during the stay of a Moroccan emissary at Marseille: slaves from Salé and other Moroccan dependencies then in French hands in contravention of treaties were hidden on an island in the harbor of Marseille, others were concealed on the upper floors of the hospital for oarsmen to delude the Moroccan visitor.[70] That same month efforts were made to force the slaves on the galleys to write letters home to Algiers misrepresenting the state of affairs at Marseille; in the approving words of the minister of marine, "It is fine [il est bon] to force the Algerian slaves on the galleys to write as the Sieur de Beaujeu requests; maltreat them for that purpose if you must, but his Majesty thinks that the threat alone will suffice."[71]

Almost a year after the treaty of 1684 was signed, the Dey of Algiers complained to Louis that very few of the Algerian slaves known to be held by the French had been released and returned. "Your officers at Marseille have kept most of those who should be delivered under [the terms of] the treaty of peace; instead they have brought us incurably sick and crippled slaves taken in the Levant, who are not from Algiers."[72] Only about a hundred and fifty Algerians had been released, and that was only a part of those actually held at Marseille. "It is not as a favor that we claim the release of the Janissaries remaining in France; they were included in the Treaty," and should be returned, complained the Dey.[73] Relations were not improved when that distinguished Knight of Malta, the French Admiral Tourville, arrived in Algiers with fifty-six Algerian slaves, declaring he had orders not to release them unless he was given fifty-six able-bodied replacements to take their places at the oars.[74] As Plantet admits, "it is certain" that the officers of the navy "showed regrettable unwillingness" in finding and delivering the slaves whose return was called for by the treaties.[75]

Infidelity on the part of officials in France was partly the product of the low esteem in which the North African states were held, but it was also related to the severity of the shortage of slaves for French galleys. The shortage of Moslem slaves was so keenly felt that officials in France even went so far as to violate treaties to avoid making it worse. When they promised the return of Algerian and Moroccan prisoners of war, they found ways to avoid returning those who were still able-bodied — still fit for the oar.

Ironically, this shortage of slaves, so keenly felt, was worsened by the high mortality among oarsmen on the French galleys themselves. Many conditions combined to raise the mortality among oarsmen: the very vigor of campaigning by French galleys was a cause, along with shorthanded campaigns, frequent and long campaigns, campaigns in the winter, rapid growth of the fleet, bad diet provided by the king for his oarsmen, even the conduct of officers toward their men — all had their effect.[76] Not all these conditions were necessarily present at any one time; but their recurrence or persistence had generally deleterious effects on oarsmen. Their aggregate effect on the rowers could be counted as part of the cost of the campaigns. Costs could also be counted in the number of men who died on the benches of galleys or the hundreds of invalids that crowded the hospital for oarsmen and overflowed onto hospital hulks in the port.[77] The cost was high, as was underscored by one senior naval officer who pointed out that "there is no slavery in all the galleys of the Mediterranean more harsh, where oarsmen perish more often than on the galleys of the King of France."[78]

By way of summary, we can say that there were many reasons why the demand for slaves exceeded the supply, and why slaves were particularly scarce for the French. Most important, of course, was that more galleys were built and maintained in the Mediterranean in the period 1670–1700 than for nearly a century past; France was the power that built the most, and needed the most oarsmen. Furthermore, French galleys campaigned with vigor, and the replacement rate for their oarsmen was extraordinarily high. Concurrently, the supply of Moslem slaves was restricted by the action of the English and Dutch and some other powers, including the French themselves, who signed treaties or truces with North African states, thereby lessening the number of ships engaged in capturing infidels who could be sold as slaves. French treaties with North African states actually reduced the number of slaves in French hands, thus increasing demand. Even the church aggravated the procurement problems of the French by opposing the purchase and use at the oar of Orthodox Christians and Christianized Turks; church opposition may also have been expressed in the Order of Malta's reluctance to sell Moslems to Louis in the early 'eighties, when his need was especially great. Africa was the one source of supply for slaves that could have been used and was not. French galley officials avoided using Negro slaves. Lacking the appeal to religious motives that Moslems had, African Negroes were rejected in the belief, or with the excuse, that they were unable to sustain the fatigues of the oar.

Facing this shortage, the minister of marine tried to get oarsmen elsewhere, from Savoy and Poland and Venice, but without satisfying French needs.[79] Louis the Fourteenth, expectedly, did not allow this shortage to limit the growth of his fleet. Since the Mediterranean sources of supply could not provide Turks, and the colonial world could not supply heathens of acceptable types, the kingdom of France would supply oarsmen of its own: criminals of various sorts were already being sent to the galleys at a high rate, but deserters and Huguenot heretics could also be used.

Louis issued new decrees that assured abundant supplies of such men. One royal decree provided that deserters from the troops, instead of being put to death, as in the past, would in the future merely be maimed by having their nose and ears cut off and by being branded on the shoulder or cheek, and then sent to the galleys for life.[80] The other legislation of importance for galleys, the culmination of a long evolution, was an attempt to enforce in France conformity to Roman Catholic belief. This was attempted by a series of acts in which the satisfaction of the navy's needs was obviously merely incidental to other, religious and more general aims. Yet many new hands were thereby produced for the oars.[81]

These laws did not solve the problems of procuring slaves; no one supposed that the random catch of deserters and Protestants condemned to the galleys were the equals of carefully selected Turks, or that the need for Turks was thereby satisfied. Needs were not satisfied even by the windfall supplies of hundreds of Moslems procured from the Balkans early in the decade of the nineties.[82] Yet condemnations of deserters and Protestants did serve to reduce the demand for slaves; in the absence of sufficient numbers of slaves, condamnés could be made to do. By serving the oar in that religio-political prison and fighting force, the Corps des Galères, deserters and Protestants served the spiritual and secular aims of church and state almost as well as the infidel did. With infidels, Protestants, deserters, and criminals working shoulder to shoulder at the oars, usually commanded by Knights of St. John of Jerusalem holding royal commissions and seeking to serve the religious and political aims of both pope and king, the galleys of Louis the Fourteenth were an impressive accommodation of the aims and forces of church and state.

NOTES

page 173

[1] In an article on "The Procurement of Oarsmen for French Galleys, 1660–1748," *American Historical Review*, vol. 65, pp. 31–48, I discussed the general problems of procuring oarsmen of various types over a long period of years; in this essay, the focus is narrowed to treat the slaves alone in the limited period 1665–1700. For views and policy on volunteers see J. B. Colbert, *Lettres, instructions et mémoires*, ed. P. Clément, Paris, 1861–1862, vol. 3, part 1, pp. 108, 218n, 242; concurring

opinions of the Duke de Vivonne: B⁶78 fol. 317 seq. Archives de la Marine, Archives Nationales, hereafter cited as B⁶(vol.) Marine.

² B⁶135 Marine fol. 227; cf. B⁶78 Marine fol. 133.

page 174

³ Series O¹ vol. 106 bis *passim*, Registre, Archives de la Marine, Archives de Port, Toulon, hereafter cited as Marine:Toulon (see note 82 below).

⁴ Knights of St. John (or *Hospitaliers*) of Jerusalem, founded in 1070, were transferred successively to Cyprus (1291) and to Rhodes (1310), there to be defeated by the Turks and, by the terms of their capitulation, spared and allowed to leave Rhodes (1522). They received Malta and other territory as a fief from the Emperor Charles the Fifth, and were established at Malta by 1530; thenceforth they were commonly called Knights of Malta, sometimes called *La Réligion* or *La Réligion de Malte*.

page 175

⁵ Abbé René Aubert de Vertot, *Histoire des chevaliers de St. Jean de Jérusalum*, Paris, 1761, vol. 1, preface, pp. 4–5 and *passim*.

⁶ Chavalier Luc de Boyer d'Argens, *Reflexions politiques sur l'état et les devoirs des Chevaliers de Malthe*, La Haye, 1739, p. 115.

⁷ The Knights made no treaty with the Infidel after their capitulation and expulsion from Rhodes in 1522. *Recueil d'actes internationaux de l'empire Ottoman*, Paris, 1897, vol. 1, pp. 28, 401.

page 176

⁸ See correspondence of François Cotolendy, French consul at Leghorn, 1670–1691, Series B¹, pp. 695–699 *passim*, Archives des Affaires Étrangères. Hereafter cited as B¹ Aff. Etr.

⁹ England with Tripoli (1676), Algiers (1682); the Dutch with Algiers (1680). Eugène Plantet, *Correspondance des Deys d'Alger avec la Cour de France*, Paris, 1889, vol. 1, p. 82n; Sir Godfrey Fisher, *Barbary Legend, War, Trade and Piracy in North Africa, 1415–1830*, Oxford, 1957, pp. 264–265, 267–268.

¹⁰ B¹814 Aff. Etr., correspondence of the Consuls at Malta with the Court. Without exception, the consuls were Knights of the Order of Malta.

page 177

¹¹ See, for example, the seniority list of captains (1674) in B⁶8 Marine fols. 1–2, where at least 19 of 25 captains were Knights of Malta.

¹² B¹814 Aff. Etr., Le Bailly D'Escrainville to Minister, November 9, 1697.

¹³ B¹814 Aff. Etr. *passim*.

¹⁴ Vertot, *op. cit.*, 1772, vol. 5, pp. 217, 220.

page 178

¹⁵ *Correspondance administrative sous le règne de Louis XIV*, ed. G. B. Depping, Paris, 1850–1855, vol. 2, pp. 912, 921–922; Colbert, *op. cit.*, vol. 3, part 1, p. 188.

¹⁶ *Ibid.*, vol. 2, p. 922.

¹⁷ Colbert, *op. cit.*, vol. 3, part 1, p. 188.

¹⁸ *Ibid.*, vol. 3, part 1, p. 503.

¹⁹ Jean Baptiste Colbert, holding several ministerial portfolios at once, destined and educated his son Colbert de Seignelay to assume navy responsibilities. Seignelay was taken into the ministry about 1672, and soon (1674) took over much of the responsibility for naval affairs.

²⁰ B¹814 Aff. Etr., Piancourt to Minister, June 8, 1674; B⁶6 Marine fol. 102.

²¹ *Ibid.*

²² B¹814 Aff. Etr., Piancourt to Minister, November 13, 1674.

page 179

²³ B⁶8 Marine fol. 157. It was a curious commentary on the navy's administration that a short time afterward, an opposite policy on Greeks was clearly indicated by the arrangements discreetly made with a certain corsair by the name of Cruvelier, whose secret contract included the promise that the navy would buy Greeks from him as slaves, but only in a ratio of one Greek to five Turks. Within a few weeks after those secret arrangements were made, they were abruptly canceled as far as the purchase of Greeks was concerned. B⁶9 Marine fols. 157–158. Religious policy opposing the use of Greeks was made to prevail, apparently, even in confidential affairs.

²⁴ B⁶12 Marine fols. 282, 284.

²⁵ B⁶10 Marine fol. 24.

²⁶ B⁶10 Marine fols. 182, 194; B⁶11 Marine fols. 30–31, 48, 72–73.

²⁷ B⁶19 Marine fols. 72, 89.

page 180

[28] According to Tincourt's reports, B¹814 Aff. Etr. Tincourt to Minister, May 19 and June 3, 1680, and *passim*.

[29] B¹814 Aff. Etr., Tincourt to Minister, May 19 and June 3, 1680.

[30] Colbert, *op. cit.*, vol. 3, part 1, p. 57n.

page 181

[31] B⁶91 Marine fol. 102–103.

[32] On corruption and illicit releases and escapes, B⁶87 Marine fols. 413–422, 427–428, B⁶89 Marine fols. 232–233.

[33] B⁶9 Marine fol. 232.

[34] B⁶10 Marine quote from Minister to Brodart, January 29, 1678; cf. March 13, 1678.

[35] B⁶10 Marine fol. 164.

[36] B⁶11 Marine fols. 90, 145.

page 182

[37] B⁶14 Marine fol. 257; B⁶ vols. 11, 12, and 13 *passim*.

[38] *The Congrégation de la mission*, an order founded by St. Vincent de Paul, whose members are variously known as Lazarites, *Missionnaires*, and Vincensians.

[39] B⁶12 Marine fol. 252.

[40] Colbert, *op. cit.*, vol. 3, part 2, pp. 154–155.

[41] B⁶11 Marine fols. 102–103.

[42] B⁶11 Marine Colbert to Brodart, September 15, 1679.

[43] B⁶12 Marine fols. 281–282.

[44] B⁶13 Marine fols. 176, 180.

page 183

[45] The king's daily ration consisted of two pounds of bread or sea biscuit a day, three ounces of beans in soup, with oil (or lard) and salt and sometimes a little wine. B⁶80 Marine "Estat des rations" (1671).

[46] B⁶90 Marine fols. 198–199.

[47] B⁶13 Marine fol. 34.

[48] *Ibid.* fol. 172.

[49] *Ibid.* fols. 172–173.

[50] B⁶14 Marine fol. 249.

[51] B⁶14 Marine fol. 257.

[52] *Ibid.* fol. 257.

page 184

[53] B⁶15 Marine fol. 20.

[54] B⁶17 Marine fol. 438.

[55] Marine:Toulon, IL 124, p. 394.

[56] M. Girouard, "L'Expédition du Marquis de Denonville," *Proceedings and Transactions of the Royal Society of Canada*, 2nd series, vol. 94.

[57] Girouard, *op. cit.*, pp. 94, 95.

page 185

[58] G. M. Wrong, *The Rise and Fall of New France*, New York, 1928, vol. 2, p. 504.

[59] B⁶19 Marine fol. 247.

[60] B⁶20 Marine fols. 3–4; Girouard, *op. cit.*, p. 93.

[61] B⁶20 Marine fol. 165.

[62] Girouard, *op. cit.*, p. 93.

[63] Chevalier de Baugy, "Journal of the Expedition of Marquis de Denonville against the Iroquois: 1687," *The Rochester Historical Society*, vol. 9, pp. 3–56 *passim*.

[64] Girouard, *op. cit.*, p. 93.

[65] Quoted in Henri Lorin, *Le Comte de Frontenac*, Paris, 1895, p. 269.

[66] B⁶21 Marine fols. 38, 44; Lorin, *op. cit.*, pp. 369–370; Girouard, *op. cit.*, p. 89.

page 186

[67] Series O, Marine:Toulon, vol. 106 bis *Registre général des Turcs*, 1682–1710.

[68] Gaston Zeller, *La Méditerranée et ses problèmes aux XVIe et XVIIe siècles*, Paris Multicopie, s.d., fasc. iv, 189–190.

[69] Zeller, *op. cit.*, fasc. iv, 189–193; Plantet, vol. 1, pp. 84–85 (notes).

[70] B⁶14 Marine fols. 91–92.

[71] *Ibid.*

[72] Plantet, *op. cit.*, vol. 1, pp. 96–97.

[73] Plantet, *op. cit.*, vol. 1, pp. 99–100.

[74] *Ibid.*, vol. 1, p. 116; according to the orders for their release, 10 of the 56 were invalids. B⁶17 Marine fols. 165–168.

page 187

[75] Plantet, *op. cit.*, vol. 1, p. 117n.

[76] For examples of these factors in actual naval operations by galleys: B⁶13 Marine fols. 11, 26; B⁶20 Marine fol. 26; B⁶83 Marine fols. 333–334; B⁶84 Marine fols. 17, 30, 49; B⁶85 Marine fols. 421–423.

[77] Louis released many hundreds of invalid Turks in the years 1684–1685, Plantet, *op. cit.*, vol. 1, pp. 97n, 105n. He still had 1,400 invalids on his hands in 1686, B⁶12 Marine fol. 276; B⁶85 Marine fol. 494.

[78] B⁶87 Marine fol. 428.

page 188

[79] B⁰17 Marine fols. 16–17; B¹1158 Aff. Etr., La Haye to Minister, December 29, 1685, January 5, 1686, and Le Blond to Minister, June 1, 1686.

[80] *Ordonnance du Roi*, December 4, 1684, A³12 Marine p. 127.

[81] *Édit portant révocation de l'Édit de Nantes*, October 1685, with the preparatory *Déclarations* dated May 12, 1682, June 16, 1685, *Recueil général des anciennes lois françaises*, ed. F.-A. Isambert, A.-J.-L. Jourdan et al., Paris, 1821–1833, 29 vols., vol. 29, pp. 388, 510, 532–534.

[82] Marine: Toulon, series O vol. 106 bis, Registre, 1690–1692 *passim*. R. F. Abler is preparing a series of maps based on this register showing the geographic distribution of slave purchases during a period of about two decades after 1682.

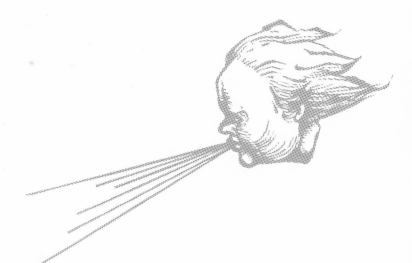

English Enterprise in the Region of the Strait of Magellan

by HELEN WALLIS

"The Str of Magellane is the gate of entry into the tresure of both the East and the West Indies. And whosoever is Lord of this Straight may account himselfe Lord also of the West Indies . . ."

The Original Writings & Correspondence of the Two Richard Hakluyts, E. G. R. Taylor, ed., London, 1935, vol. 1, p. 140.

W HEN RICHARD HAKLUYT demonstrated its importance in one of his earliest pamphlets, written in the winter of 1579–1580, the Strait of Magellan was already much in the news. Drake was known to have succeeded in finding and navigating it, although his return in the *Golden Hind* was still anxiously awaited. Her consort the *Elizabeth*, under the command of John Winter, had separated from the *Golden Hind* on October 8, 1578, two days after the ships entered the South Sea. Repassing the strait, the *Elizabeth* had returned to England in June 1579, and Hakluyt obtained the account of Winter's discoveries from the ship's steward, Thomas Griggs. With England's growing ambitions for overseas expansion seriously threatened by the impending union of the crowns of Spain and Portugal, Hakluyt set out in his pamphlet a scheme for challenging this Hispano-Portuguese supremacy. He proposed that the Strait of Magellan "be taken and fortified, inhabited and kept," by the English nation.

Magellan's discovery of the strait in 1520, symbolically portrayed in De Bry's well-known engraving, "Inuentio Maris Magallanici" (Figure 18),[1] had revealed what was still, sixty years later, the only known western passage from the Atlantic into the Pacific Ocean. Round the shores of the Pacific lay the richest empires in the world: the Portuguese East Indies, with the coveted Spice Islands, the Spanish settlements in the Philippine Islands, and, on the eastern seaboard, Spain's empires of gold and silver in Mexico and Peru. As long as the Portuguese were allowed to retain their monopoly of the route to Asia round the Cape of Good Hope, the Strait of Magellan remained the only open passage to Asia. It was the only passage by which a ship could circumnavigate the globe. Hakluyt's plan was therefore as logical a step in England's projected expansion overseas as was the search for alternative routes to Asia through northern waters.

Daniel Defoe, writing (as it seemed) the obituary of the strait in the early pages of *A New Voyage round the World, by a Course Never Sailed Before* (1725), allows his imaginary circumnavigator some critical comments on the many years of the strait's pre-eminence:

NOTES for *English Enterprise in the Region of the Strait of Magellan* are to be found on pages 217 to 220.

Figure 18. Magellan discovers and navigates the strait, 1520, between the Land of Fire and the Land of Giants; in Theodore de Bry, *America*, Part IV (1594), pl. XV (used by permission of the Trustees of the British Museum).

Such a mighty and valuable thing also was the passing this Straight, that Sir Francis Drake's going thro' it, gave birth to that famous old Wives Saying, viz. That Sir Francis Drake shot the Gulph; a Saying that was current in England for many Years, I believe near a Hundred after Sir Francis Drake was gone his long Journey of all; as if there had been but one Gulph in the world, and that passing it had been a Wonder next to that of Hercules cleansing the Egean Stable.

Of this famous place I could not but observe . . . that as Ignorance gave it its first Fame, and made it for so many Ages the most eminint part of the Globe, as it was the only Passage by which the whole World could be surrounded, and that it was every Man's Honour that had pass'd it, as above; so now it is come to the full End or Period of its Fame . . .[2]

In this assessment of the strait's importance, Defoe underestimated the wonder of Drake's voyage both to Drake's countrymen and to the world at large. It was the second circumnavigation of the globe, and the first English voyage through the strait. With Drake Englishmen entered at last the magic world of the South Seas. As William Camden records, Drake was the first Englishman to cast eyes on the Pacific. It was this view of the South Sea from a treetop on the isthmus of Darien in 1573 which fired him with his ambition to sail an English ship into those seas.[3]

The saying that Drake "shot the gulf" derived from one of the many Drake legends. Southey gives one version of the story:

To sail round the world was in the popular belief an adventure of the most formidable kind, and not to be performed by plain sailing, but by reaching the end of this round flat earth, and there shooting the gulf, which is the only passage from one side of the world to the other: Drake shot the gulf, one day: when on the other side, he asked his men if any of them knew where they were, a boy made answer that he knew, and that they were then just under London Bridge: upon which, stung by jealousy, Drake exclaimed, "Has thou too a devil? If I let thee live there will then be one greater man than myself"; and with that he threw him overboard.[4]

In its original form the story probably turned on the fact that "shooting the bridge" was the greatest danger in London, and shooting the strait the greatest danger in the world.[5] In time the story was improved on, and when the custodian at Oxford showed visitors Drake's portrait, with Drake holding a pistol in one hand, he used to say that this was the very pistol with which Sir Francis shot the gulf.[6]

On emerging from the strait, Drake found within his grasp the treasures of the Pacific. Laden with gold and silver plundered from captured galleons and from the Spanish towns of Chile and Peru, with a cargo of cloves from the eastern seas besides, the *Golden Hind* arrived home in Plymouth Sound on September 26, 1580. On October 16 the Spanish ambassador in London reported anxiously to King Philip the Second that Drake was said to be projecting a new venture to the Indies, and that "there is hardly an Englishman who is not talking of undertaking the voyage, so encouraged are they by Drake's return."[7]

In Peru the viceroy had been precipitated into panic-stricken countermeasures. While Hakluyt was writing his pamphlet and a second on the same theme,[8] the Spanish navigator Pedro Sarmiento de Gamboa, on an expedition from Peru in 1579–1580, was exploring the strait in order to intercept Drake on his anticipated return, "it being the public fame that Francisco would return by the Strait, as he now knew where it was."[9] Sarmiento, at that time the best navigator in the South Sea, was also to make a careful survey of the strait to discover the best way of closing it against Spain's enemies. He proceeded to Spain with plans for fortifying the strait and settling a colony. Encouraged by his reports, King Philip in 1581 dispatched with Sarmiento's colonizing expedition a great fleet under Don Diego Flores de Valdes, whose orders were to intercept all foreigners venturing to the strait. "These ships had the hardest hap of any that euer went oute of Spaine since the Indias were first discouered," the Portuguese Lopez Vaz recorded in his discourse.[10] Compared with the misfortunes of the English voyages to the strait, the Spanish expedition "succeeded ten times worse."[11] Of twenty-three galleons and thirty-five hundred soldiers, few ships or men returned. This loss was seriously felt when two or three years later Spain was mustering her forces for the attack on England.

The colonies of Nombre de Jesus and Don Felipe which Sarmiento settled in 1584 on the shores of the strait fared no better. Left to fend for themselves, within three years their inhabitants had starved to death. The town of Don Felipe, represented under the grandiose title of Philippopolis on the engraving "Deliniatio Freti Magellanici," 1603 (Figure 19),[12] published in Levinus Hulsius's collection of travels, part 6, survived only as a place name on the map. As Port Famine, the name which Cavendish gave in 1587 to the ruins of the deserted settlement, it commemorated "the most unhappy and unfortunate expedition that ever the Spaniards undertook."[13]

Dangers true and false. The project of blocking the strait had proved to be misconceived. There was no part less than three miles in breadth. Visiting Port Famine with Narborough in 1670, Captain John Wood wrote of it:

in truth it was to little purpose we might as well say Dover Castle could hinder all ships from passing the Chanell for at ye 1st place the Straights are 6 Leagues over Mr Cavendish fired their unhabited houses and dig'd up 4 Great Guns out of the Ground which the Spaniard had hid there we could not finde that ever there was such a place Built.[14]

The colony had failed because the inhabitants had to contend with hostile Indians and a desolate environment. That a harbor so useful in providing wood, water, fishes, and fowls was named Port Famine seemed to Wood "contrary to the quality of it." The Spaniards need not have starved if only they had been more industrous, he thought, overlooking the fact that supplies adequate for victualing a ship are not necessarily enough to sustain a settlement.

The fate of Sarmiento's colony should have convinced Hakluyt that his own plan was impracticable, but he preferred to believe that God was "enemie to the Spaniards," that their attempt to block the strait had failed because "it was not Gods will so to haue it."[15] With this reassuring thought Hakluyt echoed the Spaniards' own forebodings about their expeditions to the strait. It seemed a place of ill omen, and had proved of little use to them. Magellan's discovery had been followed by Loaysa's disastrous voyage of 1525–1527, and many years passed before the strait was navigated again. By the middle of the sixteenth century there was a saying that the strait had closed up, and a superstition that

all who were principally concerned in the discovery of the South Sea, had come to an untimely end: Basco Nunez de Balboa was beheaded; Magalhanes was killed by infidels; Ruy Falero died raving; the Mariner De Lepe, who first discovered the Strait from the topmast, turned renegado, and became a Mahometan.[16]

Lopez Vaz wrote in similar terms, as Hakluyt records: "The seeking of these Streights of Magellan is so dangerous, and the voyage so troublesome, that it seemeth a matter almost impossible to be perfourmed, insomuch that for the space of thirty yeares no man made account thereof; untill of late . . . Francis Drake."[17] On Magellan's discovery Lopez Vaz commented: "This discovery was at the first thought very profitable unto the Spaniards, but of late it hath prooued very hurtfull unto them by meanes of certaine coasters which haue sayled the selfe same course."[18]

Figure 19. Map of the Strait of Magellan, showing the Spanish fortress established by Sarmiento in 1584; in Levinus Hulsius's Collection of Voyages, Theil VI (1603) (used by permission of the Trustees of the British Museum).

The Spaniards had established trade routes more practicable for regular navigation than Magellan's long and dangerous western passage from Europe to the Moluccas: from 1565 onwards the Manila galleons were plying regularly between Manila and the Mexican port of Acapulco. The Spanish settlements in the region of the river Plate communicated with Chile and Peru not through the Strait of Magellan, but by means of what the Spaniards called "a nearer way," up the river Plate and overland, as Narborough was to learn in 1670.[19] Their interests lay in closing the strait, and keeping their charts and rutters of navigation out of foreign hands. They hoped that ignorance of the navigation would deter foreigners from using the route.

As another device for discouraging intruders, the Spaniards circulated false reports and rumors — or so it was alleged. There was truth in the allegation, but there was also enough truth in some of the reports for the Spaniards to believe their own stories. Whereas adventurers of other nations often denied the reports and accused the Spaniards of duplicity, others — sometimes members of the same expedition — would return home confirming or embellishing the original tale.

These reports were designed to give the impression that malign forces beset the adventurer to the region of the strait. The most celebrated was the story brought home by Pigafetta, the Italian chronicler of Magellan's expedition, that while wintering in 1520 at Port St. Julian in Patagonia the Spaniards had encountered a race of giants. Later Spanish mapmakers depict the giants. On Diego Gutiérrez's map of America published in 1562, "Americae sive quartae orbis partis nova et exactissima descriptio" (Figure 20), two enormous Patagonians tower over a Spanish soldier in "Tierra de Patagones," "Gigantum Regio." The giants reappear in the journals of successive voyagers, including Drake and Cavendish. Drake's chaplain, Francis Fletcher, in his manuscript journal, describes the Patagonians as of gigantic proportions: "their hands like shoulders of Mutton their eares most Large & eyes in compass to a great hand bawle or Bal." Other eyewitness reports were more restrained. Winter writes: "Here I saw first this people which they call Geannts which indede be not so allthough beinge affarre off, through the greatness of their voice a man would think them so." Adding that those nearest "seemed to us rather to be deviles than men"[20] he provided a clue to the origin of the legend. The Patagonian, as Horace Walpole's "Mrs ———" declared in a satire on the giants, 1766, had proved to be "only a well made Man."[21] Hakluyt called the men Cavendish met "a kinde of gyants,"[22] because their feet were measured and found to be eighteen inches long. The English party must have measured their great skin shoes. "Patagones," the name which Magellan gave to the Patagonians, means "big feet." Sarmiento also called the Patagonians giants. He took one home as a present for King Philip the Second, and described the man's limbs as very large.[23] Measurements of dead Patagonians "foureteene spannes long" (equal to about eleven feet, three inches) were provided by Antonie Knivet, a sailor who visited Patagonia with Cavendish in 1591, was captured by the Portuguese, and lived for twelve years with the Indians in South America.[24]

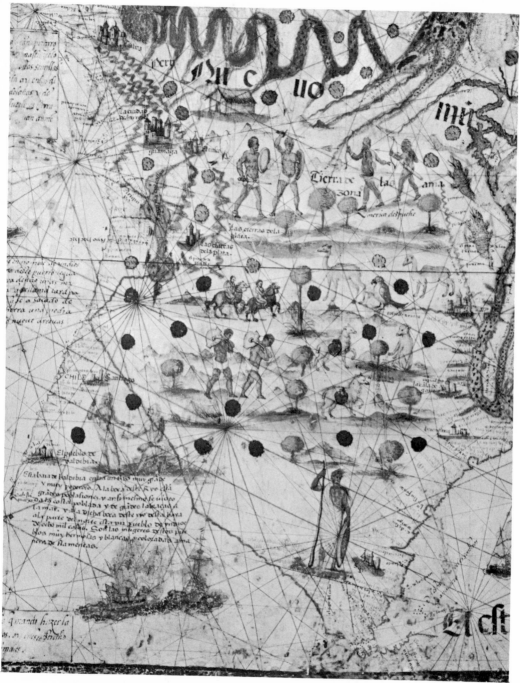

Figure 20. Patagonia and the Land of Magellan, in the map of America by
Diego Gutiérrez, engraved in 1562 (used by permission
of the Trustees of the British Museum).

That the strait was not repassable was another belief current for many years. Almost immediately after Magellan's voyage cartographers began to draw the strait as a passage between the continent of America and the southern continent. In suggesting that the strait was the only possible route round the world in the Southern Hemisphere, this delineation discouraged navigators from seeking other passages. It also deterred them from navigating the strait itself, since it provided what appeared to be a route of no return, requiring them to complete the circuit of the globe. For the Spaniards had put about the story (so we learn from the men on Drake's voyage) that a strong current, impelled by strong easterly winds, set westward through the strait, and that it was easy to sail from the Atlantic to the Pacific, but impossible to return. When Drake disproved this story, he and his men accused the Spaniards of abusing the world with untruths to prevent other nations venturing that way. They discovered that the current set eastward, not westward, and gained some indications that Tierra del Fuego, Magellan's "Land of Fire," was a group of islands. "Their is neither Continent current nor Streight," Fletcher wrote in retrospect, arguing that a strait was properly named as such only if it divided two continents.[25] On his map of Patagonia and the Strait of Magellan (Figure 21) he refers to the "Supposed Streights of Magilanus," and gives the group of islands replacing Tierra del Fuego the satirical name "Terra australis bene cognita."

The Spaniards themselves believed that the strait could not easily be passed from west to east. Because of the prevailing westerlies, the coast of Chile is a continual lee shore, Monson wrote, and "not to be enterprised without great peril." Sarmiento's instructions reveal the difficulties which the Spaniards anticipated. They believed that the western entrance to the strait was almost impossible to find from the Pacific side, "owing to the innumerable openings and channels which there are before arriving at it, where many discoverers had been lost . . ." Of those who entered the strait from the Atlantic "some were lost, and others returned, so tossed about by storms and uncertain of what could be discovered, that there was a general dread of that navigation."[26] Hakluyt claimed that Winter's return through the strait had proved the falsity of the Spanish reports; but Winter had not gone far enough out of the strait to lose the way back. At a ship's council at Guatulco, Peru, in April 1579, Drake invoked "the dangerous situation of the mouth of the streights in the South sea," as one of the two reasons why he should not return through the strait, but should proceed to the Moluccas.[27] Sent to dispel the Spaniards' "dread of the navigation" by surveying the strait, Sarmiento was the first to find and enter the western mouth of the strait on a voyage from Chile. His surveys made in 1580 might have restored the Spaniards' confidence in their ventures to the strait but for the disasters which befell the colonizing expedition. It was even claimed that in the misfortunes of his return voyage, which carried him as a prisoner to London in 1586, Sarmiento was suffering the punishment of God for the "ill usage" of his countrymen, in apparently abandoning the colonists to their fate.[28]

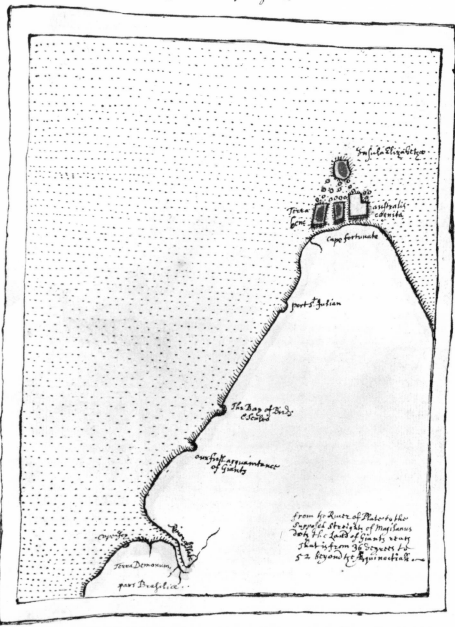

Figure 21. A sketch map of Patagonia and the "supposed Streighte" of Magellan, by Francis Fletcher, Drake's chaplain; from a copy of Fletcher's Journal of Drake's circumnavigation, made in 1680 by John Conyers, British Museum, Sloane MS 61; south is at the top (used by permission of the Trustees of the British Museum).

Drake's voyage exposed another supposed Spanish deception. The erroneous delineation of the west coast of South America on the maps of that time faced the navigator with imaginary dangers once he entered the Pacific and turned northwards up the coast. Some maps showed the coast with a northwest trend, while the best known, those of Mercator and Ortelius, displayed a large protuberance which navigators would have to negotiate almost as soon as they left the strait. Drake therefore intended to turn northwestward, but found that the coast trended northeast, as Fletcher explains:

wee following the directions of the comon Mapps of the Spanyards were vtterly deceaued for of a Malitious Purpose they had set forth the Mapp false that they might deceaue strangers if anny gaue the attempt to trauaile that way that they might perish by Running ofe to the Sea rather then Touch with anny part of the land of America . . .[29]

This distortion of the coastline, which was attributed either to a purpose to deceive, or to ignorant conjecture,[30] arose from a series of genuine errors, resulting from the difficulty of establishing longitude. To join the coast of Peru with the Strait of Magellan cartographers had to give the coastline of Chile and Peru a northwest trend such as appears on the map of America by Gutiérrez, 1562 (Figure 20). As the Spanish pilot Juan López de Velasco explained in his manuscript work, "Geografía y Descripción Universal de las Indias," written c.1575,[31] the Strait of Magellan was placed too far east of Panama. The whole of South America was about ten degrees of longitude too broad, as measured from Brazil to Peru. By the 1570s the Spaniards knew the true alignment of the west coast, as we can see from the maps which accompany López de Velasco's "Geografía." [32] Since Spanish maps and charts were still treated as state secrets, foreigners had to rely on printed maps of non-Spanish origin, notably those of Mercator and Ortelius. On these an additional error appeared in the form of the curious Chilean promontory, fully developed on Mercator's world chart of 1569, and followed by Ortelius on his world map published in the *Theatrum Orbis Terrarum*, 1570.[33] The feature had previously appeared in print on Gastaldi's world map, "Orbis descriptio," published in the 1561 edition of Ptolemy's *Geografia*. On this the western mouth of the Strait of Magellan lies some thirty degrees east of the main northward coastline of Chile and Peru, and the northwest-trending coast which links them is named, significantly, "Littus ignothum." This misconception about the direction of the coast seems to have originated in errors of compilation. Thus the manuscript world chart of Sancho Gutiérrez, Spanish Cosmographer Royal, 1551 (Figure 22), is marked with two coastlines for the west coast of South America.[34] One trends northeast from 280°E; the other bears northwest from the strait, from 305°E to 280°E, and then forms the Chilean promontory in 27°S. The map appears to represent a genuine attempt to put together material from diverse sources, with inaccurate and contradictory indications of longitude, or none at all.

The intrigues of the Spaniards and the real dangers besetting enterprises to the

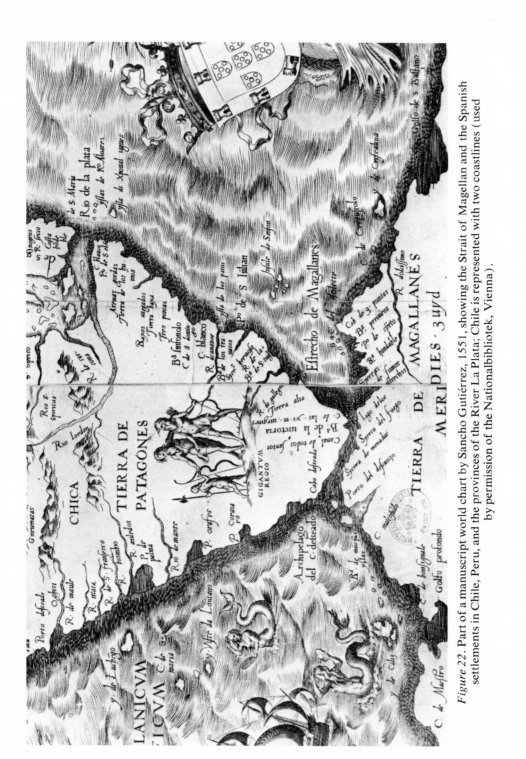

Figure 22. Part of a manuscript world chart by Sancho Gutiérrez, 1551, showing the Strait of Magellan and the Spanish settlements in Chile, Peru, and the provinces of the River La Plata; Chile is represented with two coastlines (used by permission of the Nationalbibliotek, Vienna).

strait gave the successes of Drake and Cavendish an added fame. To contemporary and later English writers it seemed that Divine Providence and native genius favored their countrymen. Cataloguing the failures and disasters of the Spaniards—and others —in their expeditions to the Strait of Magellan, the navigator Woodes Rogers in 1712 named those of Loaysa, Vargas, Cortes, Sebastian Cabot, Vespucci, and Simon Alcasara; the last three had failed to find the strait.[35] Woodes Rogers pointed in contrast to the triumphant performances of Drake and Cavendish. Other English expeditions had followed in the 1580's and 1590's: Fenton (1582), Floris (1582), the Earl of Cumberland (1586), Chidley (1589), Cavendish on his second voyage (1591), and Wood (1596). These voyages were failures, as Woodes Rogers admitted. The Spaniards' disasters in their attempts to block the strait which had seemed an encouragement to English enterprise should have been regarded as a warning. For the voyages of Hawkins in 1593 and John Davis in 1596 Woodes Rogers could claim only a partial success; but he summed up in favor of England's achievement: "so that our Countrymen, tho they did not all succeed in the Attempt, yet have been the most fortunate in passing them of any other Nation."

This was reminiscent of Hakluyt's verdict on the English enterprises to the strait. In the third volume of *The Principal Navigations* (1600) Hakluyt had published the journals of all the English voyages to the southern regions of America. He included not only those performed, but also those "intended," for much could be learnt from the account of unsuccessful voyages. For the same reason he also drew on reports of foreign voyages and other intelligence from foreign sources. Of these one of the most important was a rutter or set of sailing directions for the east coast of South America as far south as the strait. This rutter and the account of Drake's voyage were still in use when the South Sea projectors were putting forward their plans in 1709–1711. Hakluyt also encouraged the publication of Molyneux's globes, 1592, the first pair published in England and made by an Englishman. The terrestrial (Figure 23) displays the discoveries and tracks of Drake and Cavendish on their circumnavigations. In Chile and Peru the coastline and place names are evidently based on Spanish sources;[36] and the Strait of Magellan provides a record of Sarmiento's surveys and settlements, 1579–1584. The names Cabo de nombre de Iesus, Baia de gente grande, C. S. Vincent, S. Valentin, Bolecan deicae, Puerto Agosto, Puerto de la misericordia, and R. Hondo, are all recognizable forms of place names given by Sarmiento to features along the shores of the strait.[37] These names were presumably supplied by Sarmiento while he was Raleigh's honored guest during his imprisonment in London in the late summer of 1586. He gave Raleigh information about his discoveries, as we learn from the following anecdote told by Raleigh:

I remember a pretie jeast of Don Pedro de Sarmiento, a worthie Spanish Gentleman, who had beene emploied by his King in planting a Colonie vpon the Streights of Magellan: for when I asked him, being then my Prisoner, some question about an Iland in those streights, which me thought, might have done either benefit or displeas-

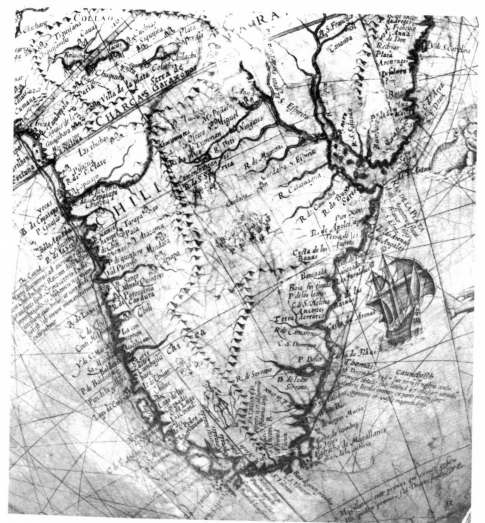

Figure 23. The southern extremity of South America, on the terrestrial globe of Emery Molyneux, 1592, revised in 1603, showing the tracks of Drake (1578) and Cavendish (1586–1587), and Sarmiento's discoveries (1579–1580); the photograph is taken from the revised edition, 1603, of which an example survives in the Library of the Middle Temple (used by permission of the Trustees of the British Museum).

ure to his enterprise, he told me merrily, that it was to bee called the *Painters wiues Iland*; saying, That whilest the fellow drew that Mappe, his wife sitting by, desired him to put in one Countrie for her; that shee, in imagination, might haue an Iland of her owne.[38]

On being captured at the Azores, Sarmiento had thrown his charts overboard, as a gesture of compliance to Spain's rigid policy of secrecy. Raleigh's anecdote gives a different picture of him. In London he seems to have been free with his maps and talk of his exploits. He did not lose the opportunity of promoting his reputation as an explorer. It is significant that he is named on the Molyneux globe as the discoverer of the Solomon Islands, to which he had sailed in 1568 as one of Mendaña's pilots. A man who boldly renames the Strait of Magellan in honor of his own expedition is obviously not backward in his claims.[39] As Peter Heylin said in 1652 of Sarmiento's jest, "I fear the Painters Wife hath many Ilands and some Countries too."[40]

Molyneux's collaborator, the mathematician Edward Wright, made further improvements in the delineation of the strait when he drew the map of the world (1599) for Hakluyt's *Principal Navigations* (1598–1600). By publishing such maps, globes, sailing directions, and journals, Hakluyt and his associates were trying to remedy what was (as the Spaniards intended it to be) one of the greatest obstacles to English enterprise overseas, ignorance of the navigation. Nowhere was this ignorance more serious than in the region of the strait. If the Spaniards dreaded the navigation, how much more daunting were the hazards to the English navigator lacking adequate charts and sailing directions. No wonder that when Spanish ships were captured, their pilots were impressed into service, and their charts were treated as a valuable prize. From the time of Magellan no Spanish fleet had made a successful voyage through the strait, and the Spaniards had had every reason to suppress the results of both successful and unsuccessful voyages. This explains why Drake and Winter carried with them as their main authority for the strait accounts of Magellan's voyage. On parting company from Drake and returning into the strait to wait for him, and then continue the voyage, Winter read Magellan's voyage to his crew, presumably from Willes's *History of Travayle* (1577), in order to encourage them to keep their course to the Moluccas.[41] A ship was in a particularly serious predicament if she separated from her "General." When John Davis lost the *Galeon* on Cavendish's second voyage in 1592, John Jane describes how Davis's skill in survey and navigation brought them safely back through the strait:

Our captaine, as wee first passed through the Streights drew such an exquisite plat of the same, as I am assured it cannot in any sort be bettered: which plat hee and the Master so often perused, and so carefully regarded, as that in memorie they had every turning and creeke, and in the deepe darke night without any doubting they conueyed the ship through that crooked chanell.[42]

The strait's "crooked channel" confronted the voyager with one of the most dangerous navigations in the world. Sailing from the Atlantic, a ship had to make her way in the face of the westerlies and of strong eastward-flowing currents. She met these in full strength after turning Cape Froward and entering the western reaches. The narrows allowed no room for maneuver. Many days had to be spent at anchor in exposed harbors, waiting for a favorable wind. This tedious passage followed a navigation of four months (or more) from Europe to the strait. If, through starting too late in the summer, an expedition had to winter on the bleak Patagonian coast, they might enter the strait after a full year's voyaging, as Magellan's did. Although Richard Hawkins maintained that the strait could be navigated all the year long,[43] the westward passage was really only practicable in the summer months, November, December, and January, when the westerlies had abated. The delays of wintering or of sheltering in the strait strained the tempers of the crew to the utmost.

At such a point the vital issue of all exploring voyages was raised: could a commander force his men to go on against their will? What authority could he invoke against a recalcitrant crew? The commander sailing under royal orders was in a stronger position than a merchant captain engaged in private enterprise, whose men had the right to refuse to continue a voyage which would endanger their lives.[44] Hence Drake's advantage in sailing (as he claimed) with the queen's sword and her mandate for its use: "We doe account that he which striketh at thee Drake striketh at us."[45]

The lawyer and author John Rastell, who was forced to turn back to Ireland when bent on a voyage of discovery to America in 1517, complained that English venturers:

> Haue cause to curse their maryners
> Fals of promys and dissemblers
> That falsly them be trayed
> which wolde take no paine to saile farther
> Than their owne lyst and pleasure
> wherefore that vyage and dyuers other
> Such kaytyffes haue distroyed

But for this, Englishmen might have been the chief discoverers of the New World.[46] Always conscious of this danger, a commander dared not overlook the slightest signs of rebellion on the part of officers and men. It was not a coincidence that Port San Julian, the last harbor for refuge and wintering before the eastern entrance to the strait was reached, was the scene of two alleged mutinies and of two acts of summary execution, by Magellan and Drake, providing "a new paire of paralells, to be added to Plutarchs."[47] When Wood visited the port in 1670 this grim fact was recalled.[48] To Lopez Vaz it seemed an accursed place.[49]

Richard Hawkins's prescription for carrying the men with him was the maintenance of iron discipline. In his *Observations* (1622), describing his voyage through the strait and into the South Sea in 1593, he advised commanders "that they goe not one foote backe, more then is of mere force; for I haue not seene, that any who haue yeelded therevnto, but presently they haue returned home."[50] He warned them against the "contradictions and murmurs of their owne people, of all calamities the greatest which can befall a man of discretion and valour, and as difficult to be overcome; for, to require reason of the common sort, is . . . To seeke Counsell of a madd man. Herein . . . they resemble a stiffe necked Horse." [51]

Winter was one of those who yielded, forced to turn back in 1579 by his rebellious master. "Callinge my whole companie together," he writes in his journal, "I made my determinaton generallie knowne, wch was for the east pte of the wourld . . . but all was in vaine for the Mr did utterlie dislike of yt." [52] By threatening to throw himself overboard the master had caused a general dislike of the voyage; and Winter had to give up his plan of making for the Moluccas and return home. Hawkins made himself "deafe to all murmurings." In the strait he kept his men occupied with training, hurling matches, wrestling, and other pursuits, so they were never idle. This diverted their minds from the "imagination" they had conceived, of returning to, and wintering in, Brazil. In 1669–1670 Narborough was to maintain the morale of his crew by observing strictly the rule of fair shares: the man who served the meat to all the officers and men was blindfolded. Dangers also were shared. Narborough promised to expose no man to more danger than he faced himself, and he held up Drake's success as an example: "Captain Drake went round the World in one Ship, when in those days there were but ordinary Navigators; and was it for us to question our good fortune, who beyond Comparison are better Seamen . . ." [53]

Narborough's survey and proposals for trade. Narborough's voyage followed more than seventy years of inactivity. For although Hawkins emerged from the strait, he suffered defeat on June 22, 1594, at the hands of the Spaniards off the coast of Peru, and he returned home after eight years in Spanish prisons. For this disaster Monson was to blame Drake and Cavendish, the first Pacific pirates. Sailing without enough force to challenge Spanish power effectively, they had set the Spaniards on the alert: "we have now discovered to the Spaniards our finding the way through the Straits of Magellan, which they thought to conceal from us; we have passed by the coast of Chile and Peru up to Panama . . . Thus have we warned, without annoying them, to strengthen themselves in those parts." [54]

In 1614 Sir James Lancaster planned an East India Company voyage to the Strait of Magellan, and thence to the Solomon Islands, and Hawkins was recommended for the command as having the "courage, art and knowledge to attempt such an enterprise," [55] but nothing came of it. The English East India Company was now challenging the Portuguese monopoly of the true route to the East, the passage by way of the Cape of Good Hope, which Monson recommended. This eastern trade and the attack on the Spanish treasure ships in the Atlantic were the chief preoccupations of Englishmen engaged in maritime enterprise until 1669, when Narborough and Wood sailed under orders from Matthew Wren, secretary to the Duke of York.

Their voyage was impelled by a new motive, the desire to tap the gold of Spanish America at its source, instead of the plundering of treasure ships. It was an American

Figure 24. John Narborough's manuscript chart of the Strait of Magellan, 1670 (western half only), with a description of the Patagonians; British Museum, K.Top.CXXIV.84; south is at the top (used by permission of the Trustees of the British Museum).

voyage. Passing through the strait into the Pacific and returning the same way, Narborough was the first to sail to Chile and back. The strait was the back door to America; the voyage was a reconnaissance for establishing trade with the Chilean Indians. Narborough brought home a meticulous survey of the strait, drawn on a large manuscript chart of 1670 (Figure 24). This displayed many details of topography and hydrography, as well as of the customs and characteristics of the inhabitants, on which Narborough had been ordered to make careful observations. An engraved map compiled from these surveys by John Thornton and James Atkinson was published in 1673; and Narborough's journal, illustrated by a similar but newly engraved map, was included in *An Account of Several Late Voyages & Discoveries* (1694). This remained for many years the standard guide to the strait.

Narborough also settled some of the doubtful points raised by the Spaniards. He reported the Patagonians to be "of a Medle Stature not taler than Generally English men are." [56] Wood wrote similarly: "they were Very Well sett Men of noe such Exterordenary Stature as is reported by Magellanes & other Spaniards . . . but I suppose they did inmaging none would come here to disprove them." [57] The voyage proved that it was possible to re-enter the strait. Narborough was the first, as Edward

[211]

Cooke noted in 1712, "to pass clear away, and repass"; [58] and he provided instructions to the inexperienced navigator for this difficult maneuver. "A Stranger that should pass out of the South-sea, and had not passed the Streights before, will find it very difficult to pass the Streights from the West to the East; for at the first entring . . . there are many Openings and Sounds on the North-side, which seem fairer for a passage than the Streight it self doth." [59] He advised the navigator to keep to the south side, and sail east from Cape Pillar. The usefulness of his directions and map is clear from the fact that the volume of discoveries was reprinted in 1711, when South Sea projectors were again active. Writers of that time, such as Cooke, Woodes Rogers, and, later, Daniel Defoe, spared themselves the description of the strait, referring their readers to Narborough's account.

Narborough also devised a plan for the development of English commerce, in the opinion "that the most advantageous Trade in the World, might be made in these parts, if it were but follow'd, and that leave were granted by the King of Spain . . ." [60] Finding that the inhabitants of the Chilean and Peruvian coasts were eager for trade, but that the local Spanish governors dared not permit it without orders, he recommended that ships should trade by force; this could easily be done by squadrons of four ships of twenty or thirty pieces of ordnance a ship.

Although Narborough did not succeed in opening up commerce in South America, his transactions were seen by Anson in 1740 as "rather an encouragement for future trials of this kind, than any objection against them." [61] Meanwhile, a later expedition had made a voyage similar to Narborough's, but remained so little known that when Woodes Rogers and Cooke sailed round Cape Horn in 1709, they wrongly believed that Narborough had been the last Englishman to pass through the strait, and the last navigator of any nation to pass and repass. In 1689–1690 Captain John Strong in the *Welfare* had made a voyage to the South Seas, bearing letters of marque for seizing French ships. He sailed from the Falkland Islands through the strait to Juan Fernandez, and returned through the strait. The astronomer Edmund Halley commended as "very well kept" the "exact journall of his proceedings" which Strong was enjoined to keep as a condition of his carrying letters of marque.[62] With the journal of Richard Simson,[63] it provided eloquent testimony of the difficulties of the strait's navigation. The westward passage, begun on February 10, 1690, lasted three months and twelve days. Simson advised accordingly that no one should attempt the passage in winter. The return passage took only seven days, during four of which the ship was at anchor in Batchelors Bay refitting with wood and water. Strong described the strait's assets and defects in these few words: "There is no want of water and wood nor cold and snow. These are ye Countries Commoditys." [64] With Drake's experience in mind Simson describes the navigation:

Returne we then to the Straits of Magelon where the first thing observable was a certain imperious Current or Tide in ye Narrows, not farr from the Entrance of the said

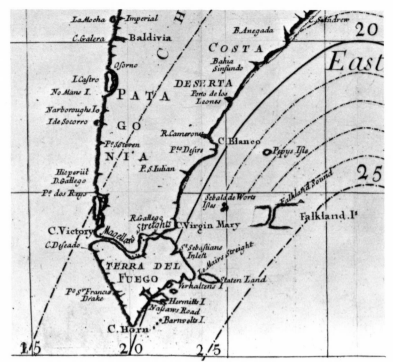

Figure 25. The southern extremity of South America, in Edmund Halley's world chart of magnetic variation, 1702 (used by permission of the Trustees of the British Museum).

Straits, Comonly called the Gulph: Hence the Uular [vulgar] tell us that S^r. ffrancis Drake shott the Gulph, that was the passage he made to the South Seas . . .[65]

On extricating themselves from the dangers of the current, Simson added: "If it had otherwise happen'd we had shott two Gulphs at once, viz. S^r. ffrancis Drakes and Charons."[66] Although Strong captured rich prizes, the promoters lost over £12,000 on the voyage. A remark in Simson's journal about the loss and "Doctor Ratcliffs share (which was one)," reveals that this was the voyage on which Dr. John Radcliffe, the fashionable Oxford physician and benefactor, lost £7,000.[67]

The accounts of this voyage remained in manuscript. To the fact that Edmund Halley secured a copy of Strong's journal and added information from it to his magnetic map of the world the Falkland Islands owe their name (see Figure 25). Robert Harley, First Earl of Oxford, who, as Lord Treasurer 1711–1714, was promoter of the South Sea enterprises, also possessed a copy.[68] To those who knew of it, Strong's navigation through the strait must have seemed merely a postscript to the closing chapter of the strait's history. In *A New Voyage* Defoe wrote critically even of the account of Narborough's voyage, describing it as

adorn'd with I know not how many Charts of the famous Streight of Magellan, a place only now famous for showing the Ignorance of Sir John Narborough, and a great many wise Gentlemen before him, and for being a Passage they had no need to have troubled themselves with, and which no Body will ever go through any more.[69]

For when at last one of the most serious problems of the navigation had been solved by the provision of a detailed survey of the strait, the solution seemed no longer relevant. Discovered by the Dutch in 1616, Cape Horn had superseded the strait as the gateway to the Pacific. After sailing round Cape Horn in 1709, Woodes Rogers and Cooke declared it far safer than the strait.[70] They doubted that the strait would be used again, and saw it as already abandoned. Defoe could envisage its further use only if that part of the world should come to be fully inhabited, an improbable contingency, conceivable only if God altered the situation of the globe so that the climates changed, or if a new species of mankind could be produced which could live in the frozen zone.[71] In the *Atlas Maritimus & Commercialis* (1728), of which he was the anonymous author,[72] he described the strait as "a Place, which may perhaps be as entirely forgotten in the World, as if it had never been known." [73]

A place to be forgotten. In the 1680's and 1690's when the South Sea buccaneers were in their heyday, the passage round Cape Horn was followed by navigators who were free to choose their route. "Our Men being Privateers, and so more wilfull, and less under Command, would not be so ready to give a watchful Attendance in a Passage so little known . . . I could not expect to find them at a Minute's call in coming to an Anchor, or weighing an Anchor." [74] Thus Dampier at the Sebald de Weerts Islands on January 28, 1684, persuaded Captain John Cooke and his company of privateers to make for Juan Fernandez by the cape route instead of through the strait. Bartholomew Sharp had already made the passage from west to east, sailing far out of sight of land and discovering what he claimed was a new route. He refers to this achievement in the legend on the manuscript chart of the strait and Cape Horn drawn by William Hack in the "Wagoner of the Great South Sea," 1682 (Figure 26). The whole passage from the island of La Plata to the West Indies had taken the record time of five and a half months. The advantage of the cape route lay in the speed of the navigation and the room for maneuver. Beset by storms and westerly winds, the passage had its difficulties and dangers, as Defoe pointed out in the *Atlas Maritimus.*[75] It was not well charted: "this being a new-discover'd Passage, we have no printed Books, Waggoners or Pilots for the Sailors Direction." Thus one of the charts used for many years, carried by Woodes Rogers and Cooke in 1708 and by Anson in 1740, was Halley's magnetic map of the world, 1702 (Figure 25).[76] Defoe could claim that despite these difficulties no ship had yet miscarried on the route round Cape Horn, in striking contrast to that round the Cape of Good Hope.

The problem of the long lines of communication remained unsolved. Freebooters moving from one American base to another were a law unto themselves. Regular traders needed established ports of call, especially if they came from Europe, and if, as Narborough prescribed, they were armed squadrons trading by force. Various ex-

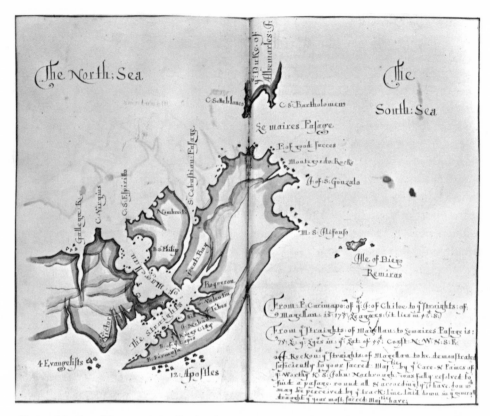

The North: Sea.

The South: Sea.

Figure 26. Cape Horn and the Strait of Magellan, in a manuscript chart by William Hack, to illustrate Bartholomew Sharp's discovery of a route eastward round the cape in 1681–1682, in Sharp's "Wagoner of the Great South Sea," 1682, British Museum, K.Mar.VIII.15 (used by permission of the Trustees of the British Museum).

peditions had made isolated acts of possession in the Strait of Magellan. In 1579 Winter had engraved Queen Elizabeth's name on a mountain of Tierra del Fuego, and he reported his act of possession in the straits to Samuel Purchas in 1618.[77] Narborough and Wood took possession of Port Desire and both shores of the strait on March 25, 1670, and recorded this fact on their manuscript chart of the Strait of Magellan (Figure 24).

In 1690 Strong's men set up an inscription on the top of a hill near Port Falkland, as they named their refuge in the strait. They also tried to win over the inhabitants, for those unhappy peoples, Simson wrote, "sat not very easy under their present Masters, who had proscribed so greate a number of them to so frightfull and cold mansions as the Straits . . ."; and Simson further suggested that "if ever a Change should happen, the English Crown might bid fair for the possession of America." [78]

On their return, Strong's men found that the inscription had been taken down, "by that small disseruice signifying they would have done us more if it had lyen in their power." [79] This was a warning of what difficulties lay in store for those attempting to establish alliance with the inhabitants of the strait.

Settlements in the strait would presuppose its continued use. With the revival of plans for South Sea trade in 1711 a different project of settlement was envisaged. Men such as Cooke, Woodes Rogers, and the London merchant Thomas Bowrey offered advice to Robert Harley, the Lord Treasurer, promoter of the South Sea project, recommending ports of call which allowed the use either of the cape or the strait. From the information provided by Hakluyt's rutter and the account of Drake's voyage (for lack of anything better), Bowrey proposed a settlement on the Atlantic coast of South America in 39°S at Anegada Bay.[80] On the Pacific coast he chose Valdivia, as the nearest port of trade to the Strait of Magellan, "and consequently nearest to us." [81] With a sufficient force the British should be able to capture this city, said to be the richest in the universe.[82] From June 1711 onwards Defoe also offered advice to Harley, proposing an even more ambitious plan for a British plantation in Chile with its capital at Valdivia, and a second British settlement between Rio de la Plata and the strait. The two colonies would be linked not only by the sea route through the strait, but also overland.[83]

Nothing came of these plans. No English seamen other than the pirate circumnavigators John Clipperton and George Shelvocke (1718–1719) ventured to these regions until 1741 when Anson made his tempestuous voyage round the cape. The lessons of that voyage produced a new formulation of the plans for settlement. Anson proposed the establishment of bases not on the continent but on the island outposts, at the Falkland Islands and Juan Fernandez. The Earl of Egmont, First Lord of the Admiralty, took this up in 1765, and a settlement was made at the Falkland Islands, "the key to the whole Pacifick Ocean." [84]

Thus Hakluyt's scheme was put into effect, belatedly, and in a modified form. For nearly two hundred years Englishmen had frequented the desolate lands and seas in the vicinity of the Strait of Magellan. That their more ambitious schemes had remained on paper is explained by the dictum quoted by Defoe that it is better to sail a thousand leagues round the Cape of Good Hope than a hundred in constant war with the elements, storms, ice, and unknown shores.[85] To understand why so many voyages were made, we need the eyes of Hakluyt, Drake, or Raleigh. We must see with their vision Tierra del Fuego and Gigantum Regio, the Land of Fire and the Land of Giants, with its tempestuous strait:

> Nor Southerne heate, nor Northerne snow
> That freezing to the ground doth grow,
> The subject Regions can fence,
> And keepe the greedie Merchant thence.
> The subtile Shipmen way will finde,
> Storme neuer so the Seas with winde.[86]

page 195

[1] "Inuentio Maris Magallanici," in Theodore de Bry, *Americae Pars Quarta*, Frankfort, 1594, pl. XV.

page 196

[2] [Daniel Defoe], *A New Voyage round the World*, London, 1725, pp. 16–17.

[3] William Camden, *Annales Rerum Anglicarum et Hibernicarum, Regnante Elizabetha, ad Annum Salutis M.D. LXXXIX*, vol. 1, London, 1615, p. 302.

page 197

[4] Robert Southey, *Lives of the British Admirals*, London, 1834, pp. 239–240.

[5] In another version, the incidents of "shooting the gulf" and of the boy being thrown overboard are two separate stories. To the question "Where are we?," the boy replied that they were at the antipodes of London Bridge, whereupon Drake threw him overboard to rid himself of a rival. Mrs. Anne E. Bray, *The Borders of the Tamar and the Tavy*, vol. 2, London, 1879, pp. 32–33. Again there is a grain of sense in the story, since London Bridge and the western mouth of the strait both lie near latitude 52 degrees, north and south, respectively, though they are not antipodes.

[6] So Mr. Davies Gilbert of Devon reported to Mrs. Bray (*ibid.*, p. 31). Bodley's librarian agrees that this story must turn on a confusion over the identity of the full-length portrait of Sir Martin Frobisher holding a pistol, presented to the Bodleian Library in 1674. For some unknown reason, the part of the inscription giving Frobisher's name had been painted over, and has only recently been revealed by cleaning, although the portrait was traditionally identified as Frobisher's. Bodley's librarian reports that as far as he knows the Bodleian Library has never possessed a portrait of Drake holding a pistol.

[7] B.M. Add. MS 28420, fol. 31r. Printed in translation in *Calendar of Letters and State Papers Relating to English Affairs, Preserved Principally in the Archives of Simancas, Vol. III, Elizabeth. 1580–1586*, London, 1896, pp. 55–56.

[8] A note written in 1580, beginning, "Ye commodity of taking ye straightes of Magellanus," in which Hakluyt offered to present the project himself to Don Antonio, Pretender to the throne of Portugal, now united with Spain. *The Original Writings & Correspondence of the Two Richard Hakluyts*, ed. E. G. R. Taylor, vol. 1, London, 1935, pp. 163–164.

[9] *Narratives of the Voyages of Pedro Sarmiento de Gamboa to the Straits of Magellan*, ed. C. R. Markham, London, 1895, p. 4. The draft plan of Drake's voyage envisaged Drake going and returning by way of the strait. E. G. R. Taylor, "The Missing Draft Project of Drake's Voyage of 1577–80," *Geographical Journal*, vol. 75, London, 1930, p. 46; and "More Light on Drake 1577–80," *The Mariner's Mirror*, vol. 16, London, 1930, pp. 134–135.

[10] Lopez Vaz in Richard Hakluyt, *The Principal Navigations . . . of the English Nation*, vol. 3, London, 1600, p. 794.

[11] Sir William Monson, expressing the views of the Spaniards themselves and of others, *The Naval Tracts of Sir William Monson*, ed. M. Oppenheim, vol. 4, London, 1913, p. 191.

page 198

[12] Levinus Hulsius, [Collection of Voyages and Travels] *Sechste Theil, Kurtze Warhafftige Relation und beschreibung der Wunderbarsten vier Schiffarten so jemals verricht worden*, 1603, Nuremberg, pl. 24.

[13] Monson, *op. cit.*, vol. 4, p. 191.

[14] Wood's journal, B.M. MS Sloane 46B, fol. 180v.

[15] Hakluyt, *op. cit.*, vol. 3, 1600, p. 806.

[16] James Burney, *A Chronological History of the Discoveries in the South Sea or Pacific Ocean*, vol. 1, London, 1803, p. 245.

[17] Hakluyt, *op. cit.*, vol. 3, 1600, p. 791.

[18] *Ibid.*, p. 789.

page 200

[19] *An Account of Several Late Voyages & Discoveries to the South and North, Towards the Streights of Magellan, the South Seas . . . By Sir John Narborough, Captain Jasmen Tasman, Captain John Wood . . .*, London, 1694, p. 20. (Hereafter cited as Narborough.)

[20] B.M. Lansdowne MS 100, fol. 19r. Taylor, *Mariner's Mirror*, vol. 16, 1930, pp. 148–149.

[21] S.T. (i.e., Horace Walpole), *An Account*

of the Giants Lately Discovered; in a Letter to a Friend in the Country, London, 1766, p. 4.

[22] Hakluyt, *op. cit.*, vol. 3, 1600, p. 805.

[23] Markham, *op. cit.*, p. 136. For comments on the legend, see Percy G. Adams, *Travelers and Travel Liars 1660–1800*, Berkeley and Los Angeles, 1962, pp. 19–43.

[24] Samuel Purchas, *Purchas His Pilgrimes*, part 4, London, 1625, lib. vi, p. 1232.

page 202

[25] Sir Francis Drake (the younger), *The World Encompassed*, London, 1628, p. 44. This work was based on Fletcher's manuscript notes. See Fletcher's manuscript printed in *The World Encompassed . . . with an Appreciation of the Achievement; by Sir Richard Carnac Temple*, ed. N. M. Penzer, London, 1926, pp. 136–137.

The manuscript was probably completed not long before 1628, when *The World Encompassed* was published. Various English authors writing about Drake's voyage after the discovery of Cape Horn in 1616 implied that Drake had discovered the insular character of Tierra del Fuego and even Cape Horn itself. Although some earlier maps, such as Jodocus Hondius's map of Drake's voyage published *c.* 1593, and Edward Wright's world map, 1599, show Tierra del Fuego as a group of islands, the discovery of islands south of the strait was only partly understood, and did not become well known.

[26] Markham, *op. cit.*, p. 4.

[27] "The famous voyage of Sir Francis Drake," Hakluyt, *op. cit.*, vol. 3, 1600, p. 736.

[28] Monson, *op. cit.*, vol. 4, p. 192.

page 204

[29] Penzer, *op. cit.*, p. 132.

[30] According to the author of the compilation "The Famous Voyage" inserted in Hakluyt, *The Principall Nauigations, Voiages and Discoueries of the English Nation . . .*, London, 1589; see H. R. Wagner, *Sir Francis Drake's Voyage around the World . . .*, San Francisco, 1926, p. 264.

[31] This work was not published until 1894: Juan López de Velasco, *Geografía y descripción universal de las Indias*, Madrid, 1894, p. 541.

[32] López de Velasco's maps were published by Antonio de Herrera Tordesillas in his *De-*

scripción de las Indias occidentales, Madrid, 1601. For a reproduction of the manuscript map of the Pacific, see L. C. Wroth, *The Early Cartography of the Pacific, The Papers of the Bibliographical Society of America*, vol. 38, no. 2, New York, 1944, pl. XII.

[33] Mercator's world map of 1538 shows no sign of the promontory, but there is a slight indication of it on his terrestrial globe of 1541. Ortelius's world map of 1564 shows a northwest-trending coastline.

[34] This chart by Sancho Gutiérrez, the father of Diego, is preserved in the Nationalbibliotek, Vienna.

page 206

[35] Woodes Rogers, *A Cruising Voyage round the World*, London, 1712, pp. 111–114.

[36] One of these sources may be an English copy (made in about 1587) of a Spanish chart captured by Cavendish, to which his discoveries were added. It later found its way to the Netherlands, where it is now in the Algemeen Rijksarchief, The Hague, MS Leupe no. 733.

[37] The globe was copied by Peter Plancius on his map of South America, *c.*1593, on which Sarmiento's names appear.

page 208

[38] Walter Raleigh, *The History of the World*, vol. 1, London, 1614, p. 574.

[39] Sarmiento renamed the strait in February 1580 as the strait of Madre de Dios. He had taken the mother of God as patron of his voyage to the strait. Markham, *op. cit.*, pp. 129, 133–134.

[40] Peter Heylyn, *Cosmographie in Four Bookes, Containing the Chorographie and Historie of the Whole World . . .*, London, 1652, book 4, p. 196.

[41] B.M. Lansdowne MS 100, fol. 20r. See Taylor, *Mariner's Mirror*, vol. 16, p. 138. This is evidence that Winter was not intending to desert. Drake's text of Magellan's voyage was probably a Latin edition of Maximilian of Transylvanus's letter, *De Moluccis Insulis*. See Wagner, *op. cit.*, pp. 41, 461.

[42] Hakluyt, *Principal Navigations*, vol. 3, 1600, p. 849.

page 209

[43] Richard Hawkins, *The Observations of Sir Richard Hawkins*, London, 1622, p. 95.

[44] This was in accordance with the Maritime Laws of Rhodes and Oleron.

[45] Drake, *op. cit.*, p. 31.

[46] John Rastell, *A New Interlude and a Mery of the Nature of the iiii Elements*, London, c.1520?, sig. c. iv.

[47] Drake, *op. cit.*, p. 33.

[48] B.M. MS Sloane 46B, fol. 154.

[49] Lopez Vaz in Hakluyt, *op. cit.*, vol. 3, 1600, p. 791.

[50] Hawkins, *op. cit.*, p. 85.

page 210

[51] *Ibid.*, p. 91.

[52] B.M. Lansdowne MS 100, fol. 20r; Taylor, *Mariner's Mirror*, vol. 16, p. 150.

[53] Narborough, *op. cit.*, p. 43.

[54] Monson, *op. cit.*, vol. 2, 1902, p. 239.

[55] *Calendar of State Papers, Colonial Series. East Indies, China and Japan, 1513–1616*, London, 1862, East Indies, pp. 288–289, doc. 706, pp. 290–291, doc. 711.

page 211

[56] From the legend on Narborough's chart, Figure 24.

[57] Wood's journal, B.M. MS Sloane 3833, fol. 20r.

page 212

[58] Edward Cooke, *A Voyage to the South Sea, and round the World, Perform'd in the Years 1708, 1709, 1710 and 1711*, London, 1712, vol. 1, p. 40.

[59] Narborough, *op. cit.*, p. 117.

[60] *Ibid.*, p. 110.

[61] Richard Walter, *A Voyage round the World . . . by George Anson*, London, 1748, p. 93.

[62] E. Halley, "Some Remarks on the Variations of the Magnetical Compass . . .," *Philosophical Transactions*, vol. 29, 1717, p. 168. There are two copies of Strong's journal in the British Museum: Harleian MS 5101 and MS Sloane 3295.

[63] Written by order of Charles Bodvile Robartes, 2nd Earl of Radnor, B.M. MS Sloane 86.

[64] B.M. MS Sloane 3295, fol. 30r.

page 213

[65] B.M. MS Sloane 86, fol. 5r.

[66] B.M. MS Sloane 86, fol. 5v.

[67] Dr. Radcliffe received the news while drinking with friends at the Bull-Head Tavern in Clare Market. When they consoled with him on account of his loss, "without baulking his Glass, with a smiling Countenance, he desir'd them to go forward with the Healths that were then in Vogue, saying, That he had no more to do, but to go up 250 Pair of Stairs to make himself whole again." [William Pittis], *Dr. Radcliffe's Life and Letters*, London, 1716, pp. 22–23.

[68] B.M. Harleian MS 5101.

page 214

[69] Defoe, *op. cit.*, p. 3.

[70] Woodes Rogers, *op. cit.*, p. 116. Cooke, *op. cit.*, vol. 1, p. 48.

[71] Defoe, *op. cit.*, p. 17.

[72] See J. R. Moore, "The Canon of Defoe's Writings," *The Library*, 5th series, vol. 11, London, 1956, pp. 167–169.

[73] Defoe, *Atlas Maritimus & Commercialis*, London, 1728, p. 316.

[74] William Dampier, "A New Voyage round the World," *A Collection of Voyages*, vol. 1, London, 1729, pp. 80–81.

[75] Defoe, *Atlas Maritimus*, 1728, p. 316.

[76] Halley's magnetic map was for many years a subject of discussion in books and periodicals, notably on the question of the longitude and configuration of the extremity of South America. For the Strait of Magellan Halley's main authorities were the observations of Captain John Wood, 1670, and Captain Strong, 1690. See Halley, *op. cit.*, p. 168. Halley placed the strait about seven degrees too far west, and this pulled the southern extremity of the continent out of shape.

page 215

[77] Purchas, *op. cit.*, part 1, lib. ii, p. 50.

[78] Simson, B.M. MS Sloane 86, fol. 8r.

[79] *Ibid.*, fol. 13r.

page 216

[80] B.M. Add. MS 28,140, fol. 31v. Bowrey's proposals form part of "An Essay on the Nature and Methods of carrying on a Trade to the South Sea," B.M. Add. MS 28,140, fol. 20r–33v.

[81] B.M. Add. MS 28,140, fol. 31r. Guildhall Library, Bowrey papers, MS 3041/2.

[82] Defoe in the *Atlas Maritimus*, p. 319, cites this statement by "one of our Geographers."

[83] J. R. Moore, "Defoe and the South Sea Company," *The Boston Public Library Quarterly*, vol. 5, Boston, 1953, pp. 175–188.

[84] A memorandum by the Earl of Egmont, July 20, 1765, P.R.O., S.P. 94/253, f. 238.

[85] Defoe, *Atlas Maritimus*, p. 280, quoting a comment of Captain Adams on the search in arctic regions for the northwest passage to Asia.

[86] Raleigh, *op. cit.*, p. 574.

De Lozier Bouvet and Mercantilist
Expansion in the Pacific in 1740

by O. H. K. SPATE

I T IS NO disparagement of the transcendent achievement of Cook to point out that the essentials of his plan for the great second voyage (1772–1775) were very clearly foreshadowed in the memoranda addressed, thirty years earlier, by De Lozier Bouvet to the Compagnie des Indes and to the minister of marine, Maurepas. It is true that Bouvet's theory seems prescientific compared with Cook's: he believed not only in Terra Australis, but even in the fantasy of Gonneville's Land; and, like his contemporaries, he confused Quiros's "Austrialia," really the New Hebrides but transferred to what is now northeast Queensland, with the Terra Australis of the old geographers. But if his strategy, as it were, was theoretically ill-founded, his tactics — his actual sailing plans — were as thorough and as seamanlike as Cook's. As for motives, his manifesto of course mentions *la gloire*, the advancement of learning, and the spread of true religion (in that order), but it is abundantly clear that his project was mainly intended as a masterstroke in Franco-British or Franco-Dutch rivalry for the Eastern trade. Since the James Ford Bell Collection is essentially devoted to the history of commerce, I propose to concentrate mainly on this trading aspect, with but secondary reference to the matter of Bouvet as a precursor of Cook, fascinating as that is.

Jean-Baptiste-Charles Bouvet de Lozier (he always signs De Lozier Bouvet) was born in 1705 or 1706, and after nine years in the merchant service (based on St. Malo) joined that of the Compagnie des Indes in 1731. In 1733, and again in 1735 and 1737, he presented memorials to the Compagnie proposing a search for a base somewhere between Senegal and the Indian Ocean islands of Bourbon (now Réunion, French since 1643) and Île de France (Mauritius) which, abandoned by the Dutch in 1710, had been claimed by France in 1715 and settled by the Compagnie in 1722.

The way stations of any known value on this long stretch were all, from a French standpoint, in hands actually or potentially hostile: St. Helena had long been British, the Dutch were solidly based at the Cape; while as for Brazil, Portugal was a British client and in any case the local officials harbored lively memories of French encroachments and aggressions, which in Rio de Janeiro itself stretched as far back as Ville-

NOTES for *De Lozier Bouvet and Mercantilist Expansion in the Pacific in 1740* are to be found on pages 235 to 237.

gagnon in 1559 and as far forward as Duguay-Trouin's successful attack in 1711. The Compagnie had considered Martin Vaz in 1730 and Ascension in 1734, but these were small and uninviting, and an expedition by two frigates to the coast of Kaffraria in 1732 produced no results. Fernando de Noronha was actually occupied, under the name of Île Dauphine, in 1734; but on second thoughts the Compagnie decided that it was near enough to Brazil to be offensive and — what is more — vulnerable, and indeed the Portuguese dislodged the few unresisting occupants in 1737. The Île de Saxembourg was also thought of, but as this does not exist it need not detain us.[1]

There remained — Terra Australis; or, more specifically, the land discovered in 1503 by the Norman Sieur de Gonneville, which haunted the imaginations of French sailors and scholars for a century and a half. Unfortunately, on his way back to France, Gonneville had fallen into the hands of an English pirate off Guernsey and so lost his records; but he brought back Prince Essormericq, son of the local King Arosca, and finding himself unable to honor his promise to return the young man to his parents, he did the next best thing and married him into his own family. Knowledge of Gonneville's voyage depended on the account published in 1663 by a priest descended from this union, and as this in some ways circumstantial account gave not a single precise location and was singularly vague even about directions, Gonneville's Land (which, from fuller versions later discovered, can be fairly confidently identified with southern Brazil) was variously located over a wide range: Virginia, Patagonia, Madagascar, New Holland, and of course Terra Australis. The possibilities for a projector of voyages are obvious.

Such projects were not new. The Archives of the Ministry of Marine contain memorials of 1699 by Sainte-Marie, Voutron, and Renan, all based more or less on Gonneville; and Bouvet's 1735 memorandum refers to a voyage projected by Pontchartrain (minister of marine and father of Maurepas) in 1708, which was dropped because the proposed commander died. Bouvet's own proposals, however, are much more detailed than those of 1699, and must have commanded more confidence; he was able to interest Orry de Fulvy, brother of Louis the Fifteenth's controller general of finances and a man high in the councils of the Compagnie, and in a letter of August 2, 1737 Bouvet was able to report that the great Dupleix himself was so far in support as to be willing (in return for trade concessions) to meet the expense himself if the Compagnie did not — as it should — undertake the enterprise.[2]

There is a good deal common to all these memoranda, although as we shall see there is very naturally a distinct shift of emphasis in those written after 1739. There are the standard citations — the land seen by Drake south of Tierra del Fuego, the Falklands in various guises, the discoveries of Quiros and Tasman, signs of land (or what could be interpreted as such) seen by Halley in the South Atlantic, the "Terre de Vüe" or "Cap des Terres Australes" shown on the maps south of Tristan da Cunha at about 42°S; but basically Bouvet relies on Gonneville's Land, conceiving it as a large temperate land mass lying southwest of the cape.[3] There are hints of opposition in the letter of August 1737, but in the upshot Bouvet got what he wanted: two ships, a picked crew, trade goods for the Gonnevilliens, and precise instructions probably drafted by himself. These envisaged a definite ocean sweep, very much in the Cook manner: from about 20°W of Greenwich to 40 or 60°E, generally in 44°S but going down to 55° at four stated intervals. In other respects too the orders were carefully worked out: for instance, when land was sighted, the crew were to be informed that they would receive an extra twenty-five per cent on their wages for each day spent on the coast — a most admirable provision doubtless inspired by the memory of some two and a half centuries of mutinies.[4]

Unfortunately for this excellently planned expedition, there was one flaw: not only was Gonneville's Land not there, but Bouvet had chosen to look for it in the sector of the Antarctic which has the greatest negative anomaly in mean annual temperature, where pack ice reaches 54°S instead of about 65° as in other sectors, and where "in a latitude equivalent to that of the mouth of the Elbe, glaciation is comparable to that in Franz-Josef Land, 25° nearer the Pole."[5] With poor ships and a crew which, despite his obvious solicitude, was inadequately clad, he was lucky to return with no more loss of life than that of a cabinboy washed overboard; and it is astonishing that on New Year's Day 1739 he should have hit upon the island, only five miles across, which bears his name and which, as Gould points out, is the only spot of land on the globe which is literally a thousand miles from anywhere. He had earned at least "a clear title to be regarded as the first Antarctic explorer on record."[6]

Bouvet's first report, written at the cape in March 1739, merely reported his safe arrival; his second, from Lorient at the end of June, frankly announces a failure: the Terres Australes, though extending much further from the pole than the geographers believed, were yet too near it to be of any use as a base on the way to the Indies. But he soon rallied, and by January 1740, was once more inditing: "According to the account which we have of his voyage, the part of the Terres Australes where Gonneville landed is distant from Madagascar by a passage of a few weeks only." But we may suspect that, while he obviously deserved and enjoyed enhanced esteem as a seaman, as a projector his credit with the Compagnie was impaired; his relations with de Fulvy seem to have remained friendly, but after some months he turned directly to the minister of marine. On September 30, 1741, he sent to Maurepas eleven documents, including copies of his letters to de Fulvy, together with a covering letter; what may well be file copies of these, made for the minister's own use, found their way into the Maurepas family archives and have been acquired by the James Ford Bell Collection, where they have the location number B 1741 fBo. This essay is based essentially on these papers.

The basic proposal is set out in memorandum A of January 1740. Since Bouvet himself had gone as far east as 37°E in latitude 51 to 52°S, and Tasman had been down to 47 or 48°S in about 72°E, Gonneville (who was thought to have rounded the cape on his way to India) could have landed only between these two routes: all that is needed is to close the gap.[7] However, in the improbable event of no land being found in these latitudes after sailing as far as 82°E, and assuming the ships to be free to carry on the exploration of the Terres Australes,

we will go to seek the southern part of New Holland, towards Nuyts Land, where what is known of it ends. We will coast it to see if it is contiguous to Van Diemens Land, and to the Terre Australe du St. Esprit, and this latter to New Guinea, and so to open the route for the ships which will go to China . . . We would take the months from April to November to explore these lands; these months are the good season in countries between the Line and the Southern Tropic. In November or December we will sail for New Zealand, in order to arrive there at the beginning of summer. We would coast this land as far as possible towards the east, and leave it altogether at the end of March in order to return by Cape Horn . . .[8]

The general planning is meticulous: the timing of arrivals and departures and the major turning points on the projected track are carefully adjusted to the regimes of the monsoons, the trade winds, and the westerlies. It will be seen that the projected circumnavigation bears a strong resemblance to that projected by Cook for his second voyage; the only significant differences are that Cook's circum-Antarctic track would lie generally some 5° further south, and his great northern sweep much further east — well to the east of New Zealand instead of along the Australian coast which he had already surveyed in the *Endeavour*. The principles, however, are exactly the same, and the credit which Cook holds as a bold, imaginative, and yet practical planner must surely be shared by Bouvet who, given well-found ships, might well have anticipated by nearly three decades the exploration of Australia's east and southeast coasts.[9]

It is perhaps unfortunate for Bouvet's reputation that historical attention has been concentrated on the Antarctic and Terra Australis aspects of his work, which to him were but means to an end — the end of attaining for France commercial parity or supremacy in the eastern seas. It is true that he never gave up faith in Gonneville's Land; he thought of the landfall now known as Bouvet Island as a mere cape — Cap de la Circoncision, from the liturgical name of the first of January — and that the mainland must stretch away to the north and east and form "as it were a barrier to the ice which we found." Nor should the low temperatures he had met be a deterrent, since Gonneville and his men had gone barefooted to Easter Mass and had left the country only in July, in the southern midwinter. Gonneville had brought away pelts, feather goods, excellent dye roots; there must be timber, which was becoming scarce in France and was costly in India, and of course other local products.

But Bouvet's primary interest was in wider commercial strategics: Gonneville's Land would be a way station to the Terre Australe du St. Esprit. The opening of a route by Gonneville's Land and the Terre Australe du St. Esprit would bypass the Dutch at the Cape and Batavia, the latter a passage "insecure in time of war, and not very honorable in time of peace, the Hollanders sending squadrons into these Straits whenever they please which compel our ships to show their papers." From the Terre

Australe, using the trades, Guam, the Philippines, and China would be reached. The return would be easy in the winter (northwest) monsoon, while even in summer the variable winds (i.e., the westerlies) could be picked up in Japanese waters until enough easting had been made to set a course through the northeast trades back to Terre Australe: home, then, by New Zealand. Of course the voyage out would be greatly shortened if New Holland, Van Diemens Land, the Terre Australe du St. Esprit, and New Guinea were not a continuous land mass.

This was the age of the Family Compacts and the War of Jenkins' Ear, and much of Bouvet's argument is predicated on Franco-Spanish cooperation: once the new route was opened, the Spanish Philippine Company founded in 1733 (and hitherto ineffectual because it could not use the Cape of Good Hope route, owing to the old Line of Demarcation with the Portuguese) could trade directly with Europe: the Manila galleons, using the Terre Australe as a halfway house, could sail to South America by the westerlies of the southern rather than the northern hemisphere. This would be a longer route, but it would avoid spells of four to six months continuously at sea, spending the winter in high latitudes, and above all, by avoiding the regularity (both in time and space) of the Manila-Acapulco run, it would render interception by hostile cruisers much more difficult — not an unimportant consideration in these years between the buccaneering of Queen Anne's day and the actual taking of the Manila galleon by Anson, who figures in Bouvet's pages.

There are other advantages: the trade of Gonneville's Land and the Terre Australe themselves, perhaps a slave trade with the Pacific coast of South America — an anticipation of the Peruvian blackbirding of the next century. Science would gain — one could circumnavigate the pole, which cannot be done in the arctic regions, making magnetic and other observations; "Religion is particularly concerned with this enterprise, which would raise innumerable peoples from the darkness of idolatry." But essentially the aim is strategic: use of the linked bases of Gonneville's Land and the Terre Australe will bypass the Dutch and English, come in on their rear, as it were, and so break their monopolistic hold on the further Indies; it will greatly strengthen connections with Spanish South America. One rather wonders why our own age has arrogated to itself the title of the "global century."

The next document (B; September 5, 1740) is a reinforcement of some of the points already made. The profits of the China trade, both directly with France and indirectly between Indian establishments and the Far East, will be lost in the event of war with the Dutch; Tasman's route shows that the Terre Australe can be reached by the south of New Holland, and to defer the expedition until an urgent need arises from the Dutch closing the Sunda Straits would mean losing the profits (estimated at over two million livres annually) for the two years that the enterprise would take. The arguments from Quiros are once more rehearsed, and (as often) with a simple eloquence: the Terre Australe has gold, silver, pearls, spices,

provisions in abundance, all the necessities for a base, all the commodities for the navigation. This report is that of Quiros, who speaks from having seen it, whose testimony is confirmed by that of his crews, who speaks to his king, and who asks to return . . . It is in these original documents that we must see the advantages of this land, and the trustworthiness of him who gives the account of them.

Like calls to like; previously, in so many words, Bouvet had said that the very naivety of Gonneville's story carried conviction. Before we make too much of the naivety, we should perhaps recall that pearling is still important in Torres Strait, and that several of Queensland's goldfields are not far inland from the coast that Bouvet regarded as the Terre Australe.

Strategic arguments are stressed: this land is within reach of the Philippines, China, Japan; a base for the protection of Spanish posts and trade from Dutch attacks; or conversely, the case arising, a base whence to cruise against the Manila galleon. "Thence we can go on to see what joins or what separates Asia and America, and explore the islands discovered last year by the Russians of Kamchatka."

By this time (winter 1740–1741) Bouvet seems to have recognized that the attraction of Gonneville's Land was becoming worn out: spices and the China trade were better cards to play, and the third memoir (document C; February 1, 1741) ends with the suggestion that the Île de France will do for the time as a base, "putting off to another time the discovery of Gonneville's Land." From the point of view of mercantilist commercial strategy, this third memoir, avowedly produced to answer objections, is perhaps the most revealing of the documents, and warrants an extensive summary.

Bouvet begins with a straightforward commercial estimate: France consumes annually perhaps three millions' (livres?) worth of nutmegs, cloves, and cinnamon. This money could be retained in the kingdom did the Compagnie control the trade; and if it could secure a surplus over home consumption large enough to market competitively, it could sell much more both in Europe and in India, where the Dutch distribute twice as much as they bring to Europe. Altogether, the trade could bring in six millions.

There is no current claimant to the Terre Australe du St. Esprit, and Quiros "assures us in the most credible manner that he saw spices there. Must we wait for some European nation to take it before we believe him?" Should it be feared that the Dutch, faced with this threat to their profits, might intervene, the plants could be introduced to the Île de France and Bourbon before they even learnt of the design; there is no difficulty at all in growing them, and there is plenty of unused land in these islands. Bouvet then gives examples of small islands, such as Amboyna and the Bandas, which produce a large part of total output; he does not consider the risk of overproduction. Eventually, perhaps, spices could be grown in Senegal for the European market, the Île de France and Bourbon supplying India, and the Terre Australe selling to China and the Philippines. All this is very much like the usual eighteenth-century projector's pipe dream: but it is worth noting that later, when he became governor of Île de

France (1752–1755), Bouvet enthusiastically supported Pierre Poivre's efforts to introduce the clove and the nutmeg.[10] The idea was not new, and when in 1714 Pontchartrain had given orders for the occupation of Mauritius (Île de France) it seems that this was done in connection with proposed plantations of pepper and cinnamon from Malabar; but nothing came of the spicery project.[11]

It is not likely that the Dutch, once they have seen that France has assured herself of a spice supply, will want to interfere with the Terre Australe base, but even if they do so, they are unlikely to succeed: the distance from Batavia is over twelve hundred leagues, and except by rounding the south of New Holland (eighteen hundred leagues), the voyage between the two is by favor of the monsoon. They could learn of the enterprise only by way of Europe (this seems to take an optimistic view of "security") and by the time they could mount an attack, the French would be firmly entrenched: good relations with the native peoples will ensure rapid completion of fortifications and assembly of supplies, and finally "the contacts which we shall have made with these people, the experience of these regions which we shall have gained, and the knowledge we shall have acquired, will give us a real advantage against enemies to whom the sea, the land, everything, will be new."

The locational advantages are again driven home by the argument that the China trade can be carried on from the Terre Australe during the four or five months when the summer monsoon closes the approaches from the Indian Ocean. It might even be possible to reopen trade with Japan: "M. Caron, who was the director there for the Dutch, proposed to return there for the French Company in 1665, a time still close to the first fury of the Japanese against the Christian Religion. One may believe that present circumstances would be more favourable." At all events one could feel out the attitude of the emperor through Chinese intermediaries.

At the very least, even if other powers should intervene in the Terre Australe, the China trade would be secured, spices procured for home consumption and for competitive trade in world markets, and the Dutch Indies trade (a third of their commerce) seriously diminished; in fact, however, French priority will give a commanding advantage. It may not even be necessary to share the trade with the Dutch: transplanted spices would cost the French only for cultivation, as with coffee in Bourbon, whereas the Dutch have the vast expense of considerable fortresses to overawe their Indies: "if they decrease these precautions to decrease the expense, they will expose themselves to a general defection of the Natives of these Islands, who regard them as Tyrants."[12] In many parts of the world, spices are so much in demand as to be in effect the equivalent of current coin; France is in a position to exploit this demand.

The third memoir closes with so classic a statement of the cold war implied by mercantilism that it deserves to be quoted almost in its entirety:

The new traffic has also this advantage, that it will be as firmly based as the Colonies which will give rise to it, unlike a part of the English and Dutch commerce, which is based only on the inactivity of other European nations and would collapse if Spain prevented the smuggling trade they carry on with America, and if Muscovy and other Powers liberated themselves from the habitual servitude they are in, of receiving from them the foreign merchandise they consume and allowing them in return to carry off the products of their own growth which they need, and carried on trade in their own ships . . . [As for the Dutch,] the power of these Republicans is perhaps ten times greater than it was a hundred and fifty years ago. That of the English has also greatly increased, while during this period the European possessions of these countries have not changed. This augmentation of strength comes entirely from trade. It is no longer permissible that France should neglect this means of increasing her own power. Nothing but a great commerce can support a great navy. The ease with which the Dutch and even the English can equip and run their shipping more cheaply than we can, gives them the advantage in trades which are well known and lie near at hand, where the returns are small. This advantage disappears in new trades and long-distance voyages, which ordinarily bring in large profits; thus our trade with the Indies is as flourishing as theirs as regards those types of merchandise which we possess in common with them. It is perhaps by new trades that France should begin to counterbalance these neighbors, called by distinction the Maritime Powers. At all times she should take great care not to allow herself to be anticipated in trades which could become monopolies in favor of those who first seize upon them. The Dutch undertook the Indies trade in the middle of a war in which their liberty was at stake. The English have declared war, and carried it on for a year, to secure a greater share of the trade with America. That which the Terres Australes offer us is perhaps inferior only because it is less known . . .

The next three papers deal largely with matters of machinery; documents D and F (February 8, 1741, and April 22, 1741), on the choice of ships and sailing dates respectively, need not detain us; more interesting is the memorandum E (April 12, 1741). Much of it is concerned with details of crews and equipment needed; despite the cynical note that the article assuring the continuance of wages and emoluments, even in the event of accident to the ships, "can be kept secret, and only produced in case of necessity," there is once more evidence of Bouvet's obviously sincere solicitude for his men. But the bulk of the memorandum concerns the instructions needed and the principles which should govern relations between the expedition and native peoples. There is some suggestion that Bouvet felt himself cramped by his previous instructions, which forbade absolutely any gifts of arms, the bringing away of any "Australiens," or the leaving of any member of the expedition in the new lands. Bouvet argues that exceptions might be made in special cases and that advantage might be taken of local wars to build up a position of strength: he was clearly of the school of Dupleix and Bussy. On the question of supplying arms, he is delightfully characteristic of his times (and yet, are our times of military missions, MIG contracts, and U2 bases so very different?):

it does not seem that there would be any harm in furnishing small quantities of [muskets and cannon] to Princes as powerful as the Mogul, the Emperor of China, and other Kings of the Indies; on the contrary, it is to be feared that a refusal would lead them to call upon other Europeans, and perhaps prefer them to us, who would not fail to supply them with these things. One can have less consideration for less civilised Peoples.

Bouvet also discusses the action to be taken should the poor state of ships or crews prevent the direct return around the world to France: if both ships were to go to the Île de France or Bourbon, the news would soon reach Batavia; it would therefore be better to leave the smaller vessel at the new base and set up a small station to gather further information, spread French influence, and generally build up a position which would make the assertion of prior possession and occupation both valid and effective. In such a case Bouvet, since he requests the chief command of any new establishments, should stay in the Terre Australe with the smaller ship so as "not to pass on to another the initial difficulties, which will perhaps be the greatest."

These three papers date from spring 1741: by summer, the attention of those who might have helped Bouvet's plans was hopelessly involved in the confusions of the War of the Austrian Succession; seen from his distance, a crazy patternless congeries of double and triple dealings, and, in a rather pathetic way, Bouvet tries to hitch his wagon to these anything but fixed stars. Britain and Spain had been at war since October 1739; in September 1740 Anson had sailed for the Pacific; in December Frederick of Prussia invaded Silesia. As yet Britain and France were not principals; indeed, on the best "cold war" principles, hostilities were not formally declared until nine months after George the Second's spectacular (and, considering the tactical situation, preposterous) victory over French troops at Dettingen in June 1743. But by the summer of 1741 the anti-Austrian party was clearly in the ascendant in France, a Franco-Spanish convention for joint action in Italy and the Mediterranean had been made in May of that year, and indeed even in 1740 Fleury had ordered a fleet to support the Spanish position in American waters.[13] The international situation, then, gave renewed urgency to Bouvet's pleadings — in his own eyes; for Fleury and Maurepas the priorities were different.

Document G, dated June 10, 1741 — less than a week after France and Prussia entered into a definite alliance — is addressed to de Fulvy, but already Bouvet is aiming higher: "if you, Sir, do not wish to speak to the King, I could make an excerpt from the memoranda . . . for M. le Comte de Maurepas or M. le Cardinal [Fleury]." The matter is surprising: "What is said in the public prints, that the Muscovites in concert with the English design to attempt once more the passage to the Indies by the North, seems to me worthy of attention." Clearly, it is a genuine interest for the Russians, and it is astonishing that they wish to enlist English aid when a memorandum of a few lines would have given them all the information they needed to carry it out with their own resources; but the British aim is only too clear:

to carry their commerce into those rich regions of the East, to do what they please there . . . to seek the spiceries, in a word to establish their influence and (to use their own notions and language) their hegemony and their empire in these seas. These advantages seem to them so great that to secure them they do not fear to form the

Russian marine and to introduce them, and perhaps other competitors, into the Indies. If there is such a passage and it is not commanded by some straits, then all nations trading to the Indies will use it, and even towns such as Ostend and Hamburg.[14]

It is important that France should not allow herself to be anticipated; if the Compagnie cannot undertake the enterprise, it must be at the expense of the state.

This was a long shot indeed: a month later (July 15) Bouvet has found a more immediate target (document H). Anson is in the Pacific, he will fall upon the Manila galleons; if we had firm knowledge of eastern New Guinea, the Terre Australe du St. Esprit, and New Zealand, the Spaniards would no longer be tied to their fixed trans-Pacific routes and timings. The king of Spain could help in the discovery by allowing the ships to refit and to trade in Peru: the profits of this trade will amply repay the cost of the expedition, and "the Court of Spain in granting this permission at the present time, gives nothing but what it cannot itself enjoy"; but the exploration rights will still belong to France.

By August Bouvet seems almost desperate. Document I (August 4, 1741) begins dramatically: "The Galleons blockaded in the ports of America have not returned for three years. The Atlantic is covered with English ships." Gonneville's Land, even the Terre Australe, are all forgotten now: the task is to get the treasure of Peru to Europe, either out and back by La Plata and the Falklands, or out by Cape Horn and home by the Red Sea, the Court of Spain taking appropriate measures to have the silver forwarded from Suez. In the former case, the homeward course will be set out of sight of the Azores, to make a landfall between Ushant and Finisterre in January or February. This for tactical reasons: "In winter ships have difficulty in maintaining station in our seas; and the long nights, the fogs, the squalls, the bad weather of this season, almost always furnish opportunities to make feints and to avoid the enemy, if one finds them in force."

There is at this point a marginal insertion: "one need not fear the English at all at this time"; the "not at all" has been corrected to "not much" — one would like to know whether by Bouvet's hand or no.

The rest is diminuendo. A long letter (document K, August 31, 1741) takes up the idea of a M. de Sales that it would be better to get the silver which the Compagnie uses for its India trade direct from America, rather than bear the risks and charges of first bringing it to Europe; this could be done by opening a route from Peru by New Guinea and New Britain and between Amboyna and Celebes, thence north or south of Java. As Bouvet says, the seas between New Guinea and Gilolo are full of shoals and reefs, and the Dutch would certainly interfere: his own plan (not divulged to M. de Sales) is better, but it would still be good business to get the silver in Peru. It would be of reciprocal benefit were France and Spain to reach an agreement for a direct trade in merchandise payable with silver in America; the English will openly oppose it, but then they cannot be everywhere.

The last document (L, September 30, 1740) provides a sad anticlimax: it is a copy of an earlier memorandum and we are back where we came in, with a discussion of South Atlantic bases. The Île de Saxembourg[15] is preferred; and — merely in passing — it would also serve for voyages to the Terre Australe du St. Esprit and the South Sea.

On this unsatisfactory note the once bold project dwindles away. If one needed a reason for the failure, it would probably be enough to point to the obvious if reluctant admission of naval inferiority, a leitmotif running through at least two centuries of French writing on maritime affairs, just as the assertion of superiority is a commonplace of contemporary British publicists, often raised to grotesque heights or ranting, as in Edward Young's *Imperium Pelagi* (1730). Perhaps the most diverting example of this antireciprocity, if I may so term it, is Callander's complete and impudent transposition of de Brosses:

Vain are the repeated exhortations of the *French* Writer, addressed to a nation which . . . by the ruin of their marine, seem totally disabled at present to attempt anything of moment in this way. Far other is the case of this happy Island. United among ourselves, respected by foreigners, with our marine force intire and (humanly speaking) invincible, aided by a set of naval-officers superior in every respect to those of the nations around us.[16]

The climate, then, was unfavorable. The voyage, considered simply as a physical achievement, was feasible enough, as Cook and others were to show, and Bouvet's plans were well laid. But even setting aside the war, one may doubt that so lightweight a minister as Maurepas would have given even a successful expedition the solid and sustained backing it would need if it were to be more than reconnaissance. But in any event the war intervened, and Bouvet had his moment of glory: in June 1748 he commanded a convoy taking troops and funds to Dupleix, and, by seamanship universally admitted to be brilliant, brought these succors safely to port under the eyes of a much superior British squadron, an action which may well have been decisive in enabling Pondicherry to repel Boscawen's besieging forces.

For nearly fourteen years after 1750, Bouvet was governor either of the Île de France or of Bourbon, except for another Indian expedition, to Malabar in 1757, which again was carried out with his accustomed ability. After the Peace of Paris (1763) he returned on leave to France, and in 1767 he again broached the scheme of Austral discovery. He recalled that after his return in 1739 he had been led to hope that his first sally might be followed up: the minister, the cardinal, seemed to wish it, and he had been told that Louis the Fifteenth himself had said (with matchless kingly platitude): "So they are making Discoveries in my Reign. That gives me pleasure." However, the Compagnie was not in a position to incur expenses which did not directly affect its trade; he waited three years in Paris, and then resumed his ordinary voyages in its ships.[17]

The France of Choiseul might well seem more propitious than that of Fleury and Maurepas; as Bouvet himself puts it, "What period, Monseigneur, could be more favorable to the most important enterprise I know of, than that of Your Excellency's Ministry?" But Bouvet was past sixty; his career, though not undistinguished, was one of merit only, owing little or nothing to birth or influence; he had been out of France — and out of Paris was out of mind, in that century! — for fifteen, perhaps twenty, years. It is a familiar figure: the tough, weathered sailor-governor, an old Indies hand, wholly admirable but more than a bit of a bore. The new project seems to have been but the old memorial, Gonneville's Land[18] and all; the letter to the minister seems almost routine, as if his heart was not in it. There have been other memorialists, heartsick with hope deferred, in this Pacific field: Godinho de Erédia, Quiros, Dalrymple.

Younger men were coming up, and one at least had birth, influence, a polished education, for his years a wide experience in arms and affairs, and no less merit — Bougainville. There is perhaps a touch of bitterness in one paragraph of Bouvet's 1767 letter:

The voyage which I propose is quite different from that which M. de Bougainville is making to the South Sea, although that may have been based on my writings which I had communicated to M. Trehat, secretary of the Academy of Belles Lettres, and which I have reason to believe to have fallen into the hands of M. de Bougainville, who succeeded him in that position.

And indeed there may well be an echo of Bouvet's memoranda in Bougainville's instructions.

The letter ends with a request for an interview: it is endorsed "M. Dubuq — reply, thanking him and saying that we cannot see our way to take up the project." Even so had Erédia's memorials, which could have led to a Portuguese discovery of Australia in 1602, been endorsed: "As for the business of Manuel Godinho de Erédia, there is nothing to be done about it; but I recommend that you should favor him in accordance with his capacities, etc." [19]

The prize went to Bougainville, but Bouvet has not been without honor, based on his achievement, which was small in comparison with his vision. Narratives of his voyage naturally figure in the works of de Brosses and Alexander Dalrymple;[20] he certainly influenced Kerguelen in the discovery of the group which bears the latter's name, and Edward Heawood states categorically that "The reports brought back by Bouvet had an important influence on the plans of Cook's second voyage." [21] This, however, would seem to refer simply to the question of Cap de la Circoncision, which Cook searched for but missed, rather than to Bouvet's broader plans. These remained in the French archives, though we may be very sure that had Cook seen them he would have been highly appreciative. As it was despite the soundly-argued support of Le Monnier in 1776 and 1779,[22] the very existence of his island was doubted, despite occasional sightings by sealers, until the definitive rediscovery by the German exploring ship *Valdivia* in 1898. It was indeed the oddest of chances that led him to this lost speck of land, the farthest-flung scrap of solid earth on the globe.

In a sense, Bouvet was before his time — but so little before! He did not die until 1786, after Cook and Bougainville had carried out the work he had so longed to do. Beaglehole has pointed out the element of colonial rivalry evident in the placid scholarly speculation of de Brosses, to say nothing of the vulgar commercial plagiarism of Callander and the part that it played in the motivation of the great Pacific voyages of the second half of the century; Bouvet very clearly anticipates this rivalry — as it were a "conquest of space" to secure a hegemony — and, a quarter of a century earlier, he goes far to meet Beaglehole's point that "We have no formal memoranda, no cabinet papers or grand debate to unroll before us a deliberate plan of action." [23] Formal memoranda and a deliberate plan of action are just what Bouvet provides.

Concentration on the Antarctic Terra Australis aspect of his work, rather than the Terre Australe aspect — the planning for a Pacific base for purposes of war and trade — has obscured his significance as a systematic planner of discovery and tactician of trade rivalry. So excellent a scholar as Beaglehole seems to some extent to fall into this trap of confusing, instead of just connecting, an Antarctic Terra Australis with its northern reaches or outliers in the Terre Australe du St. Esprit. Hence he is a little less than fair to Bouvet, who admittedly was "rapt by the story of Quiros" but who fully recognized that Cap de la Circoncision could not be Quiros's Austrialia del Espiritu Santo, though the two might well be connected by a land mass running north and east (roughly along the Marion-Crozier-Kerguelen line), with New Holland lying separately to the north and west of this passage. And in the context of contemporary geographical knowledge, ignorance, and theory, this was by no means an unreasonable proposition.[24]

Had Bouvet secured two good ships and good crews, the results might of course have been startling, even though one may feel that Maurepas, if not Choiseul, would have been incapable of exploiting them. There is no question whatever, given the facts of Bouvet's career, of either his seamanship or his leadership; he had the considerable advantage, rare among long-distance exploring navigators between Da Gama and Cook, of knowing exactly where he wanted to go; and that included the east coast of New Holland. He would certainly not have found Terra Australis; his grandiose schemes for commercial warfare might never have succeeded; but he would almost certainly have discovered — shall we say Nouvelle Galles du Sud? Or perhaps, since Bouvet's roots were in St. Malo, it might have been, by a final irony, Nouvelle Bretagne.

NOTES

page 224

[1] For Bouvet's project in general, and its antecedents, see A. Rainaud, *Le Continent austral*, Paris, 1893, pp. 394–405, and E. Marthe, *La France et l'exploration polaire*, vol. 1, Paris, 1959, pp. 220–242. Franco-Brazilian relations, generally hostile, are referred to *passim* by F. A. de Varnhagen, *História geral do Brasil*, 5th ed., São Paulo, 1956; see, e.g., vol. 4, pp. 58–62, for Fernando de Noronha.

[2] All the documents quoted in this paragraph are in the Archives du Service Hydrographique de la Marine, vol. 105[3], bundles 1–18; most are cited in Rainaud, *op. cit.*, pp. 394–405, and Marthe, *op. cit.*, pp. 220–242. I have used the copies, collated by T. Dunbabin, in the National Library, Canberra, and filed as "France Marine Department Transcripts" (also to be found in the Mitchell Library, Sydney). I wish to acknowledge the assistance of Mr. J. W. Forsyth of Avalon and Mr. Colin Jack-Hinton of the Department of Pacific History, Australian National University.

[3] It is known that the Ministry of Marine under Maurepas (possibly influenced by Bouvet) had searched the archives of Dieppe and other towns of Normandy for further information on Gonneville's voyage. See C. de Brosses, *Histoire des navigations aux terres australes,* vol. 1, Paris, 1756, p. 107n.

page 225

[4] The instructions are in Archives du Service Hydrographique, vol. 105, bundle 5, and are summarized in Marthe, *op. cit.*, pp. 225–227.

[5] E. Aubert de la Rüe, *Les Terres australes,* Paris, 1953, pp. 7, 98; cf. M. Zimmermann, *Régions polaires australes,* vol. 10, Paris, 1930, p. 298, and O. Nordenskjöld and L. Mecking, *The Geography of the Polar Regions,* New York, 1928, p. 285 (fig. 94), p. 320.

[6] R. H. T. Gould, *Oddities,* 2nd ed., London, 1944, pp. 136–137. As Gould points out, it was unlucky for Bouvet's reputation that Cook, misled by his predecessor's faulty longitude, missed the island by beginning his search for it about two and a half degrees too far east.

page 226

[7] Bouvet's longitudes, reckoned by the full round of three hundred and sixty degrees eastwards from Ferro (Hiero) or Teneriffe, have been given their approximate equivalents east or west of Greenwich. It may be mentioned that Bernard de la Harpe, in a letter of May 5, 1738, generally supporting Bouvet's earlier proposals, had refuted the claim that Gonneville had rounded the cape, though it does not follow that he reached only as far as Virginia.

[8] "Terre Austrole du St. Esprit" is of course Quiros's Austrialia del Espiritu Santo, which was generally held to occupy a position roughly corresponding to the east coast of the Cape York Peninsula, Queensland; see for a standard representation Vaugondy's general and Australasian maps in de Brosses, *op. cit.* In this essay, "Terra Australis" refers to the concept of a sub-Antarctic continent, the Great Southland; "Terre Australe" to Quiros's Austrialia del Espiritu Santo.

[9] See J. C. Beaglehole's introduction to *The Journals of Captain James Cook,* vol. 1, Cambridge, England, 1955, p. cxiv; vol. 2, Cambridge, England, 1961, pp. xxi–xxii and Figure 2.

page 229

[10] See Madeleine Ly-Tio-Fane, *Mauritius and the Spice Trade: The Odyssey of Pierre Poivre,* Mauritius Archives Publication Fund, no. 4, Port Louis, 1958.

[11] Ly-Tio-Fane, *op. cit.,* p. 3.

[12] The French Marine Transcripts in the National Library, Canberra, have an amusing misreading in an analogous document: "qui les regardent comme des Titans" for "comme des Tirans."

page 231

[13] *Cambridge Modern History,* old series, vol. 6, 1909, pp. 158, 231.

page 232

[14] There is probably a side glance here at the intermittent and ineffectual imperial attempts at opening up an eastern trade from the Austrian Netherlands by means by the Ostend Company, spasmodically active from 1722 to 1744.

page 233

[15] For an account of this mythical island, placed in 30°30′S. and 355° longitude (= 23°W of Greenwich) see R. H. T. Gould, *op. cit.,* pp. 132–136.

[16] J. Callander, *Terra Australis Cognita,* vol. 1, London, 1766, pp. ii–iii; cf. de Brosses, *op. cit.,* vol. 1, p. 10.

[17] De Lozier Bouvet to Monseigneur Le Duc de Praslin, January 10, 1767; MS in Bibliothèque Nationale, Nouvelles Acquisitions Françaises, No. 9407, 52; Rainaud, *op. cit.,* p. 397, fn. 1, refers to a memoir of this date, unsigned and in another hand, in Archives du Service Hydrographique de la Marine, vol.

105³, bundle 5, no. 30. The copy of the covering letter to Praslin in the French Marine Transcripts in the National Library, Canberra, is fully signed. Praslin was Choiseul's brother and took his place as Minister of Marine (1766–1770); he was a strong supporter of Bougainville.

page 234

[18] Gonneville's Land makes a last appearance, spectral as it may seem, as late as 1783, in a memoir addressed to the former Minister of Marine, Sartine, by a Baron de Gonneville. See Charles A. Julien, *Les Voyages de découverte et les premiers établissements*, Paris, 1948, p. 18.

[19] For Erédia, see Rainaud, *op. cit.*, pp. 350–356; O. H. K. Spate, "Manuel Godinho de Erédia: Quest for Australia," *Meanjin*, Melbourne, vol. 16, 1957, no. 2, pp. 109–122.

[20] De Brosses, *op. cit.*, vol. 2, pp. 255–259;

Dalrymple included a detailed chart of Cap de la Circoncision, from Bouvet's bearings, in the memoir to accompany his "Chart of the Ocean between South America and Africa. With the Tracks of Dr. Edmund Halley in 1700 and Monsʳ Lozier Bouvet in 1738," London, 1769.

[21] *Geographical Discovery*, Cambridge, 1912, p. 208.

[22] See Rainaud, *op. cit.*, pp. 405–406. The subsequent "history" of Bouvet Island may be found in Gould, *op. cit.*, p. 22, and C. Vallaux, "Le Roman géographique de l'île Bouvet," *Mercure de France*, n.s., vol. 193, 1927, pp. 85–100.

page 235

[23] Beaglehole, *op. cit.*, vol. 1, pp. lxxviii–lxxxi.

[24] J. C. Beaglehole, *The Exploration of the Pacific*, London, 1934, p. 224; cf. Bouvet's memoir (document A) of January, 1740.

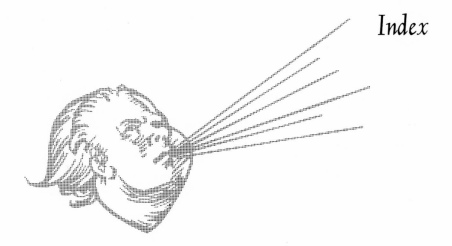

Index

Abdorians, 80
Abler, R. F., 191n82
"Abstract of the Journall of Henry Hudson, An" (in *Purchas His Pilgrimes*), 94
Acapulco, 200, 227, 228, 232
Account of Several Late Voyages & Discoveries, An, 211
Addington, Surrey, 133
Admiralty, High Court of, 138
Afonso V, king of Portugal, 14, 15, 18
Africa: slave trade in, 6, 37, 187; Portuguese expeditions down west coast of, 12, 24; part of *orbis terrarum,* 13; circumnavigation of, 14, 23; in Ptolemy's geography, 23; opening up of, 40
Age of Discovery, 3, 11–13
Agnese, Batista: reviser of Ptolemy's atlas (*1525*), 75
Agriculture: Brahmadeyas and, 54; sugar-cane growing, 145–170
Aihole, Bijapur district, Mysore state, 50
Ailly, Pierre d' (*Imago Mundi*), 21, 23
Akimiski Island, 100
Albany River: described in *Arctic Pilot*, 100
Alberti, Leon Battista (*Descriptio Urbis Romae*), 18
Albuquerque, Afonso d', 40
Alcasara, Simon, 206
Alexander, columns of, 81
Algiers: treaty with France about slave trade, 185–186
Alvares, Father Francisco: leads envoys from Negus to pope, 38

Amaram: warrior's fief in Coromandel, 58
Amazon River, 4
Amboyna Island: 232; spice production cited by Bouvet, 228
America, North and South: 121, 202, 215, 228, 230, 232; belief in a navigable water route through, 6, 90; Toscanelli's ignorance of existence of, 14; opened up, 40, 42; western part of shown on Gerritsz's "Great Chart of the South Sea," 104; English patent to control colonization, 120; treatise on colonization, 138; Diego Gutiérrez's *1562* map of, 200; *1562* map of, 204; journals of English voyages to southern regions of, 206; Rastell's voyage to, 209; the back door to, 211. *See also* North America; South America
America (de Bry), 196
"Americae sive quartae orbis partis nova et exactissima descriptio" (Gutiérrez map, *1562*), 200
Amherst Island, 124, 125
Amou, 78, 79
Amsterdam: 70, 92, 93, 106; Weymouth's logbooks seen by Hudson in, 91; book fair in, 98; the *West-Indische Spieghel* published there, *1634*, 105
Amu-Darya (Oxus), 75, 78, 79
Anageda Bay, 216
Anbil, 55
Andeghen (Andizhan), 82
Andhra Pradesh, 52
Anglo-Dutch relations of late *16*th c., early *17*th c., 89, 92, 104, 112n2

Animal-driven mill in sugar production, 157, 166
Anne, queen of England: buccaneering during reign of, 227
Anson, George: quoted, 212; uses Halley's magnetic map, 214; lessons of voyage round Cape Horn, 216; proposal for settlements, 216; in the Pacific, 231, 232
Antarctic: Bouvet's exploration, 225, 226, 235
Anticosti, 128, 136
Antigua windmill (sugar production), 156
Antilles, British, 154
Antilles, French, 154
Antipodes, 217n5
Antwerp, 42, 69, 70
Arabs: 38; geographic contributions of, 12; Samarkand a center of culture and trade, 83
Aral Sea, 75, 78
Arctic: ice from blocked Hudson's *3*rd voyage, 90, 91; Anglo-Dutch dispute over commercial rights in, 104; exploration of, 108, 111
Arctic Ocean, 68, 74, 78
Arctic Pilot (book): on Cape Digges-Cape Wolstenholme region, 99; on the approach to Albany River, 100
Aristotelian philosophy: 19; influence on natural sciences, 42
Arnoul, Nicolas (Intendant des Galères at Marseille), quoted, 178
Arosca, king from Terra Australis, 224
Arrash River, 79
Arsow (Acsow, Ak-su, Akhsi), 82

INDEX

INDEX

foe's obituary of, 195; dangers of navigating, 198–210, 212, 214; on maps, 199, 202, 204, 205, 206; the expeditions after Drake, 206; Sarmiento renames, 208, 218n39; voyage of East India Company to, 210; Narborough-Wood voyage to, 211; as "a place to be forgotten," 214–216; an engraving of, 215; settlement projects near, 216
Magnetic map, Edmund Halley's, 213, 214, 214n76
Magnetic observations: as advantage of Bouvet's enterprise, 227
Magnetic pole: position in *1610–1611*, 101
Magnetical compass, 219n62
Magnifique et somptueuse pompe funèbre faite aus obseques et funeralles du très grand et très victorieus Empereur Charles V., La: 70; printed by Plantin, 69
Magnus, John: meets Góis, 38; interested in Ethiopian issue, 38–39; describes Nordic countries, 41
Magnus, Olaus, 41
Maharaja Ganapatideva: edict of, 52
Mahasabha (Brahman assemblies), 54, 61n25
Mahasahasa, 52
Malabar: Bouvet's *1757* expedition to, 233
Malaya, 51
Malaysia, 50
Malta: as center of slave trade, 176, 177, 178, 179, 180
Mangusla (Mangyshlak), 82
Mangyshlak, 83
Manigramam: Tamil merchant association, 50, 56
Manuel, king of Portugal: receives gifts, 35; sends letters to pope, 41
Mapmaking. *See* Cartography
Marco Polo: 20; and Southeast Asian islands, 23; on Mutfili's diamonds and cotton, 52; in Catalan atlas, 75
Mare Caspium, 67, 68, 75, 78–79, 84, 85, 86n24
Mare de Zabachae, 75
Mare Dulce, 91
Mare Euxinum, 79

Mare Glaciale (Arctic Ocean), 68, 74, 78
Mariage, M.: and slave trade, 182, 183, 184
Marigold (Strong's ship), 127
Marine, Ministry of: in French slave commerce, 178, 180, 181, 182, 183, 184, 186, 188, 224
Marion-Crozier-Kerguelen line, 235
Maritime Powers, 230
Maritimes, 130, 139
Markham, Clements R., 103–104
Marot, Clément, 38
Marseille: base for galley slave trade, 173, 174, 178, 180, 181, 182, 183, 186
Martin, Samuel (sugar production), 148
Martin Vaz (island), 224
Martinique (sugar production), 148, 156
Martins, Fernão, canon of Lisbon cathedral: gets letter and chart from Toscanelli, 13–14, 15, 16, 18, 20
Martyr, Peter, 41
Mary (Merv), 82
Massachusetts, 139
Matanzas (sugar production), 156
Maurepas, Comte de, Minister of Marine, 224, 225, 231, 233
Mauritius: 223, 231; Bouvet as governor of, 228–229, 233
Mayer, C. A.: quoted, 38
Medes, 83
Medici, Cosimo de, 17, 19
Medici, Lorenzo de, 22
Medicis, 29n25, 36
Menquit. *See* Ramea
Medieval trade organizations (India), 53
Mediterranean, 68, 121, 126, 149, 174, 176, 187, 188
Meli (Tamil for plowshare), 55
Menan, Bay of (Bay of Fundy), 130, 139
Mendaña de Neyra, Álvaro de, 208
Mercator, Gerardus and Rumoldus: 204; world map of *1569*, 74, 84; maps of Europe, 75–76, 79, 80; on columns of Alexander, 81; "Mare Dulce" on maps of, 91

Merchants Iles: first appearance on maps, 105, 111
Merick, Richard: ships walrus tusks to Russia for sale, 128
Merv, 82
Mesena (Mezen), 78
Mexico: sugar industry in, 147; Spanish empire in, 195
Mezen, 78
Michaelmass Bay, 100
Michow, H., 65
Middle Ages: 12, 20, 40; geographers of, 23, 24; religious faith in, 37
Mill (sugar production), 154–157
Mines: copper, 130; in the Maritimes, 140; in Spanish possessions, 147
Mississippi River, 4
Modiford plantation, Barbados (sugar production), 163
Mohammedans. *See* Islam
Molasses (sugar production), 162–163, 165, 166, 168, 169n19
Mologa, the Mosko (Moskva)–Oka–Desna (Klyazma) system, 78
Molgomaiana (tribe), 80
Moluccas, 200, 202, 208, 210
Molyneux, Emery: terrestrial globe, 206, 207, 208, 218n36
Mongol threat to Russia, 66
Monson, Sir William, 202, 210
Monsoons, 226, 227, 229
Montreal, 185
Monts, Sieur de, 140
Mordoviti, 68
Mordva, 75
More, John, 42
More, Sir Thomas, 42
Morison, Samuel Eliot: quoted, 14
Moroccan emissary: and French slave trade, 186
Moscho (Moscow), 80
Moscovia, 68
Moscovia der Hauptstat in Reissen (Herberstein), 76
Moscow: 65, 66, 68, 70, 80, 81; Chancellor and, 67; Herberstein on, 67; on Van Deutecum map, 74, 76–77; burning by Tartars described by John Stow, 80
Moskva River, 77
Moslems. *See* Islam
Mosquito Bay: 101; on Gerritsz